DAY BY DAY
WE MAGNIFY THEE

D0393694

DAY BY DAY
WE MAGNIFY THEE

Daily Readings for the Church Year
Selected from the Writings of Martin Luther

FORTRESS PRESS   PHILADELPHIA

First Paperback Edition in the United States by Fortress Press 1982

Reprinted by permission of the Epworth Press, London, England

Compiled and translated by Margarete Steiner and Percy Scott

Third printing 1985

Library of Congress Cataloging in Publication Data

Luther, Martin, 1483–1546.
   Day by day we magnify thee.

   1. Devotional calendars. I. Steiner, Margarete.
II. Scott, Percy. III. Title.
BR331.E6 1982   242′.3   82–2481
ISBN 0–8006–1637–5 (pbk.)   AACR2

2115J85   Printed in the United States of America   1–1637

PUBLISHER'S FOREWORD

CONSTANCY in prayer and worship is regarded by Christians of all traditions as a hallmark—and a safeguard—of faith. Thus was Martin Luther able to write about Mary, who first sang the hymn, "My soul doth magnify the Lord": " . . . Mary's heart remains the same at all times; she lets God have His will with her and draws from it all only a good comfort, joy, and trust in God. Thus we too should do; that would be to sing a right Magnificat."

This collection of brief daily readings, arranged according to the Year of the Church and gathered from the enormous writings of Luther, had great impact when it first appeared in the United Kingdom in 1946 and in North America in 1950. It is again made available, near the observance of the five-hundredth anniversary of Luther's birth in Eisleben, November 10, 1483. The collection is itself a classic and the anniversary noteworthy, but this re-publication is offered chiefly in the conviction that these writings—words of "spiritual counsel"—can help Christians of all traditions remain constant in prayer and worship.

Users will note that the book's organization, of 1946, remains. For example, designations for the Sundays before Lent and for the Sundays after Pentecost (Whitsuntide) are according to earlier custom, and biblical passages are rendered in King James English. References to the original German editions of Luther's writings are noted by the customary W.A. for the Weimar edition and E.A. for the Erlangen edition; "Tischreden" refers to the "Table Talk" of the reformer.

Martin Luther was a child of his times, the sixteenth century, and this is born out in the way he wrote. Yet the writings included in this book—alongside his accomplishments as theologian and reformer of the evangelical catholic church—retain a robust reality even centuries later. Anchored firmly in faith's life in the world created by God, *Day by Day We Magnify Thee*—that title being a phrase from the *Te Deum*—through its daily readings can in our time remind us again and again of our Baptism. That Baptism, as Luther affirmed in *The Small Catechism*, "signifies that the old Adam in us, together with all sins and evil lusts, should be drowned by daily sorrow and repentance and be put to death, and that the new man should come forth daily and rise up, cleansed and righteous, to live forever in God's presence."

*The Presentation of
    the Augsburg Confession
June 25, 1982*

Fortress Press
Philadelphia

PREFACE

AT all times translators, both scholars and poets, have affirmed that their endeavour is a striving after the impossible. In the process of translation the intimate connection of thought and wording is broken up, and idioms, periods, and sounds suggestive of certain accompanying visions and general experience can hardly ever be reproduced. Yet those very visions and experiences lend the peculiar and endearing flavour to thought which in itself is abstract and general. An idea expressed in the mother-tongue strikes us differently from the same idea expressed in a foreign tongue. Thought is all that can truly be got across. The more poetic the original, the greater the difficulty entailed in translating it into another idiom.

This being so, I have here made it my first endeavour to remain true to the spirit of Luther. Thereafter I have thought to keep close to the German in order to preserve the forcefulness and ruggedness of his style. This is essential in a translation from Luther, because with him the very mode of expression is the arresting factor.

Yet often enough thought and syntax are so involved, or the wording so intrinsically German, that a literal translation could not be attempted. In such cases, whenever possible, I have replaced Luther's own words by a quotation from the Authorised Version, as this seems to be truest to the spirit and the style of the original. In translating the Bible into German, Luther's own style has become altogether a biblical style.

On the other hand, ample use has been made of the great religious writers of the Middle Ages. Luther's mode of expression is at times not at all unlike that of the Anchoress Rule, Walter Hilton, or Mother Julian, and others of that period.

I have used St. John of the Cross's well-known metaphor of the burning log united with the fire in order to translate the word: 'durchottet' (cf. *The Living Flame of Love*, Prologue, v. 4).

Wherever Luther's German translation of the Bible differs from the Authorised Version, I have translated his German into English.

The sections taken from Ellwein's German translation of Luther's *Romerbrief-Vorlesung* and Justus Jonas' German translation of *Vom unfreien Willen* have been translated from the Latin. For translating the one section taken from Menius' German translation of the *Galater Kommentar* and for other sections from Luther's *op. lat.*, for which Dr. Witte does not give the German translation, I have translated the German as it stands.

Wherever the wording of the translation touches upon theological problems, the advice of theologians, both English and German, has been sought. I am greatly indebted to my friends Pastor Franz Hildebrandt, Ph.D., the Rev. A. M. Ramsey, M.A., Canon of Durham and Professor of Theology, Dr. Sidney R. Smith, Cambridge, and Miss Olive Wyon for their generous help and interest in the work.

I also wish to thank most warmly my friend Mrs. Charis Hort and my daughter Hendrikje for many valuable suggestions, and for their untiring help in reading both manuscript and proofs.

If a translator had any right to make the work a dedication to a friend, this book should be dedicated to the late Master of Selwyn College, Cambridge, the Rev. J. O. F. Murray, D.D., Canon of Ely.

M. S.

THE COMING OF THE LORD

Sunday: MATTHEW xxi. 1–9

Rejoice greatly, O daughter of Zion; shout, O daughter of Jerusalem: behold, thy King cometh unto thee: he is just, and having salvation; lowly, and riding upon an ass, and upon a colt the foal of an ass. ZECHARIAH ix. 9.

Yea, of a truth, He will be a king, but a poor and wretched king who has in no way the appearance of a king if He is judged and esteemed by outward might and splendour, in which worldly kings and princes like to array themselves.

He leaves to other kings such things as pomp, castles, palaces, gold, and wealth; and He lets them eat and drink, dress and build more daintily than other folks; but the craft which Christ the poor beggar-king knows, they do not know. He helps not against *one* sin only, but against *all* my sin; and not against *my* sin only, but against *the whole world's* sin. He comes to take away not sickness only, but death; and not *my* death only, but *the whole world's* death. This, saith the Prophet, tell the daughter of Zion, that she be not offended at His mean advent; but shut thine eyes and open thine ears, and perceive not how He rides there so beggarly, but hearken to what is said and preached about this poor king. His wretchedness and poverty are manifest, for He comes riding on an ass like a beggar having neither saddle nor spurs. But that He will take from us sin, strangle death, endow us with eternal holiness, eternal bliss, and eternal life, this cannot be seen. Wherefore thou must hear and believe.

Sermon for first Sunday in   W.A. 37. 201 f.
Advent, 1533.

*And he shall reign over the house of Jacob for
ever; and of his kingdom there shall be no end.*
LUKE i. 33.

He is thy king, the king promised to thee, whose own
thou art. He and no other shall rule over thee, but in spirit
and not after worldly rule. This is He for whom thou didst
long from the beginning. This is He for whom thy dear
forefathers were yearning and crying with heartfelt desire.
From all the things which until now have burdened, oppressed, and imprisoned thee, He will redeem thee and will
set thee free.

O, what comfortable words unto a believing heart, for
apart from Christ a man is thrown under the heel of many
furious tyrants, who are not kings but murderers, under
whom he suffers great pain and fear; of such are the devil,
the flesh, the world, sin and the law withal, and death and
hell; by the which the wretched conscience is oppressed, and
held in harsh confinement, leading a bitter and fearful life.

But when a man with strong faith receives this king into
his inmost heart, he is saved. Sin, death, hell, and all distress
he dreads no longer; for he knows well, and does not doubt,
that this king is a master over life and death, over sin and
grace, over hell and heaven, and that all things are in His
hands. Lo, what great things are contained in these few
words: 'Behold, thy king'. Such superabundant great blessings does the poor ass-rider and disdained king bestow, and
these things neither reason nor nature can comprehend, but
faith alone.

Sermon for the first Sunday in   W.A. 10. 1 (ii). 27 f.
   Advent, 1522.

*. . . I will come in to him, and will sup with him, and
he with me.* REVELATION iii. 20.

He cometh, cometh unto thee. Yea, verily, thou goest not
to Him, neither dost thou fetch Him. He is too high for thee,
and too far away. All thy wealth and wit, thy toil and labour,
will not bring thee near Him, lest thou pride thyself that thy
merit and worthiness have brought Him unto thee. Dear
friend, all thy merit and worthiness are smitten down, and
there is on thy side nothing but sheer undeserving and unworthiness, and on His side is pure grace and mercy. Here
come together man in his poverty and the Lord in His unsearchable riches.

Therefore learn here from the Gospel what happens when
God begins to build us into the likeness of Him, and what
is the beginning of saintliness. There is no other beginning
than that thy king comes unto thee, and begins the work in
thee. Thou dost not seek Him, He seeks thee; thou dost not
find Him, He finds thee; thy faith comes of Him, not of thyself; and where He does not come, thou must stay outside;
and where there is no Gospel, there is no God, but sheer sin
and destruction. Therefore ask thou not where to begin a
godly life; there is no beginning but where this king comes
and is preached.

Sermon for the first Sunday in   W.A. 10. I (ii). 78 ff.
Advent, 1522.

3

> *Blessed be the Lord God of Israel; for he hath
> visited and redeemed his people.* LUKE i. 68.

In His first advent God came in a cruel, thick, black cloud
with fire, smoke, and thunder; with a great sound of trumpets, so fierce that the children of Israel were filled with fear
and dread, and said unto Moses (Exodus xx. 19), 'All that the
Lord hath spoken we will do. But speak thou with us . . . ,
but let not God speak with us, lest we die'. At that time He
gave them the Law. The Law is cruel; we do not like to hear
it. The Law is such a terror to our reason that at times we
fall into instant despair. It is so heavy a burden that the
conscience knows not where to turn, or what to do.

Christ *in His advent* is not terrible like that, but meek; not
fierce like God in the Old Testament, but meek and merciful
like a human being; He does not come on the mountain, but
in the city. On Sinai He came with terror, now He comes with
meekness; there He was to be feared, there He came with
thunder and lightning; here He comes with hymns of praise.
There He came with the great sound of trumpets, here He
comes weeping over the city of Jerusalem; there He came
with fear, here He comes with consolation, joy, and love;
there He spoke: 'Whosoever toucheth the Mount shall be
surely put to death', here He says: 'Tell the daughter of Zion,
her king cometh unto her'. Behold, herein findest thou the
difference between the Law and the Gospel, to wit, that the
Law commands while the Gospel gives all things freely. The
Law causes anger and hate, the Gospel gives grace. At the
first advent the children of Israel fled before the voice of God,
but now our desire to hear it cannot be stilled, because it is
so sweet. Therefore, when ye are in anxiety and tribulation,
ye shall not run to Mount Sinai, that is to say, look to the
Law for help, neither shall ye think that ye yourselves have
power to atone, but rather shall ye look for help in Jerusalem,
that is to say, in the Gospel which saith: 'Thy sins are for
given thee, go thy way, from henceforth sin no more'.

Sermon for Palm Sunday, 1522.   W.A. 10. III. 67.

4

But when the fulness of the time came, God sent forth his Son, born of a woman, born under the Law.
GALATIANS iv. 4.

Because the Law can give us neither justification nor faith, and nature with all its toil can gain us nothing, St. Paul now preaches Him who in our stead has won for us such faith, and who is a master in justification, for justification did not come to us easily, but at great cost, namely, it was paid by God's own Son. Hence the Apostle writes 'when the fulness of the time came', that is, when the time of our bondage had come to an end.

For the Jews that time was fulfilled with Christ's advent in the flesh, and in like manner it is still being fulfilled in our daily life, whenever a man is illumined through faith, so that his serfdom and toil under the Law come to an end. For Christ's advent in the flesh would be useless, unless it wrought in us such a spiritual advent of faith. And verily, for this reason He came in the flesh, that He might bring about such an advent in the spirit. For unto all who before or after believed in Him thus coming in the flesh, even to them He is come. Wherefore, in virtue of such faith, to the fathers of old His coming was ever present.

From the beginning of time to the end of the world everything must needs depend upon this coming in the flesh, whereby man is set free from bondage, whensoever, wheresoever, and in whomsoever such faith is wrought. And the fulness of time is come for every man when he begins to believe in Christ as the One whose advent was promised before all times and who has now come.

Sermon for the Sunday after   W.A. 10. I (i). 352 ff.
Christmas, 1522.

Lift up your heads, O ye gates; and be ye lift up, ye everlasting doors; and the King of glory shall come in. PSALM xxiv. 7.

Hail, amen! That selfsame glory is hidden, therefore to Him the gates are locked, and no man desires to let Him in. Those in high places resist Him with all their strength, but it does not help them. He is a mighty king of the Cross, yet under this very Cross His glory is hidden.

'Who is the king of glory?' Thus it will happen to Him: 'Who', they will say, 'is this heretic, this stirrer-up of the people?' By such names do they call the king. Who is the king of glory? They speak these words with bitterest scorn, and show the greatest contempt for that king. How absurd a thing it is that He is called a king of glory!

Christ still comes, in those who are the least of His servants, to those who are the greatest of this world; in those who are despised, to those who are praised; in His fools, to the wise. But not only do they keep Him out and shut the door, they even hunt Him down and scoff at Him; they still oppose Christ and His word, but they will never overpower Him. For He is the Lord Sabaoth, the Lord of Hosts. He is now the king of glory, for He remains the king of glory eternally, and the heavenly hosts and the saints on earth worship and serve Him.

Exposition of the first 25   W.A. 31. I. 373.
Psalms, 1530.

> *But as many as received him, to them gave he power*
> *to become the sons of God, even to them that believe*
> *on his name.* JOHN i. 12.

Here ye hear what a great glory is wrought by the Son of God in His advent amongst those who receive Him, have faith in Him, and believe Him to be the man sent by God to help the world. This is to be the new work and way, that He shall give the power and the right to become children of God even unto them who believe in His name.

There thou hast it in sum and substance, that by no other way, manner, or means may we come to such high honour, such wondrous freedom and power, as to be made children of God, save alone through the knowledge of Christ, and through faith in Him. This glory is preached and offered unto us year by year, and day by day, and it is so great that no man, whoever he may be, can meditate enough upon it, much less tell it in his own words—that we, through our first birth from the time of Adam, poor, condemned, and miserable sinners should come to this high honour and glory, that the eternal and almighty God should be our Father and we His children, Christ our brother and we His joint-heirs, and that the dear angels should be—not our masters—but our servants and our brothers. Lo, it is so great and overwhelming that any man who ponders it deeply is so astounded that he says: 'Beloved, can it be so, and is it true?'

Therefore the Holy Ghost must needs be Master in this matter. He must write this knowledge in our hearts, and witness to our minds, that it is Yea and Amen, that we through faith in Christ are children of God, now and for evermore.

Exposition of John i, 1537.   W.A. 46. 610 f.

Second Week in Advent

HE COMETH AT THE JUDGEMENT DAY

Sunday: LUKE xxi. 25–36

*For the Lord himself shall descend from heaven with
a shout, with the voice of the archangel, and with the
trump of God: and the dead in Christ shall rise first.*
1 THESSALONIANS iv. 16.

When such a voice and the last trump of God resound, the
sun and the moon and all the creatures will cry: 'Strike them
dead, dear Lord, strike them dead!' There are the godless
who know Thee not, and the false confessors who obey not
the word of Christ; they have all blasphemed Thy Name;
on earth they have persecuted Thy saints and have killed
them. Strike them dead, it is high time. Make an end of the
woe and the wickedness! For there will be a terrible and
unheard-of tempest, the like of which has never been since
the beginning of the world, and all creatures will run wild
with fear because the end is upon them.

The thunders which occur now are but a prelude of that
last thunder which will make the whole world pass away,
whereat all creatures shall cry: 'Yea and Amen!' For that will
be the true war and battle which Christ in His glory will
wage against all the devils in hell and all the godless on earth,
the battle in which He will dash in pieces with lightning and
with thunder all His adversaries. Then will be fulfilled the
word which He spake: 'And he gave him authority to execute
judgement because He is the Son of man' (John v. 27).

Sermons from the year 1545.   W.A. 49. 740.

8

And take heed to yourselves, lest at any time your hearts be overcharged with surfeiting, and drunkenness, and the cares of this life, and so that day come upon you unawares. LUKE xxi. 34.

God in His great mercy does not will that the Day of Judgement should suddenly overtake us, wherefore in His grace He honours us with a merciful warning. He causes His word to be preached unto us, He calls us to repentance, and offers us in Christ forgiveness of all our sins. He gives a sure promise that pain and guilt shall be abolished if we believe in His Son; He commands us to continue in our calling and to do our work well. If we obey Him therein, He in no way grudges us food and drink, and that we are happy and of good cheer. For eat and drink we must if we are to live on this earth. But we must not be forgetful of God and the life to come. Is not He a good and holy God, in that He looks on us with so fatherly a love? He ever speaks to us like a father to his children, and He says: 'Dear children, repent; believe in My Son whom I have sent unto you. Be holy and obedient, and faithful servants in your work; thereafter eat and drink, and use the earthly goods with which I have blessed you. But take care that you use the world and its passing goods like a man who is awaiting the last trump; so that when it peals and when the last thunders resound you are prepared and ready, walking in holy ways and with a godly spirit. If you live like that, you are in no danger'.

Sermons from the year 1545. W.A. 49. 743.

9

Thy kingdom come.   MATTHEW vi. 10.

This prayer does two things: it humbles us and it uplifts us.

It *humbles* us in that it makes us confess openly that God's kingdom is not yet come to us. The which, if it is earnestly contemplated and thoughtfully prayed, is a dreadful thing to us, and will grieve and pain every devout heart; for it follows that we are still cast out, bereft of our most beloved fatherland. These are two woeful and deplorable losses: the first, that God the Father is bereft of His kingdom in us, that He who is and should be Lord of everything, should through us alone be kept from such lofty power and honour. This must without doubt pain all who love God well and truly. The other loss is ours: that we should still be kept in misery, in foreign lands amongst such mighty foes.

Further, when such thoughts have humbled us and have made our wretchedness manifest unto us, *consolation* follows, and our kind Master, the Lord Christ, teaches us that we should ask and crave to be taken out of that wretchedness, and not despair; for those who confess that they themselves are hindering God's kingdom from coming, and plaintively pray that it may come, God will reward for their sufferings and prayers.

And that is why we do not pray: Let us come to Thy kingdom, as if we should run after it; but thus: Thy kingdom come to us. For the grace of God and His kingdom, with all the virtues thereof, must come to us, if ever we are to inherit it. Of ourselves we can never come to the kingdom, just as Christ came from heaven to us who are on earth, and we did not ascend from earth into heaven, to Him.

When God reigns in us and we are His kingdom, that is blessedness.

Exposition of the Lord's Prayer for   W.A. 2. 95 f.
simple lay-folk.

And when these things begin to come to pass, then look up, and lift up your heads; for your redemption draweth nigh. LUKE xxi. 28.

Behold, this is the true Master, who can interpret the signs aright, not like astrologers and fortune-tellers, who read nothing but evil in them, and so frighten people. For He tells nothing but good. And in those signs, which unto wit and world betoken but destruction, which man must flee and fear, He can discern all that is good, and can find there that blessed word 'your redemption', and so have a comforting picture for which the heart should long above all things. For what else mean these words 'your redemption' than that thou who art now in bondage under the might of Satan, who attacks thee with all his arrows so that thou art beset and oppressed by the world, and holden in all manner of peril and want, out of which neither thou thyself nor any man may help thee, shalt be saved and set free by thy Lord Christ in heaven, and shalt be brought where thou wilt be a master over devil, hell, and death, so that they all must lie at thy feet? Why then shouldst thou be afraid of those signs and fear them? Why shouldst thou not rather greet them most happily?

But this comfort we should willingly receive, that we know that He will surely come and showeth by these signs that He is nigh.

Sermon for the second Sunday in Advent, 1531.　　　　　W.A. 34. II. 470 ff.

Let us walk honestly, as in the day.   ROMANS xiii. 13.

No man does dark deeds while it is day; every man would stand abashed before his neighbour. Hence all men appear to be honest. Men say: 'Night knoweth no shame'. This is true and is the reason why we do by night deeds at which we should blush by day. The day is chaste and makes us to walk in the way of honour. Likewise also should a Christian live his life and so behave that he need feel no shame at any of his works, even though all the world should see them. For if a man's life and works are such that he is loath to let his deeds be seen or heard openly, and before every man, of a truth he is not living the Christian life.

Hereby thou seest how needful is such an exhortation and warning to be wakeful and to put on the armour of light. How many true Christians may there be found at this moment who could suffer all their doings to come to light? But what manner of Christian life is it that we hypocrites live, if we cannot suffer to have our ways laid open before our neighbours, when, of a truth, they are long since laid bare before God, and His angels and all creatures, and at the Day of Judgement will be known to every man? Therefore a Christian should live as he would wish to be known by all men and at the Last Day. (Ephesians v. 8): Walk as children of light.

Sermon for the first Sunday in   W.A. 10. I (ii). 13.
Advent, 1522.

*And then shall that Wicked be revealed, whom the
Lord shall consume with the spirit of his mouth, and
shall destroy with the brightness of his coming.*
                              2 THESSALONIANS ii. 8.

Thus do the Christians, that little band, following their
Lord and Master, speak even today unto the devil: 'Satan,
get thee hence! for it is written: thou shalt worship the Lord
thy God, and him only shalt thou serve'. That is to say, the
Word of God is always with them, they live in it, they study
it unceasingly, reading, teaching, preaching, punishing,
exhorting, comforting, and the like, whereby they have
wrought so much amongst the chosen people of God that
henceforth that people trusts no longer in any self-appointed
work or services however wondrous be their name, however
radiant their light. Henceforth they build on God's unfathomable grace and mercy alone which are promised and
made manifest to us in Christ. . . .

Thus is slain the spiteful fiend by the breath which cometh
forth from the mouth of God, which is the Word preached
by His ministers. This, I say, is going forth now and for evermore until the blessed hour of our final redemption for which
we wait.

We all who have the mind of Christ hope that this same
joyful and comforting appearance of the glory of the great
God and of our Saviour Jesus Christ (who is now weak, poor,
and disdained, and in His followers is more and more mocked,
blasphemed, spat upon, crucified, and slain) is nigh and at
our door, and that there will be an end to the numberless
horrors. In His appearing Christ, who is our life and our hope,
will manifest and reveal Himself as we now preach and believe
Him to be. That is, He will save us from the woe and
wretchedness, which we, because we confess His precious
Word and holy Name, must now suffer both in body and
soul, from the evil and deceitful world, and from its father,
the devil, and the Antichrist, which causes nought but sin,
and provokes sheer destruction.

Sermons from the year 1537.   W.A. 45. 43 f.

> *Let your loins be girded about, and your lights burning.* LUKE xii. 35.

He who sets out on a journey must lay aside his long, wide garments; he must gird his loins, for thus Christ speaks: 'Be ye prepared and attentive to the game, have candles alight in your hands, be cunning and skilful, for there is nothing certain. Death comes to your homestead, but the hour thereof remains unknown to you. Work as if ye were to live without end, yet be of such a mind as if ye were going to die at this hour. Such is the true meaning of the girding of our loins, that we live in expectation of Christ, the Bridegroom. But such teaching casts us down, and calls us to repentance. For there will be no man thus prepared that he may expect the Day of the Lord with a joyful heart. We love so dearly our most wicked foe the flesh, that we do not wish to die.

And if thou dost not yet know that thou art not thus girded, cry to thy God and sigh unto Him, and He will forgive thee; whereas those that despise His Word and are sure of themselves God will not forgive; nay, of a truth, He will count their wickedness unto them for evil. God can suffer weakness, but wickedness and contempt He cannot endure. Therefore, who perceiveth that he is not thus inclined, let him confess unto God and pray for His help, that we may become thus girded; and God will forgive him and help him graciously.

Sermons from the year 1537.   W.A. 45. 384 ff.

Third Week in Advent

THE GOSPEL IS PREACHED TO THE POOR

Sunday: MATTHEW xi. 2–10

The blind receive their sight, and the lame walk, the lepers are cleansed, and the deaf hear, the dead are raised up, and the poor have the gospel preached to them. MATTHEW xi. 5.

We should diligently mark these words of Christ and His kingdom, and should let their peal ring on amongst us, namely, that Christ has such a kingdom and is such a King that He wills to help poor wretched people in body and in soul, and without Him not all the world with all its might and means can help. For never before has there been such a doctor with such skill, that he could make the lepers clean, and cause the blind to see. Just as there was never before a preacher who could preach the Gospel to the poor, that is, who could turn and point to himself the sad and wretched, and affrighted souls, and succour them and give them comfort, and fill with joy the fearful hearts, which before were drowned in heaviness and sorrow.

This is the good and happy news, that Christ has paid for our sin, and through His suffering has redeemed us from eternal death. It is His kingdom and His ministry, to preach the Gospel to the poor; that is His purpose. For to the great and holy He cannot come. They do not wish to be counted sinners, and therefore do not need His Gospel.

Sermon for the third Sunday in Advent, 1544. W.A. 52. 24 ff.

And the angel answered and said unto her, The Holy Ghost shall come upon thee, and the power of the Highest shall overshadow thee: therefore also that holy thing which shall be born of thee shall be called the Son of God. LUKE i. 35.

These words the angel spoke to the saintly Virgin, so that she should rejoice in the Babe and cast off all fear and sorrow. Yet these words do not apply to the Virgin only, but also to us. Wherefore, although this saintly Virgin is alone the mother of the child, we too belong under His rule and kingdom. Otherwise we should fare ill. All that is ours passes away and lasts but a short while. For what are forty years, or fifty, or even a hundred? But with a man who belongs to an everlasting kingdom all is well, and it is fitting that he should dance through life for evermore.

Thus the angel's saying reminds us of our passing life, wherein there are so many dangers, sin and death, and helps us to endure it, in that he shows us a kingdom the like of which is never come on earth, an everlasting kingdom which has no end.

Sermons from the year 1544. W.A. 52. 639 f.

That which we have seen and heard declare we unto you. 1 JOHN i. 3.

Thus, then, is Christ, our Lord, true God and true Man whom the Father has appointed and ordained thereunto. For He is to be the chief source and fountain from which spring grace and truth, and justice, in order that we may receive and enjoy grace and truth from Him and may be given by Him grace for grace and truth for truth. 'He is the man', saith the Evangelist, 'whom we have seen, heard, and touched, with our eyes, ears and hands; and by His words and deeds we have perceived that He is the Word of Life, and the unspeakable fountain of all truth and grace'. If any man desires to partake of it, be he Abraham, Moses, Elijah, Isaiah, John the Baptist, or whosoever he be, let him come here and receive it from Him, and from no other man; otherwise he will be lost eternally. For we all without exception, saith the Evangelist, 'received from His fulness grace for grace and truth for truth'. Thus all Holy Writ points from the beginning to the end to Christ alone, and directs our minds to Him, and makes in this matter no mention of all the other saints, in whom we might seek and find grace and truth. If any man attains to grace and truth, it is the fulness of Christ that does it. Our morsels, drops, bits, and pieces will not do it.

Exposition of John i.   W.A. 46. 643.

He made himself of no reputation, and took upon him
the form of a servant, and was made in the likeness of
men. PHILIPPIANS ii. 7.

The soul may not and must not find contentment in any
other thing but in the highest Good, which has made her
and is the fountain of her life and blessedness. Therefore God
wills to be the One to whom the soul shall cleave and in whom
she shall believe. Neither is there aught but God alone to
whom belongs the honour that all creatures should believe
in Him. Therefore God is come and was made Man, and has
sacrificed Himself for man, has drawn him to Himself and
called him by His name, that he should believe in Him. For
God did not need to come and be made Man, but rather was
it needful and profitable for us.

God's nature is too high and incomprehensible for us.
Therefore for our good He submitted Himself to the nature
which is best known to us, that is, our own. There He waits
for us, and there He may be found, and nowhere else. Here
is the throne of grace from which no man will ever be shut
out, if he only comes.

Sermons from the year 1526.　　　　　W.A. 10. I (ii). 354.

Though the Lord be high, yet hath he respect unto the lowly. PSALM cxxxviii. 6.

Behold the picture painted here of God, who makes known to us His true nature in that it shows Him as looking *downward*. *Upward* He cannot look, for there is nought above Him; *beside* Him He cannot look, for there is nought like unto Him. Therefore He can only look downward, beneath Himself. Wherefore, the simpler and the lowlier thou art, the brighter do God's eyes see thee.

In short, this verse teaches us rightly to understand God's nature in that it shows Him as looking down upon the lowly and despised, and he knows God aright who knows that He looks upon the lowly. From such knowledge springs forth love of God and faith in Him, so that we willingly abandon ourselves to Him and follow Him.

The truly humble never think of the result of their humility, but with a simple heart they look at what is lowly, live gladly with it, and are never aware of their own humility. But the hypocrites wonder why their honour lingers so long on the way; and their hidden and deceitful pride is not content with humble ways, but secretly they think higher and higher of themselves. Therefore a truly humble soul never knows of her own humility, for if she knew, she would be proud because she is aware of that noble virtue within her. But with her heart and mind and all her senses she cleaves to the lowly things, for she has them unceasingly before her eyes. They are the images which dwell with her, and while she keeps her eyes on them, she cannot keep them on herself or be aware of herself.

Sermons from the year 1523.   W.A. 12. 612.

Blessed is he, whosoever shall not be offended in me.
MATTHEW xi. 6.

Yea, truly blessed! For this King and His Word, in which men should find great joy, are a stumbling-block for all the world. The world takes offence and is provoked by the Gospel of Christ, because it will not trust in the grace of God, but rather in its own works and merits. And again the world takes offence at Christ because He is so utterly poor and wretched. And again, that, as He carries His cross and lets Himself be hanged upon it, He admonishes His followers to take their cross and to follow Him through all manner of temptations and afflictions. To this the world is especially hostile.

Thus is our dear Lord Christ everywhere in the world an annoying preacher. The Gospel will never fare otherwise. It is and it will be a message at which offence is taken, not by the lowly, but by the most saintly and most pious, the wisest and the mightiest on earth, as experience teaches us. Blessed are those who know and trust that it is truly the Word of God, for they are healed, and they are comforted and fortified against all such offence.

Sermon for the third Sunday in   W.A. 52. 27 ff.
Advent, 1544.

Rejoice in the Lord alway: and again I say, Rejoice.
PHILIPPIANS iv. 4.

Such joy is the fruit and the consequence of faith. Where there is no faith, there is sheer fright, flight, dread, and wretchedness, when God is remembered or named. Yea, in such a heart are hatred and enmity against God, because it finds itself guilty in its conscience, and the soul cannot believe that God is good and gracious unto her, because she knows that He hates sin and punishes it severely. And if thou wouldst talk to such a soul about great joy in the Lord, it would be like telling water to catch fire. None but the just and righteous souls can joy in God, the Lord. Therefore is this epistle not written for sinners, but for saints. Sinners must first be taught how they can be freed from sin, and receive the grace of God. Then the joy will follow of its own accord as soon as they are rid of their bad conscience.

But what is the promise of the Gospel other than this: that Christ is given unto us in order that He take upon Him our sin? When such faith in God's Word lives truly in our hearts, God becomes to us dear and sweet, for the heart now trusts fully and feels there is nought but grace and favour with Him, and dreads His punishment no longer. But it is filled with hope and confidence that God has given in Jesus Christ such surpassing grace. Therefore from such faith must follow love, joy, peace, singing, thanksgiving and praise, and man must feel a great and hearty joy in God as his dearest and most gracious father. Behold, of such joy speaketh St. Paul here. And that is why he calleth it a joy in God, the Lord.

Sermon for the fourth Sunday in   W.A. 10. I (ii). 170 f.
Advent, 1522.

Fourth Week in Advent

THE FORERUNNER

Sunday: JOHN i. 19–28

Thou, child, shalt be called the prophet of the Highest.
LUKE i. 76.

Because Christ was to come in such simplicity, without splendour and ostentation of which our worldly hearts are so very fond, so that the world might be won through His Word and wondrous deeds, and not by muskets, swords, and earthly power, He sent (as Moses and all the prophets, priests, and Levites tell us) not an angel but a man. This man's name was John, who was more than a prophet (as Christ testifies of him), who came not of his own accord, but was sent from God. And he was sent before the Lord, that he should knock at the hearts of the Jews, and awaken them, and testify to the Lord, saying: 'Open gates and doors, for He is come, your Saviour, for whom you have been waiting so long. Awake! Behold the light, which was with God from the beginning and was eternal God, and is now Man, and is present here. Take heed and let not this thing pass you by'.

Therefore he has a precious name the which is John, which means: full of grace. And he could not be called by any random name like other people, but by a name which signifies his message, and bears with it what it indicates, like all the names which God has made and given. And likewise was His own beloved Son not in vain called Jesus, but because He should deliver His people from their sins. And for that self-same reason John hath not been given his name for his own person's sake, but that it should make manifest his testimony and ministry.

Exposition of John i.   W.A. 46. 573.

22

*He was not that Light, but was sent to bear witness
of that Light.* JOHN i. 8.

I do not reject John the Baptist, I honour him, and I exalt
him highly. But I must make a difference between him and
his ministry and life, and Christ to whom he testifies. He is a
bondman and a servant, not the Lord. He points and leads
to the true light, but is not the light itself. His ministry is
greater and nobler than that of all the prophets, for he not
only prophesies about the coming of the Lord, that He will
come sooner or later; the rather he points to Him at this
moment with his finger: Lo, this is He.

Therefore I think so highly of his ministry, and I give
thanks to God, our beloved Father, that He has given unto
us so faithful a witness, so blessed a mouth and finger to testify
before us to the true light, and lead us thither, that through
that selfsame light we may be enlightened, and that it may
shine radiantly in our hearts for evermore. Behold the man,
who points with his finger to the Lord, the Lamb of God.

But as for my salvation, I will not and I cannot trust in
John, neither can I cling to his holiness, his austere living and
his saintly works; for he is not God's Christ (as he himself
confesses) who is alone the light and life of men. He is a witness to the light, and he helps us through his ministry to
become children of the light. Therefore he shines like a
radiant and lovely light.

Exposition of John i.   W.A. 46. 590.

Prepare ye the way of the Lord, make his paths straight.   MATTHEW iii. 3.

This, then, is the way made straight for Christ, and this is the true ministry of John, that he shall humble men and tell them that they are all sinners, lost, and condemned, poor, miserable creatures, and that there is no life, nor work, nor standing so holy, great, and good, that it is not under condemnation, unless Christ dwell, and work, and walk therein, and both is and does all things through His faith. And they all need Christ Jesus and should earnestly desire to partake of His grace.

Behold, where this is preached, that all the work of man and all his life is counted nought, there sounds the true voice of John in the desert, and the pure and full truth of Christian teaching, as Paul says (Romans iii. 23): 'They have all sinned, and come short of the glory of God', which means that man is completely humbled, that his pride is cut out from his heart and altogether abolished. And this may truly be called the straightening of the path for our Lord, making the rough places plain for Him, and making way for Him.

Sermon for the fourth Sunday in   W.A. 10. I (ii). 198.
    Advent, 1522.

WITH EAGER ZEAL, O MAN, PREPARE IN THEE THINE HEART

Repent ye: for the kingdom of heaven is at hand.
MATTHEW iii. 2.

If ye would know: I am the voice calling, I am the angel which is sent before the Lord to announce to you that you are to prepare and to make straight the way for Him, the Lord, who is following close after me. Lay, then, aside all that may hinder His way. Put away the gross and open sins, but above all the sins of the spirit which have the appearance of holiness but which most impede His coming to you. Receive Him with rejoicing, obey Him and believe in Him, and come to be baptised. If you do this, you will be blessed by God, will receive the forgiveness of your sins, and will truly become His people, saved and holy. But if you will not let yourselves be taught, intending rather to abide by your old nature, all hope will be gone, and your doom will be upon you before you expect it. For the axe lies not beneath the bench, neither does it hang on the wall, 'but even now it is laid at the root of the tree'.

Thus the man to whom I point and witness is not so weak and contemptible as you may think. Verily, I say unto you: He is stronger than I am. He is so great and holy that 'I am not worthy to unloose the latchet of His shoes', for He Himself is God, the Lord. Behold, He comes to you full of grace, that He may help you out of all your need and make you just and blessed. If ye receive Him, all will be well with you; if not, He will soon finish with you.

Sermons from the year 1540.   W.A. 49. 114 f.

Behold the Lamb of God, which taketh away the sin of the world. JOHN i. 29.

Herewith begins the other part of St. John's teaching where he turns the people away from himself towards Christ, saying: 'Behold the Lamb of God, which taketh away the sin of the world'. Through my teaching, he says, I have first made you sinners, condemning all your works, and telling you that you must despair of yourselves. But in order that you should not likewise despair of God, behold, I will now show you how you can rid yourselves of all your sins and attain salvation.

Strip yourselves free from sin, you cannot; neither can you make yourselves holy through good works. That is another man's work. I cannot do it either, but I can point to Him who can. He is this Jesus Christ, the Lamb of God. He, and He alone, and no one else in heaven and on earth, takes sin upon Himself, so fully that even thou canst not atone for the smallest sin. He must take upon Himself alone not only *thy* sin, but the *whole world's* sin; not some of the world's sin, but all the sins of the world, be they great or small, many or few. This, then, is preaching and hearing the true Gospel, and behold the finger of John, that he may show thee the Lamb of God.

And if thou canst believe that this voice of John is a harbinger of truth, and follow the direction of his finger, and behold the Lamb of God bearing thy sin, thou hast won the victory, thou art become a Christian, a master over sin and death, and hell, and all things. Thereby thy conscience is gladdened, and thou wilt love the gentle Lamb of God.

Sermon for the fourth Sunday in   W.A. 10. I (ii). 206 f.
Advent, 1522.

And without controversy great is the mystery of godliness: God was manifest in the flesh, justified in the Spirit, seen of angels, preached unto the Gentiles, believed on in the world, received up into glory.

1 TIMOTHY iii. 16.

O, what a ridiculous thing, that the one true God, the high Majesty, should be made man; that here they should be joined, man and his Maker, in one Person. Reason opposes this with all its might.

Here, then, those wise thoughts with which our reason soars up towards heaven to seek out God in His own Majesty, and to probe out how He reigns there on high, are taken from us. The goal is fixed elsewhere, so that I should run from all the corners of the world to Bethlehem, to that stable and that manger where the babe lies, or to the Virgin's lap. Yes, that subdues the reason.

Do not search what is too high for thee. But here it comes down before my eyes, so that I can see the babe there in His Mother's lap. There lies a human being who was born like any other child, and lives like any other child, and shows no other nature, manner, and work than any other human being, so that no heart could guess that the creature is the Creator. Where, then, are all the wise men? Who could ever have conceived this or thought it out? Reason must bow, and must confess her blindness in that she wants to climb to heaven to fathom the Divine, while she cannot see what lies before her eyes.

Sermons from the year 1533. W.A. 37. 42 f.

Christmas

THE WORD WAS MADE FLESH

In the morning of December the Twenty-fourth

*And she brought forth her firstborn son, and wrapped
him in swaddling clothes, and laid him in a manger;
because there was no room for them in the inn.*

LUKE ii. 7.

Behold, how simply these things happen on earth, and yet
they are so highly esteemed in heaven. On earth it happens
thus: there is a poor young wife, Mary, at Nazareth, thought
nothing of and regarded as one of the lowliest women in the
town. No one is aware of the great wonder that she bears.
And she herself keeps silent, does not pride herself, and thinks
she is the lowliest woman in the town. She goes up with
Joseph, her master. They have probably neither man-servant
nor maid-servant, but he is master and servant, and she is
mistress and maid. Perhaps they left their homestead to look
after itself, or they may have given it into a neighbour's care.

As they are thus drawing nigh to Bethlehem, the Evangelist
presents them to us as the most wretched and disdained of all
the pilgrims, being forced to give way to everyone, till at last
they are turned out into a stable, and made to share shelter,
table, and bedchamber with the beasts, while many a wicked
man sits in the inn above and is treated like a lord. Not a soul
notices and knows what God is doing in that stable. He leaves
empty the manors and stately chambers, and leaves the people
to their eating and drinking, and their good cheer. But this
comfort and great treasure remains hidden from them.

O, what a thick, black darkness was over Bethlehem then,
that she failed to apprehend so great a light! How truly God
shows that He has no regard for the world and its ways, and
again, how the world shows that it has no regard for God, for
what He is, and has, and does.

Sermon for Christmas, 1522.   W.A. 10. I (i). 62 ff.

On Christmas Eve

LUKE ii. 1–20

Fear not: for, behold, I bring you good tidings of great joy, which shall be to all people. For unto you is born this day in the city of David a Saviour, which is Christ the Lord. LUKE ii. 10-11.

The little word 'you' should make us joyful. For unto whom does He speak? Unto wood or stones? Nay, verily, He speaks unto men; and not unto one or two, but unto all the people. How then shall we understand these words? Shall we yet doubt the grace of God and say: 'St. Peter and St. Paul may well rejoice that their Saviour is come, but I may not, I am a wretched sinner; the dear and precious treasure is not for me!'? My friend, if thou wilt say: He is not mine, then shall I say: Whose is He then? Has He come to save geese and ducks and cows? Thou must look here who He is. If He had come to save another creature, yea, of a truth, He had assumed the likeness of that creature. But now He hath been made the Son of Man.

And who art thou, and who am I? Are we not likewise sons of men? Yea verily, we are! Who, then, but men should receive this child? The angels do not need Him. The devils do not want Him. But we need Him, and for our sake was He made Man. Thus it behoves us to receive Him joyfully, as here the angels say: 'Unto you is born a Saviour'. Is it not a great and marvellous thing that an angel should come from heaven with such good news? and that afterwards so many thousands of angels are filled with overflowing joy, which makes them desire that we should also be glad, and should receive such grace with thankful hearts? And therefore we should write this little word (with flaming letters) in our hearts: 'For You!' and should joyfully welcome the birth of this Saviour.

Sermon for Christmas Day, 1544.   W.A. 52. 46.

Christmas Day

The Word was made flesh. JOHN i. 14.

Christ has a holy birth, immaculate and pure. Man's birth is unclean, sinful, and accursed, and man can only be helped through the holy birth of Christ. Yet Christ's birth cannot be shared out to us, nor would it help; but it is offered spiritually unto every man wherever the Word is preached. He who firmly believes and receives it will not suffer harm because of his own sinful birth.

That is the way we are cleansed of our wretched Adam's birth, and that is why it was Christ's will and pleasure to be born as man, so that in Him we might be born again. 'Of His own will He brought us forth by the Word of truth, that we should be reborn unto a new creation.' Behold, in this manner Christ takes our birth away from us and sinks it in His own birth and gives us His birth, that we may be made new and clean, as if it were our own birth. Therefore shall every Christian man rejoice in this birth of Christ, and glory in it, as if he too were born of Mary. He who does not believe that, or doubts it, is no Christian.

O, this is the great joy of which the angel speaks. This is God's comfort and His surpassing goodness, that man (if he believeth) may glory in such a treasure, that Mary be his very Mother, Christ his Brother, and God his Father. For all these things have truly happened that we might believe in them.

See, then, that thou make this birth thine own and dost change with Him, so that thou mayest be rid of thy birth, and mayest take over His, which comes to pass if thou believest. Thus dost thou surely sit in the Virgin Mary's lap, and art her darling child. But thou must learn to have such faith and to exercise it throughout thine earthly life, for it can never be strong enough.

Sermon for Christmas Day, 1522.   W.A. 10. I (i). 71.

The day after Christmas

Fear not! LUKE ii. 10.

Thereby is shown that this King is born unto those who live in fear and trembling, and such alone belong to His Kingdom. Unto them shall be preached, as the angels preached unto the poor, affrighted shepherds: 'Behold, I bring you good tidings of great joy'. And, of a truth, such joy is offered to all men, but only those can receive it who are affrighted in their consciences, and troubled in their hearts. These are they who belong to me and to my preaching, and unto them shall I bring good tidings. Is it not a wonderful thing that this joy is nearest to those whose conscience is the most restless?

The world is happy and of good cheer when it has loaves and fishes, means and money, power and glory. But a sad and troubled heart desires nothing but peace and comfort, that it may know whether God is graciously inclined towards it. And this joy, wherein a troubled heart finds peace and rest, is so great that all the world's happiness is nothing in comparison. Therefore should such good tidings be preached to wretched consciences as the angel preaches here: Hearken unto me, you of a sad and troubled heart, I bring you good tidings. For He hath not come down to earth and been made Man, that He might cast you into hell, much less was He for that end crucified and given over unto death for you. But He has come, that with great joy ye might rejoice in Him. And if thou wouldst truly define Christ and properly describe who and what He is, mark well the angel's word, how he defined and describes Him, saying that He is and is called: 'Great Joy'. O, blessed is the man who can well understand the meaning of this word, and hold it truly in his heart; for therein dwelleth strength.

Sermon for Christmas Day, 1531.   W.A. 34. II. 505.

THE HEART AND THE CHILD

*For unto us a child is born, unto us a son is given:
and the government shall be upon his shoulder: and
his name shall be called Wonderful, Counsellor, The
mighty God, the Everlasting Father, the Prince of
Peace.* ISAIAH ix. 6.

This Child is sent to fill thine heart, and for no other reason
is He born. And when the heart thus gives itself up through
faith, it finds what His name is, namely this: 'sweet Jesus'.
Thereafter the heart lifts itself up unto the Father, who in His
grace has given the Child into the heart. No word can say nor
understand that so small a thing should hold so great a
treasure. Thus the great and wonderful sign is repeated and
the heart is made sweet and glad and fearless, for it is at peace
with all the suffering that may befall it. For what should cause
it woe? Where the Child is, all will be well. The heart and
the Child cannot be parted.

But mark this well, that it is impossible for the heart to
receive the Child and taste His sweetness, unless it has first
cast out all earthly joy, all things that are not Christ's. The
Child will never suffer that the heart cares for anything else,
for He would dwell therein alone. We must part with all
things which are good in our sight: voluptuousness, love of
property, fame, our life, and piety, and wisdom, and all our
virtue. And when we have thus fully abandoned all that we
have, and have denied it to ourselves, then the Babe comes to us,
but He brings with Him everything that slays our old Adam.

Thou must bring to the Child a single soul, and he can best
do this who is cast down under much sadness, grief, and
suffering, and has nothing to his liking, in such a way that
he still bears willingly all adversities. Never will Christ be
sweet to thee, until thou hast first become bitter to thyself.
If a man feels not this within his heart, he may as well keep
away.

Sermon on the birth of Christ,   W.A. 7. 190 f.
Christmas Day, 1520.

HE BEHOLDETH THE LOWLY

He hath put down the mighty from their seats, and exalted them of low degree. LUKE i. 52.

How could God have revealed His lovingkindness more divinely than by sinking Himself so deeply into our flesh and blood, by not despising natural secrecy and by honouring nature most where Adam and Eve had most disgraced it?

All evil lust and all evil thoughts fall away, however strong they are, if we but turn our eyes to that nativity, beholding how the most high Majesty is creatively at work in the flesh and blood of such a lowly Virgin. As deeply as she is despised on earth, so highly, yea, a thousand times higher, is she glorified in heaven.

Behold, how very greatly God glorifies those who are despised by men and who rejoice therein. Open thine eyes and see what the Lord beholds! Only downward doth He gaze into the deepest lowliness, as it is written: 'He is throned above the Cherubim and gazeth into the deepest depth, even into the abyss'.

Neither did the angels find princes or the mighty, but the untaught lay-people and the lowliest on earth. Might they not have brought their message to the high priest, the scholars at Jerusalem who have so much to tell about God and the angels? No, not they, but the poor shepherds were found worthy of such great grace and honour from heaven, they, who on earth have no honour. Yea, verily, God casteth out all that is lofty.

Sermon for Christmas, 1522.   W.A. 10. I (i). 68 ff.

SIMEON

*Then took he him up in his arms, and blessed God,
and said, Lord, now lettest thou thy servant depart
in peace, for mine eyes have seen thy salvation.*
LUKE ii. 28–30.

Simeon is old, sees death before him, yea, he feels death
in his very bones, in every limb, as death approaches day by
day, and daily he grows weaker after the manner of old people. But it does not grieve him. He desires only that it be soon,
says that he is not affrighted by his departing, yea, that death
is welcome unto him, since his eyes have seen his Saviour.
For were this not so, there could be no joy, nor could there
be happiness in dying. Therefore the godly Simeon wanted
to warn every man and to lead us thither (because we must
all confess that we need a Saviour), that we should accept
Christ Jesus, whom our fancy has not created but whom God
Himself has ordained. For with His help we cannot fail. For
this reason alone the child is come. God, His heavenly
Father, has prepared Him for us, that He shall help us. And,
of a truth, if any man possesses this Saviour, who is God's
Saviour, that man is still and peaceful in his heart.

It all depends on this, that we with the dear old Simeon
open our eyes and see the Babe, take Him into our arms, and
kiss Him, which means, that He is our hope, joy, comfort,
and our life. For where this faith is firm and sure in our hearts,
that this Child is God's Saviour, there, of a truth, it must follow that the heart is content and is not afraid of sin or death,
for it has a Saviour who delivers it from them.

Sermons from the year 1544.   W.A. 52. 157.

UNTO YOU I HAVE GIVEN ALL MY GRACE

This is my beloved Son, in whom I am well pleased.
MATTHEW iii. 17.

With these words He says to us nought else than this: there I give unto you all My grace, love, and blessing, which I have in My heart and My power. For, that you may not and cannot doubt it in your minds, I offer unto you here—not Moses, nor a prophet, nor an angel, nor a saint, nor a treasure of gold and silver, not great earthly or heavenly gifts—but My beloved Son, that is: My very heart, the true, eternal fountain of all grace and good, which no angel nor any creature in heaven and on earth can fathom. He shall be the token and pledge of My grace and love against your sin and fear. And inasmuch as He is by birth and right the true heir and Lord of all the creatures, so shall ye in Him become my children and joint-heirs, and inherit all that He possesses in His power. For in addition to giving us His privilege, and inheritance which are His by nature, He has merited and bought us through suffering and death as our priest and bishop, that we may be His chosen children, and eternally joint-heirs of all His goods. What more could He have given or done for us, and what greater or better thing could man's heart desire or conceive?

Sermon on Holy Baptism,   E.A. 16. 85.
Epiphany, 1535.

The New Year

JESUS CHRIST THE SAME YESTERDAY, TODAY, AND FOR EVER

Morning of St. Sylvester's Day

HOLDING FAST OUR PROFESSION

Let us hold fast our profession. HEBREWS iv. 14.

And if I were to live another hundred years, and if I were given power by the grace of God to overcome all assaults, and assaulters, past, present, and future, I see very clearly that this would not establish peace for our descendants, for the devil is still alive and reigning. Therefore I crave for life no longer, and I pray that God may have mercy upon me in the hour of my death. And you, who come after us, pray too with great earnestness, preaching and teaching the Word of God with diligence. Keep God's little lantern alight. Take heed to the warning, be prepared, for you must expect at any moment that the devil may knock out a window-pane, or tear open roof and door, so that he may blow out the light.

Therefore be sober and vigilant; he does not sleep, nor take a holiday, and he will not die before the Judgement Day. You and I must die, but when we are dead he will remain what he always was, and he cannot stop his raging. May Christ, our Lord, who has bruised his head, come at long last and deliver us from his raging. Amen.

Faithful and earnest warning to devout and   w.a. 48. 226.
   God-fearing hearts.

39

ASCRIBE GREATNESS UNTO OUR GOD

*I will publish the name of the Lord: ascribe ye great-
ness unto our God.*   DEUTERONOMY xxxii. 3.

This means: I will sing a song beginning on a high note,
so high that no man on earth shall begin higher, nor sing
better. And my finest song and subject shall be God's first
command, that men should worship the one true God alone,
should fear and love Him from the heart, should trust in Him
and build on Him alone.

And thus my song runs: ascribe to the Lord all honour
and give to Him all praise, which means, that to the One,
True, Living God all praise and honour in heaven and on
earth belong. He alone is God above all gods, Lord above all
lords, the Maker of heaven and earth and the sea and all that
in them is, who holds in His hand all the kingdoms of the
earth. He lifts them up and casts them down as He pleases;
He gives the breath of life to all mankind; He shapes and
guides the inmost thoughts of the hearts of all kings and of
every man on earth, as He pleases. He alone is the giver of
all good gifts for body and soul, and without Him no man
can have body or life, wisdom or strength, health, power or
riches, or any good, or hold them for a moment.

Learn and remember this then, that we should give all
honour to Him alone, should earnestly look to Him for all
earthly gifts, and all spiritual help and comfort, give Him our
whole hearts, trust in Him for better, for worse, for life and
death, flee to Him in all temptations, seek Him in all distress
and grief, and call on Him alone. This is the highest and most
pleasing service.

None but the little company, the true believers, and the
saints on earth, give such glory to the Lord God. They trust
in Him with all their heart and build on Him. They know that
their every good comes from Him, and that they could not
stand before the devil for one moment, if Thou, O God,
didst not defend and preserve them.

Exposition of the Song of Moses, 1532.   E.A. 52. 404 f.

IN GOD ALONE WILL I PUT MY TRUST

The God of my rock, in him will I trust: he is my shield, and the horn of my salvation, my high tower, and my refuge, my saviour; thou savest me from violence. 2 SAMUEL xxii. 3.

I believe in God the Father, Maker of Heaven and earth. I put my trust in no man on earth, not even in myself, nor in any power, skill, possession, saintliness, or whatever else may be mine. I trust in no creature, whether in heaven or on earth. I regard and put my trust in the One, True, Invisible, and Incomprehensible God alone, the Maker of heaven and earth, who is above all creatures. And again I do not take fright at the wickedness of the devil and his band, for my God is above them all. I believe not less in God even though I am abandoned or persecuted by all men. I believe none the less, though I am poor, foolish, untaught, and despised, and lacking all things. I believe none the less, although I am a sinner. For this my faith must hover above all that is and is not, above sin and virtue and above all things, so that it remains immaculate and pure in God, as the first commandment urges.

Neither do I entreat Him for a sign or token, for I would not tempt Him. I trust continually in Him, however long He tarries, and I set Him no term nor time, no measure nor means, but in a true and trusting faith I leave all things to His divine will.

Since He is almighty, what could I want, that He would not give or do for me? Since He is the Maker of heaven and earth, and Lord of all things, who will rob me or do me harm? Yea, why should not all things work together for my good, since I have found favour with Him, to whom they all are subject in obedience?

Because He is God, then, He is able to make all things work for my good. Because He is Father, He desires to do so and gladly does it . . . .

A short form of the Apostles' Creed, 1520. W.A. 7. 215 f.

January the Second

Whether we live, we live unto the Lord; and whether we die, we die unto the Lord; whether we live therefore, or die, we are the Lord's. ROMANS xiv. 8.

Yes, certainly, we are the Lord's, and this is our greatest joy and comfort, that we have as a Lord Him unto whom the Father has given all power in heaven and on earth, and into whose hands He has given all things. Who, then, can and will harm us? The devil may well rage with wrath, but he cannot tear us out of His hands. Further, are not we who believe in Jesus Christ our Lord, and live under His protection, also in Him and through Him, ourselves made lords over the devil, sin, and death? For He was made man for our sake (that He might win for us such lordship). For our sake He entreated the Father, and so loved us that He became a curse for us and gave Himself a sacrifice for us. With His dear blood He bought us and washed us clean from sin. And again He has given us in our hearts the pledge of our inheritance and salvation, the Holy Spirit, and has made us kings and priests before God. In short, He has made us children and heirs of God, and joint-heirs with Himself. Yes, truly, this is a faithful saying. O Lord, strengthen our faith and suffer us not to doubt Thy Word.

Comment on Romans xiv. 8.　　　　　　　　　W.A. 48. 206.

January the Third

THE LORD IS OUR STRENGTH

The Lord is my strength and song, and is become my salvation. PSALM cxviii. 14.

In nothing should we put our trust but in the Lord, who will be our strength, and will work all things in us. Therefore should we praise Him and thank Him, that He alone may be our song. So shall we truly be blessed in Him. It follows, that this Lord is Jesus Christ, true God, eternally born of the Father, and also true Man born of Mary, in the fulness of time, because He is here praised as our strength and power, our psalm and Saviour.

But Christ cannot be our strength until we, in our own selves, are made weak, and through much suffering crucified. Then He becomes our praise and song and psalm. Then follows victory, and salvation unto eternal life.

Comment on Psalm cxviii. 14.   W.A. 48. 65.

January the Fourth

THE TRUSTING HEART

I am the Lord thy God.   Exodus xx. 2.

That is: thou shalt have as thy God none but Me. What is the meaning of this word, and how is it to be understood? What does it mean to have a God? Or what is God? Answer: God is the One unto whom we should look for every good, and with whom we should seek refuge in all distress: thus, to have a God means nothing other than to trust Him and believe in Him with the whole heart. For this I have often said, it is the heart's trust and faith alone that makes both, God and idols. If your trust and faith are right, your God is right; and again, if your faith is wrong and false, the true God is not present. For these two, Faith and God, are inseparable, and wherein you put your heart and trust, that I say is properly your God.

Therefore this is the meaning of this commandment, that it demands of us true faith and trust of heart, which are directed to the one true God and which cleave to Him alone. It means: see that I alone am your God, and seek no other, that is to say: whatever good you may lack, look to Me and seek it from Me. And if you are weighed down by distress and woe, keep to Me and hold fast to Me. I, your Lord, will give unto you abundantly and help you out of every distress, if only you will set your heart on no other.

The Larger Catechism.   w.a. 30. I. 132 f.

Epiphany

KINGS AND PRIESTS

Ye are a chosen generation, a royal priesthood, an holy nation, a peculiar people; that ye should shew forth the praises of him who hath called you out of darkness into his marvellous light. 1 PETER ii. 9.

Thus it fares with a Christian: through faith he is so highly exalted above all things, that he becomes spiritually lord of them all. Nothing can jeopardise his salvation, but everything must be subject to him and help him towards his salvation. Not that we are made master of all things to possess them and to use them after the manner of this earth, for after the flesh we must all die, and no man may escape death. We are likewise subject to many other calamities, as we may see in Christ and His saints. For this is a sovereignty after the spirit, which reigns in us while we are still oppressed in the flesh, which means that I can use all things to purify and to uplift my soul. Even suffering and death must help towards my salvation. This is a high and wonderful excellence, and where there is nothing, however holy or evil, but it must serve for my good, that is, if I have faith and do not depend on these things but let my faith suffice. Such precious freedom and power do Christians enjoy.

But further, we are priests, which is more than kings, for priesthood makes us worthy to stand before God and to pray for others. For it behoves none but priests to stand before God. Thus Christ gained this privilege for us, so that we might stand and intercede for one another in spirit, as a priest stands before his people in the flesh making intercession.

Who then will fathom the honour and glory of a Christian? Through his kingdom he is a lord over all things, through his priesthood he has power over God, for God has promised to fulfil all that he asks and desires, as it is written in the Psalm (cxlv. 19): 'He will fulfil the desire of them that fear him'.

On the freedom of a Christian, 1520.   W.A. 7. 27 f.

WE BEHELD HIS GLORY

When they saw the star, they rejoiced with exceeding great joy. And . . . they presented unto him gifts; gold, and frankincense, and myrrh.

MATTHEW ii. 10–11.

The first thing that we should learn from this story . . . is that when the wise men went to search for Christ, the new-born king, they did not . . . find Him in Jerusalem. Indeed, if they were to find Him at all, they had need to listen to the Prophet Micah. Thereafter, when they had received the *Word* . . . they . . . took the road to Bethlehem. Thereupon God gave them the consolation that the star returned as soon as they had got outside Jerusalem, and it shone brightly before them right to Bethlehem, to the door where the Babe was. And, of a truth, they were in need of such a comfort, for they found nothing there but poverty and beggary. That is not Mary and Joseph's home; the Babe is lying in a manger; there is hardly a drink of water. Can this be in truth a king's abode?

But the saintly men are not misled. . . . Heedless of the poverty and wretchedness, they fall down before the Babe and worship Him, and open their treasures and present them to Him.

The second thing that we should learn from this story is how to bear ourselves aright towards our Lord Jesus Christ, that is, that we should cast aside all offence, and together with these wise men witness before the world to the Lord Christ, seek Him from the bottom of our hearts, and adore Him as our Saviour. And because His reign on earth is so poor and wretched, we should with our gold, goods, and whole possessions gladly help to further and increase His kingdom, which is in so many ways suppressed and hindered by the devil and the world. For on this very day we can still open to Christ our treasures and present them to Him, as the wise men did. And how? Behold, His word is written (Matthew xxv. 40): 'Inasmuch as ye have done it unto one of the least of these my brethren, ye have done it unto me'.

Sermon for Epiphany, 1544. W.A. 52. 92 f.

THE KINGDOM OF HEROD AND THE KINGDOM OF GOD

When Herod the king had heard these things, he was troubled, and all Jerusalem with him. MATTHEW ii. 3.

To all outward appearance Herod was a mighty king, fortunate in war. Wherever he struck with his sword, all went well. He was wise, keen-witted, powerful, and wealthy in trade with foreign lands. But in his house he was frail and weak, a hapless man. Thus Herod was outwardly fortunate but inwardly miserable. But Christ, our true king, was outwardly utterly poor, wretched, despised, and cast away; yet He was inwardly utterly filled with joy, comfort, and courage.

Now we must strive that Herod, who is outwardly and in the world so fortunate, steal not away from us our true and gracious king, which is Christ. Although He lies in a manger as a poor and wretched babe, we must go thither to Him.

Therefore, if we desire happiness and want a pure and happy conscience, we must forgo King Herod's manner of living and follow another king, which is Christ; and that means, that we must not be so bold as to seek justification through works, nor place our hopes therein, but that we must blazon on our hearts the image of Christ alone, the gracious Lord, who comes without any show. For when the three dear holy kings had left all human works behind and all help of man, and (trusting in the holy Word of God through Micah, the Prophet, v. 2) went forth towards Bethlehem, immediately they saw the star again.

Sermon from the year 1521. W.A. 7. 239 f.

TWOFOLD PERCEIVING

We beheld his glory. JOHN i. 14.

There is a twofold manner of hearing and seeing, one which comes to pass through our bodily ears and eyes alone, in which the spirit has no part, just as all the Jews knew Christ with the five senses, that He had come from Nazareth and was the son of Mary. That is merely natural and physical perceiving. But in this manner Christ cannot be known (nor His Christians either), not even if we could see Him before our eyes and hear Him at all times. The other kind is a spiritual perceiving, and this Christians alone possess. It is called forth by faith rooted in the heart, whereby we likewise, if we are Christians, perceive and understand each other.

In that manner you must behold Christ if you would know Him, and understand who He is, not as your eyes and senses direct but as His Word reveals and portrays Him to you: born of the Virgin, dying for you, risen and made Lord above all things. Therein you behold not only His body, which your eyes see, but the strength and power of His death and resurrection, and He is no longer called the son of Mary and Joseph of Nazareth, as the Jews thought Him to be, but He is now called our one true Saviour and Lord over all.

And this He wrought alone by passing through suffering into that life in which He rose again from the dead and was transfigured, so that all things in heaven and on earth must be subject unto Him, and He is a powerful king over all who believe in Him, and against all that is against them.

There is a great difference between this beholding of Christ and that which the world beholds. For now our eyes are made single through faith and our understanding is made new.

Exposition of John xiv.   W.A. 45. 490 f.

SEEK GOD IN CHRIST ALONE

He that hath seen me hath seen the Father.
JOHN xiv. 9.

Begin your search with Christ and stay with Him and cleave to Him, and if your own thoughts and reason, or another man's, would lead you elsewhere, shut your eyes and say: I should and will know of no other God than Christ, my Lord. Behold, if He is sent by the Father, He must have something really great to say and do for us, by the Father's will, so that we should hear Him as the Most High Himself. And what then is the word we hear? No other than that He came to help the world and to make the Father our friend.

What is the deed? No other than that He preaches and suffers and in the end dies on the cross. Behold, the Father's heart, and will, and work lie open before me, and I perceive and know Him fully, and this no man could ever see or reach by his own wise and penetrating thoughts, however high he might climb with his speculations.

But if you abandon this clear prospect, and climb up into God's Majesty on high, you must stumble, fear and fall because you have withdrawn yourself from God's grace, and have dared to stare at the Majesty unveiled, which is too high and overpowering for you. For apart from Christ, Nature can neither perceive nor attain the grace and love of God, and apart from Him is nothing but wrath and condemnation.

Sermons on John xvi-xx.　　　　　　　W.A. 28. 101 f.

THE GOSPEL IS NOTHING BUT CHRIST

*Let not your heart be troubled: ye believe in God,
believe also in me.* JOHN xiv. 1.

Here, then, and elsewhere I hear that all His words are
esigned to comfort me, indeed all His thoughts and words
nd works are pure kindness and comfort.

Therefore this must be true and cannot be false: if a man
1as a heavy, dull, and frightened heart, it cannot be from
Christ. For He is not the man to make hearts fearful, sad, and
heavy. For He came and wrought His work and ascended
into heaven to take away from our hearts all fear and sadness
and give us in their stead a joyful heart and conscience, and
joyful thoughts. But, you say, does not Christ Himself often
threaten and frighten us in the Gospel, as when He says:
'Repent!', and again in Luke xiii: 'I tell you, nay, but except
ye repent, ye shall all likewise perish'?

Behold, this is the very meaning of such words of Christ,
that a sad and heavy conscience should care for nothing but
that it find Him, and say to Him: Say what Thou wilt, these
are Christ's own words, who can ignore them?

And behold, if we could understand and discern aright,
both things would be true, namely, that Christ comforts
those whom the devil has frightened into despair, and again,
that He frightens those whom the devil has made sure and
presumptuous. For these two will always wage war the one
against the other; what the devil spoils, Christ must build up
and set right; and again, what the devil builds, Christ
destroys.

Exposition of John xiv.   W.A. 45. 472 ff.

THERE IS NO OTHER WAY

*I am the way, the truth, and the life: no man cometh
unto the Father but by me.* JOHN xiv. 6.

Behold, make, and seek what you will, when the hour is
come to enter another life and leave this behind, you must
choose this way above or be lost eternally. For (says He)
I am the way by which you come to the Father, and there is
no other. 'I am the Truth and the Life, I, and no other',
you must hold fast to this Man, and remain steadfast in your
faith and confession, practising it always in suffering, and in
dying, and saying: I know of no other help or counsel, succour or comfort, path or way, but alone my Lord Christ,
who for my sake suffered, died, rose again, and ascended into
heaven. To this I cling, and I will persevere, even if nothing
but hell, death, and the devil are beneath me and before me.
For this is the right way and bridge, firmer and surer than
any built of iron or of stone, and heaven and earth would
burst before this would fail or deceive me.

Exposition of John xiv.   W.A. 45. 493.

THE GLORY OF GOD SHINES OVER THE CHILD

Sunday: LUKE ii. 41–52

*And he said unto them, How is it that ye sought me ?
wist ye not that I must be about my Father's business ?* LUKE ii. 49.

What does this mean: I must be about My Father's business? Are not all creatures His Father's? Yes, everything is
His. But He gave the creatures to us for our use, that we
should have dominion over them in this earthly life, as we
know. But one thing He has kept to Himself, . . . His holy
Word. . . . And the Temple is called His Sanctuary or holy
dwelling-place, because He causes His Word to be heard and
shows Himself present therein.

He does not wish to be found amongst our friends, or
acquaintances, or in anything apart from the ministry of the
Word. For He does not wish to be of this world, . . .

Do you know that Christ will not be found in what is not
His Father's? Not in what you or any other man is or has?
And that is why such dire distress befell the mother of Christ
and Joseph, so that their wisdom, thoughts, and hope failed
them, and they thought that all was lost, as they searched for
Him in pain and sorrow, wandering from place to place. For
they did not seek for Him as they ought. They searched for Him
as flesh and blood are wont to do. Here everything must be
abandoned; friends, acquaintances, the whole City of Jerusalem, all skill and human wit, and what they and all other
men are of themselves, for all this gives and helps to no true
comfort, until He is sought in the Temple, where He is about
His Father's business. There He will certainly be found, and the
heart will be joyful again. There is no other means of comfort
for the heart, for it can find none in itself or in any creature.

Sermon on the first Sunday after   W.A. 17. II. 24 f.
Epiphany, 1525.

And he went down with them, and came to Nazareth,
and was subject unto them.   LUKE ii. 51.

In these words the Evangelist gathers up all the years of
our dear Lord's youth.

But what does it mean: He was subject unto them? Simply
that He walked in those works enjoined in the fifth commandment. Such works are those which father and mother need
done in the house, namely, that He fetched water, bread, and
meat, that He minded the house and did other things of that
kind as He was told to do, like any other child. All that the
dear, sweet Child Jesus did. Therefore all good and god-
loving children should say: Alas! I am not worthy of such
honour that I should be made like the Child Jesus in that I
do what my Lord Christ has done. He picked up shavings
and did other such tasks as His parents told Him, menial tasks
such as need to be done in any household. Yes, and what
good children we should be, if we would follow His example,
and do as our parents tell us, however poor and lowly the
task may be.

Christ is a Lord above all things, and yet, as an example
for us He condescends to obey father and mother. Therefore
we shall take great pains to learn this story and shall deem
ourselves blessed, when we walk thus obediently, for we perceive that Christ Himself did not find such duties irksome.

Sermons from the year 1534.   W.A. 37. 257 f.

*Children, obey your parents in all things: for this is
well pleasing unto the Lord.*   COLOSSIANS iii. 20.

To fatherhood and motherhood God has given praise
above all ranks and callings which are ordained by Him.
Therefore He commands us not only to love our parents but
to honour them also. Towards our brothers and sisters and
all our neighbours He commands no more than love. Thus
He sets father and mother apart and gives them preference to
all other persons on earth, in that He places them beside Himself. For to love is not so high a thing as to honour, as this
comprises not only love but also obedience, humility, and awe,
as towards Majesty. Neither is this the only demand, that we
address them kindly and with reverence, but above all that
we should show by our bearing and behaviour that we esteem
them highly and regard them as, next to God, the highest. If
we are to honour them with all our heart, we must certainly
think of them as high and great. Thus should it be graven on
the heart of the young, to regard their parents as representing
God and as appointed by God to be their father and mother,
however lowly, poor, weak, and quaint they may be. They
are not bereft of honour even if they have faults and if their
ways are foolish, for it is not a case of regarding persons, but
of God's will which ordains it thus. Before the eyes of God
we are all equal, but amongst ourselves we cannot live without diversity and proper distinctions. Therefore it is ordained
by God that I, thy father, should be thy master, and thou
shouldst be obedient unto me.

Exposition of the fifth Commandment.   W.A. 30. I. 147 f.

TO MERIT HEAVEN AND HELL THROUGH ONE'S CHILDREN

And whoso shall receive one such little child in my name receiveth me. But whoso shall offend one of these little ones which believe in me, it were better for him that a millstone were hanged about his neck, and that he were drowned in the depth of the sea.
MATTHEW xviii. 5–6.

Thus it is true that parents, even if they had nothing else to do, might attain eternal blessedness through their children. And if they bring them up in the true service of God they will have both hands full of good works to do. What else are the hungry, thirsty, naked, the prisoners, the sick and the strangers here but the souls of your own children (Matthew xxv. 35–36), for whose sake God makes your house a hospital, and appoints you the master of it, that you may tend them, feed them, and quench their thirst with good words and works, so that they learn to trust in God, believe in Him, fear Him, and place their hope in Him; to honour His name, neither swear nor curse, be diligent, worship God and hear His Word, that they learn to despise the kings of this world, to bear misfortune meekly, not to fear death or to love this life! O, what a blessed home and wedlock where such parents live; truly, it is like a true church, a select monastery, yea, like paradise.

And again, there is no easier way for parents to merit hell than through their own children, in their own home, when they neglect to teach them these things. What does it help them if they bring themselves to the verge of death through fasting, praying, going on pilgrimage, and doing good works? On the Day of Judgement God will not ask about such things, but will demand of them the children He has given and committed to them.

Sermon on Good Works, 1520.   W.A. 9. 279.

> *He took them up in his arms, put his hands upon*
> *them, and blessed them.*   MARK x. 16.

Why does He not embrace some mighty man, or a king,
or some great saint? No, but He takes a little child, which
has so little understanding, and embraces it. Thus He shows
that His Kingdom belongs to children, that He, the Lord, is
a duke and prince of children, and that He wills to be found
among children. By this He means to say: If you want to
know who is the greatest, I will tell you; if you listen to Me,
you are great, for I am all in all, and whosoever receives Me
receives the Father, the Maker of heaven and earth, yea, he
receives heaven and earth at the same time. He receives God,
with all His heavenly gifts and glory.

Thus it comes to pass that we first receive Christ, the Babe,
and then through Him the Father in heaven, for, He says,
you will not always see Me with your physical eyes. Therefore I will set something else before you, which you are to
value as equal to me, namely: 'Whosoever receiveth such a
child in my name, receiveth me, and whosoever receiveth me
receiveth the Father'.

Why, then, should I search far and wide or even run towards heaven to find Christ? I see here so many Christians
and their children, who are the mirror and dwelling-place of
my dear Lord Christ, and when I see them, I see the Christ;
when I hear them, I hear Christ; when I give them a drink
of water, I give it to Christ; when I feed them, I feed Christ;
and when I clothe them, I clothe Christ, and thus I have
within the Christian Church the world full of God and full
of Christ. Wherever I look and see Christian children, I see
Christ, if only I could believe it.

Exposition of Matthew xviii-xxiv.   W.A. 47. 243 f.

*Jesus saith unto her, Woman, what have I to do
with thee? mine hour is not yet come.*   JOHN ii. 4.

He sounds bitter and hard, but I know He is sweet. Notice
here, how hard He is even with His own mother, thus con-
firming that in the things which are God's we must know
neither father nor mother. For although there is no greater
authority on earth than that of father and mother, yet it ends
where God's Word and work begin. For in the things which
are God's, neither father nor mother, let alone a bishop or
any other person, shall teach and lead us, but alone God's
Word. And if your father or mother should command or
teach, or even beg you to do anything for God, and in God's
service, which is not clearly commanded by God, you must
say to them: 'What have I to do with thee?' For fathers and
mothers are bound, and for this very purpose they are appointed by God to be father and mother, to teach and guide
their children, not according to their own conceit and pious
ideas, but according to God's commandment.

Sermon on the second Sunday after   W.A. 17. II. 67.
   Epiphany, 1525.

Verily I say unto you, Except ye be converted, and become as little children, ye shall not enter into the kingdom of heaven.   MATTHEW xviii. 3.

Of a truth, dear Lord, Thou dealest too harshly with us. O that Thou wouldest deal more considerately, and not exalt those little foolish children so highly! Where didst Thou command and teach that a foolish child should be esteemed greater than a wise man? How can our Lord God assert His justice and righteousness, which St. Paul praises so highly: 'God's righteousness, God's righteousness'?

Is this the righteousness, that Thou cast out the wise and takest up fools? The rule is here: Thou shalt believe in the Word of God, and shalt give thyself up, a prisoner to it. Our Lord God has purer thoughts than we humans. He must therefore take away our coarseness. He must hew off rough twigs and branches, before He can make such children, such little foolish ones, of us. Behold, what pure and lovely thoughts the little children have when they look heaven and death full in the face, without any doubts. They are as in Paradise. And the children, who are destined to be so great, have wonderful and peculiar ways.

O dear Lord God, how well art Thou pleased with the life and the playful ways of little children. Yea, all their sins are soon forgiven.

Miscellaneous Writings.   E.A. 57. 258 f.

Second Week after Epiphany

THE NEW SANCTITY

Sunday: JOHN ii. 1–11

*And there were set there six waterpots of stone, after
the manner of the purifying of the Jews.* JOHN ii. 6.

The six water-pots of stone out of which the Jews performed their ritual washings are the books of the Old Testament, which through Law and Commandments cleansed the
Jewish people only outwardly. Therefore the Evangelist says
that the pots stood there after the manner of the purifying of
the Jews, as if he would say: it means purification through
works without faith, which never purifies the heart, but
makes it impurer still. . . .

To turn water into wine means to make lovely the understanding of the Law, which is brought about as follows:
Before the Gospel comes every man understands the Law as
meaning that it demands works, and that we are to fulfil it
with our works. From such understanding come, either stub-
born and arrogant hypocrites, harder than any pot of stone
can be, or anxious and uneasy consciences. But the Gospel
transfigures the Law in that it demands more than we can do,
needing a man very different from us to fulfil it. That is, it
calls for Christ, driving and pointing towards Him, that
through His grace we may first by faith be made like Him
and other Christians, and then really do good works. So
the gracious Gospel comes and makes the water wine. Yes,
it is now a precious thing, and has a lovely taste, for the Law
is at once so deep and lofty, so holy, true and good, that it
is praised and loved for evermore because it demands such
great things. Thus, that is become sweet and easy which was
previously hard and difficult, yes even impossible, for
through the Spirit it is now alive within the heart. . . .

Sermon on the second Sunday after   W.A. 17. II. 69 f.
Epiphany, 1525.

*But after that the kindness and love of God our
Saviour toward man appeared.*   TITUS iii. 4.

Thus God has shown Himself in His Gospel altogether
loving and kind toward us, willing to receive every man,
despising none, forgiving all our wickedness, never driving
any away with severity. His Gospel proclaims pure grace,
with which He succours and surrounds us in the most benevo-
lent way, so that no man is treated according to his merit
and deserts. This is the time of grace, where every man may
draw nigh to the throne of God with complete trust and
confidence.

In the Gospel God has revealed to us His kindness not only
in that He will help men and suffer them to be near Him, but
yet more holds to them, seeks to be with them, and offers
them unceasingly His grace and friendship. These are two
sweet and comfortable words and promises of our God,
namely, that He offers His grace to us and does not leave us,
and that He receives in a most loving way all who desire to
draw near to Him. What more could He do? Behold then,
why His Gospel is called a comfortable and lovely message
of God in Christ. What sweeter word could be spoken to a
wretched, sinful conscience?

Sermons from the year 1522.   W.A. 10. I (i). 97 ff.

Therefore we conclude that a man is justified by faith without the deeds of the law. ROMANS iii. 28.

Here we learn that all Holy Writ is divided into two different parts, which are: one, God's Law and Commandments; the other: His pledged Word and Promise.

The Commandments teach us and prescribe for us many kinds of good works, but the works are not yet done when they are commanded. The Commandments direct us well, but they do not help us. They tell us what we ought to do, yet do not give us the strength to do it. They were given for no other end than that man through them should perceive that he is incapable of doing good, and should learn to despair of himself. For that reason the Commandments are called the Old Testament and belong to the Old Testament, just as: 'Thou shalt have no evil desires' shows that we are all sinners, for no man is able not to have evil desires, strive as he may, and therefore he learns to despair of himself, and to seek help elsewhere in order that he may be set free from evil desires, and thus by the help of Another fulfil the Commandment, which he could not do of himself. And in the selfsame manner it is impossible for us to keep the other Commandments.

Now when a man has learned his own impotence, through the Commandments, and is anxious about how he is to keep them (and keep them he must or be damned), he is truly humbled and undone in his own eyes, and can find nothing in himself whereby he might be saved. Then comes the other word, the divine *Promise*, and says: 'If thou desirest to fulfil all the Commandments, and to be set free from sin and lust as the Commandments demand and insist, behold, thou must believe in Christ in whom I promise thee all grace, righteousness, freedom, and peace. If thou believest this, thou hast it; if thou believest not, thou hast it not. In Faith I have gathered up all things, so that whosoever believes shall be blessed and have all things, but whosoever does not believe shall have nothing'.

On the freedom of a Christian, 1520.   W.A. 7. 23 f.

> *But we know that the law is good, if a man use it lawfully; knowing this, that the law is not made for a righteous man.*   1 TIMOTHY i. 8–9.

In order to understand truly how to use the Law you must divide man into two parts and keep the two clearly separated, namely, the old man and the new man, as St. Paul divided man. Leave the new man completely undisturbed by laws, but the old man you must unceasingly spur on with laws, and must give him no rest from them. In that way you use the Law well. The new man cannot be helped through works, he needs something higher, namely, Christ, who is neither Law nor works, but a gift and present, of the sheer grace and goodness of God. When through faith He comes to dwell in your heart, God makes you saintly. But if you should ever think of becoming acceptable through some deed of your own, such as entering some order, or pursuing some vocation, you would have failed to use the Law aright, and denied Christ. He wills to help you without any work of yours, but if you desire to help yourself through your works you have carried the Law too high and too far. For you drive Christ out of your heart where He should be seated and reign alone, and in His place you put the Law and your own works.

In this manner (I say) the new man carries in his heart Christ and all His heavenly goods, and has everything he should have and is in need of nothing, whether in heaven or on earth.

Sermon on 1 Timothy i. 8-11.   W.A. 17. I. 122 f.

> *For sin shall not have dominion over you: for ye are*
> *not under the law, but under grace.* ROMANS vi. 14.

This is the main article which we have to learn. It gives
us authority, even if we feel the lust of our flesh or even fall
into sin, to say: 'Howbeit, it is my will to be rid of the Law,
neither am I still under the Law or sin, but I am devout and
righteous'. If I cannot say this, I must despair and perish. The
Law says: 'Thou art a sinner'. If I say, 'Yes', I am lost; if I
say 'No', I must have a firm ground to stand on, to refute
the Law, and uphold my 'No'. But how can I say it, when
it is true and is confirmed by Holy Scripture that I was born
in sin? Where then shall I find the 'No'? Of a truth, I shall
not find it in my own bosom, but in Christ. From Him I must
receive it and fling it down before the Law and say: Behold,
He can say 'No' against all Law, and has the right to do, for
He is pure and free from sin, and He gives me the 'No', so
that though if I look on myself I should have to say 'Yes'
because I see that I am a sinner and could not stand before
the Law, and feel there is nothing pure in me, and see God's
wrath, yet I can say that Christ's righteousness is my
righteousness, and henceforth I am free from sin. This is the
goal, that we should be able to say, continually, we are pure
and godly, for evermore, as Christ Himself can say, and this
is all wrought through faith.

Sermons from the year 1525. W.A. 17. I. 155 f.

And looking upon Jesus as he walked; he saith,
Behold the Lamb of God!   JOHN i. 36.

This is our greatest certainty, that we know where our sins are laid. For the Law lays them upon our conscience, but God takes them from us and lays them upon the shoulders of the Lamb. For, if they were to lie upon me and upon the world, we should be lost, because sin is so strong and powerful. And God says: 'I know your sins are far too heavy for you to bear. Therefore, behold, I will lay them upon My Lamb, and will take them from you'. Believe in this promise, and if you believe, you are free from sin. For sin has only two places where it can be: it is either with you, so that it lies on your shoulders, or it lies upon Christ, the Lamb of God. And if it lies on your back, you are lost, but if it rests on Christ, you are free and blessed. Choose then, and take which you will: that your sins remain with you, which is right and meet according to the Law: but by grace they are cast on Christ, the Lamb. For if the Lord would deal with us according to the Law, we should be eternally lost.

These are strong words and a clear and luminous text.

Exposition of John i.   W.A. 46. 683 f.

*This is a faithful saying, and worthy of all accepta-
tion, that Christ Jesus came into the world to save
sinners.* 1 TIMOTHY i. 15.

Christ means: 'My ministry is to save people'. And, He
can certainly speak gloriously of His handiwork as a true
master, for where a man has learned every detail of his trade
he has a right to speak of his work so that all men must
acknowledge he is a master craftsman. In such a manner is
Christ a master of His craft. He speaketh most assuringly
about His ministry. 'I have come to help every one who is
lost; that is My craft and ministry. I have not been sent to
bring a new law to burden the world.' There are laws enough
in the world, more than people can keep. The state, fathers
and mothers, and school-masters, and warders all exist to rule
according to laws. But the Lord Christ says: 'I am not come
to judge, to bite, to grumble, and to condemn people. The
world is too much condemned because it lies under the power
of the devil and hell. Therefore I will not rule people with
laws. I have come that through My Advent and death I may
give help to all who are lost, and may release and set free
those who are overburdened with laws, with judgements, and
with condemnation'.

This is a comforting saying in which the Lord Jesus portrays His dear sweet self, and it agrees with John, who in the
third chapter says, 'God hath sent his Son into the world,
not to condemn the world, but that the world through him
should be saved'. I am come into the world which was condemned already, and has enough to do with judges and judgement; but I will take away that judgement, that all who are
condemned may be saved.

Such sayings we must have because of our desperate need.

Exposition of John iii.   W.A. 47. 27.

Third Week after Epiphany

GOD IS GLORIFIED IN OUR BODIES

Sunday: MATTHEW viii. 5–13

When Jesus heard it, he marvelled . . .
MATTHEW viii. 10.

In this example, as the text clearly says, two kinds of miracle have taken place, or one twofold miracle, one which the Lord does, and the other which the centurion does. For the text clearly says that Jesus Himself marvelled at the centurion that he had such a strong faith. And what Christ regards as a miracle, we too must surely regard as such.

People deem it a great miracle that He made the blind see, the deaf hear, and the lepers clean. And certainly, they are great miracles. But Christ thinks much higher of that which comes to pass within the soul than of that which happens to the body. Therefore, by so much as the soul is more precious than the body, so great and so much greater is the miracle to be regarded which He praises here, than other miracles that happen to the body.

Thus have two kinds of miracle come to pass here, and so it has remained and so it will remain to the Day of Judgement, that Christ daily performs miracles and will do so for ever. Those to the body He rarely performs, as He rarely performed them while He was on earth, . . . Those miracles were only performed in order that the Christian Church should be founded, . . . But those signs which He regards as miracles happen still today and remain eternally, and are such as the faith of this Roman centurion at Capernaum. It is a miracle, a great miracle, that a man should have such fine strong faith; therefore Christ exalts this centurion's faith as if it were a miracle above all miracles.

Sermons from the year 1535.   W.A. 41. 18 ff.

The Spirit of God hath made me, and the breath of the Almighty hath given me life.   JOB xxxiii. 4.

This is my firm belief, that I have been created by God, that is, that He has given and sustains unceasingly, my body, life, and soul, limbs small and great, all my senses, reason and understanding, and likewise food and drink, clothing, wife and child, servants, house and home, and over and above makes all the creation serve us for the good of our life: the sun, moon, and stars in heaven, day, and night; also fire, water, and earth, and all that the earth brings forth: birds, fish, beasts, corn, and every kind of plant. Also, what other temporal goods there are: good rulers, peace, and security. Therefore we learn from this article that none of us either has, or could maintain, of himself, life or any of the aforementioned things, or any others that might be named, however small and insignificant, for they are all gathered up in the one word: 'Creator'.

There would be much to relate here if we wished to show how few there are who believe this article, for we all pass it over. We hear it and repeat it, but do not perceive what these words mean, neither do we meditate upon it. For if we believed in it from the bottom of our hearts we should live in accordance with it, and should not go about so proudly and defiantly, and give ourselves airs, as though we had our life, wealth, power, and honour of our own selves, so that we must be feared and ministered unto, as the wicked and perverted world will have it. Therefore this article ought to humble and alarm us all, if we really believed it. For every day we commit sins with eyes, ears, hands, body and soul, money and possessions, and with all that we have. And that is why we must daily practise this article, engrave it on our hearts, and remember it in everything which comes before our eyes, and in every good thing which we meet. And likewise, when God has brought us through distress and calamity, we should discern His fatherly grace and abounding love towards us. . . .

The Larger Catechism.   W.A. 30. I. 183 ff.

And they bring unto him one that was deaf, and had
an impediment in his speech; and they beseech him
to put his hand upon him . . . And looking up to
heaven, he sighed, and saith unto him, Ephphatha,
that is, Be opened. MARK vii. 32, 34.

He was not concerned about the tongue and ears of this
poor man alone, but this was a general sighing over all
tongues and ears, yea, over all hearts, bodies, and souls, and
over all mankind from Adam till the last man that shall be
born. So He does not sigh chiefly over the many sins which
this man will still commit; no, but best of all, the Lord Jesus
sees all mankind's flesh and blood, and how in Eden the devil
had brought it into deadly peril, making man dumb and
plunging him into death and hell-fire.

This is the vision which Christ had before His eyes, and
He looked around and beheld the great evil which the devil
has wrought through one man's fall in Eden. He looks not
on those two ears alone, but on the whole multitude of men
which have been born of Adam and still are to be born. So
that this Gospel paints Christ as being the one man who
cares for you and me, and for us all, as we ought to care for
ourselves, as if He were plunged in the same shame and sin
as we are, and tells how He sighs over the horrible devil who
wrought all the ruin.

Sermons from the year 1534.   W.A. 37. 509.

And he took him aside from the multitude, and put his fingers into his ears, and he spit, and touched his tongue.   MARK vii. 33.

He singles out these two organs, ear and tongue, because the kingdom of Christ is founded upon the Word, which cannot be perceived and comprehended except with these two organs: ears and tongue. The kingdom reigns in the human heart by faith alone. The ears comprehend the Word and the heart believes it. Therefore, if tongue and ears are taken away, there remains no marked difference between the kingdom of Christ and the kingdom of the world.

For in the outward life a Christian goes about like an unbelieving man: he builds, tills the ground, and ploughs like other men. He does not undertake any special task, neither as regards eating, drinking, sleeping, working, nor anything else. These two organs alone make a difference between Christians and non-Christians: that a Christian speaks and hears in a different manner and has a tongue which praises God's grace and preaches Christ, declaring that He alone can make men blessed. The world does not do that. It speaks of avarice and other vices, and preaches and praises its own pomp.

Sermons from the year 1534.   W.A. 37. 512.

> *Sarah died. . . . And Abraham came to mourn for Sarah.* GENESIS xxiii. 2.

That Abraham came to mourn and weep for her is written in order to show that it is not wrong to grieve, and weep, and mourn when those whom we love die. Although we must all die, we are so made by love that we rejoice in each other's life, just as we are all linked in that we are poor and eat our bread in the sweat of our brow. Indeed, so long as we live we shall care for each other and be mindful of our neighbour's poverty and other sorrows.

It is not God's will that His Gospel should destroy nature; rather He upholds what is natural and leads it into the right way. It is natural that a father should love his child, a wife her husband, and be happy when all is well with them; and again: a Christian is not content to stand before God as a man of faith simply when someone's world collapses, but we should interest ourselves as if it were our own trouble, and act with love. He would not have ordained it should be written that the great Patriarch Abraham wept for Sarah, if it were not meant to serve us to that end. Thus God ordains that such feelings of the heart remain with us, yet it is His will that we should overcome them through faith and not despair or fall from Him.

Exposition of Genesis xxiii.   w.a. 24. 408 f.

*Now if we be dead with Christ, we believe that we
shall also live with him.*   ROMANS vi. 8.

Behold, in this way, St. Paul understands the life of
Christians on earth entirely in relation to the death of Christ,
and pictures them as now dead and lying buried in a coffin,
which means that they have died to sin and have no part in
it for evermore. That is to say, that sin is dead unto them and
they are dead unto sin, because they are no longer found to
be walking in the sinful ways of the world. Yea, now they
have died twice, or in a twofold manner; once spiritually
unto sin, which is a blessed dying, full of grace and comfort
(although to flesh and blood it is painful and bitter) and a
lovely, sweet death, for it leads to an entirely heavenly, sure,
perfect, and eternal life; and once physically, which is no
death but rather a pure and gentle sleep laid upon the flesh,
because while we are here on earth the flesh never ceases to
resist the spirit and life.

As long as the flesh lives here on earth, it spreads and drags
sin behind it. It resists and will not die. Therefore in the end
God must put it to death, that it may also die to sin. And
this is again a pure and gentle death and really nothing but
a sleep, for it will not remain in death (because the soul and
the spirit are no longer in death); but will come forth on the
Day of Judgement cleansed and purified, and will return to
the spirit, where it will be a clean, pure, and obedient body
without any sin and evil lust.

Sermon on Romans vi. 3-11.   W.A. 22. 99 f.

*As ye have yielded your members servants to un-
cleanness and to iniquity unto iniquity; even so now
yield your members servants to righteousness unto
holiness.* ROMANS vi. 19.

Even reason teaches you that since you are no longer subject to sin and iniquity you should no longer serve them nor
obey them with your bodies and members, that is, with your
whole physical life and nature. And again: having given yourselves up to obey God and His righteousness, it is your duty
to serve Him with your whole body and being. This means,
to put it as simply and clearly as possible: any man that previously did evil and lived in opposition to the will of God and
his own conscience shall now live devoutly and serve God
with a good conscience, or, as St. Paul says elsewhere
(Ephesians iv. 28): let him that stole steal no more.

Previously, he says, all your members, eyes, ears, mouth,
hands, feet, and the whole body, served to uncleanness. In
the same way you allowed your members to serve iniquity,
or every manner of evil in life and work, for you committed
iniquity after iniquity with all kinds of trickery and cunning.
Turn this now round, according to your own judgement and
understanding. Where formerly you liked to see, hear, and
talk about what was lewd and obscene, or where you pursued
such things and made your bodies servants to uncleanness,
it should now hurt your eyes and ears to see and hear, and
the whole body should flee from them and be chaste in words
and deeds, so that all the members and the whole body, in
the things it does and leaves undone, shall serve righteousness.

And for this reason: that your members and bodies become
holy, that is, God's property, used alone in His service, so
that they all, the longer the more and the more gladly, serve
obediently to the honour of God in everything that is godly,
praiseworthy, honourable, and virtuous.

Sermon on Romans vi. 19-23.   W.A. 22. 112 f.

Fourth Week after Epiphany

GOD IS GLORIFIED IN HIS CREATION

Sunday: MATTHEW viii. 26–27

Why are ye fearful, O ye of little faith? Then he arose, and rebuked the winds and the sea; and there was a great calm. MATTHEW viii. 26.

This Gospel places before us an example of trust and the lack of trust. Let us consider the experience of the disciples in order to learn what they really felt in their hearts. First, when they entered the boat with Christ everything was calm and they felt nothing in particular. If at that moment any man had asked them whether their trust was firm, they would have answered: 'Yes'. But they were unaware that their hearts trusted in the stillness of the waters, and in that there was no storm, and that their faith was thus founded on what they could see. But when the storm arose and the waves broke over the boat, their faith collapsed, because the peace and stillness to which they clung had gone. Thus their faith disappeared with the peace and calm, and in their souls nothing was left but despair.

And what does that despair do? It perceives nothing more than it feels. It feels neither life nor safety, but only the waves breaking over the boat, and the sea presenting all manner of danger and death. And because they are conscious of those perils and keep their minds fixed on them and never turn away from them, their hearts become filled with anguish, fear and trembling. Indeed, the more they feel and look at the storm, the harder are they beset by trembling and death.

But if there had been true faith in their hearts, it would have swept their minds clean of the tempestuous blast, the waves and the waters, and instead of the storm it would have set up before their eyes the power and the grace of God as they are promised in His Word. . . .

Sermons from the year 1525.　　　　　　　　　W.A. 17. II. 104 f.

Jesus answered them, My Father worketh hitherto, and I work. JOHN v. 17.

God the Father through His Word began and completed the creation of all creatures, and through His Word He upholds them for evermore. And He maintains His work of creating until He wills that it shall cease to be. How long could the sun and the moon and the heavens run so perfectly as they have done for many thousand years; how could the sun rise and set year after year at a certain time and place, unless God, who created them, should also daily sustain them? If God should withdraw His hand, houses and everything would very soon crash in a heap. The wisdom and power of man and of all the angels could not sustain them, not for an instant. The sun would not long remain in the sky and give his light; no child would be born; no seed nor herb would grow on earth, unless God were unceasingly at work.

And if the Creator who works forever, and His Son and the Holy Ghost who work with Him, were to withdraw Their hands, all things would soon collapse in ruin. Therefore we confess in our Christian Creed: 'I believe in God the Father Almighty, Maker of heaven and earth'. If He did not uphold and sustain us after He had made us, we should long since, yes, even in our birth and cradle, have perished and died.

Exposition of John i. w.a. 46. 558 f.

He is before all things, and by him all things consist.
COLOSSIANS i. 17.

The article concerning the Creation from nothing is more difficult to believe than the article concerning the Incarnation of Christ.

Through His Incarnation Christ leads us back to the knowledge of the Creator in which the angels rejoice. This could not happen unless through His own Person, which is the image of God, He took away sin from us, which is the kingdom and the victory of death. For sin has so blinded human nature that it no longer knows the Creator, although it catches a hint of His works, especially in the order of the world! Man does not even know his own sin, and thinks his blindness is the highest wisdom.

If only Adam had not sinned, men would have recognised God in all creatures, would have loved and praised Him so that even in the smallest blossom they would have seen and pondered His power, grace, and wisdom. But who can fathom how from the barren earth God creates so many kinds of flowers of such lovely colours and such sweet scent, as no painter or alchemist could make? Yet God can bring forth from the earth green, yellow, red, blue, brown, and every kind of colour. All these things would have turned the mind of Adam and his kin to honour God and laud and praise Him and to enjoy His creatures with gratitude.

Table-Talk.   W.A. Tischreden 4. 198.

He upholdeth all things by the word of his power.
                                                HEBREWS i. 3.

Here the Apostle says that He upholds all things. If He upholds all things, He is not upheld Himself and is a Being above all things, which none can be but God alone. The upholding means that He nourishes and sustains all things, so that all things were not only made by Him but continue in Him and are sustained by Him, as the Apostle Paul says: all things consist in Him and through Him. And what a fine and lovely word that is he uses when he says: 'God upholds'. He does not drive, or hunt or roar; He gently upholds and lets all creatures enjoy His lovingkindness, as it is written in the book of Wisdom viii. 1: 'The wisdom of God reacheth from one end of the world to the other with full strength, and ordereth all things graciously'.

The meaning of this text is that Christ upholds all things by the Word of His power, that is by the working of His power. For by the working of His power all things are upheld, and all that has being and power has it not itself but of the active and creative power of God. And here especially the power and the Word must not be sundered, for the power and the Word are one, which means there is one active or powerful Word, so that power is the essence and the nature of the Word which worketh in all things.

Sermons from the year 1522.   W.A. 10. 1 (i). 158 f.

How terrible art thou in thy works! PSALM lxvi. 3.

A housewife should stand in sheer amazement if she really thought about this: today she has a set of fifteen eggs and she places them under a hen or goose. In four or six weeks' time she has a basket full of little chickens or goslings. They eat, and drink, and grow until they are full grown. Where do they come from? The eggs open when the time is come, and inside sit the chicks or goslings. They poke their little beaks through the shell and at last creep out. The mother hen or goose does nothing but sit on the eggs and keep them warm. It is God's almighty power that is at work within those eggs, making them turn into hens and geese.

Similarly with the fish in the water and with all the plants which grow from the earth. Where do they come from? Their first beginning is the spawn which floats in the water, and from this grow, by the Word and power of God, carp, trout, pike, and all kinds of fish, so that the water is swarming with fish. An oak, beech, or fir-tree grows out of the earth many feet thick and many yards high. What is its first beginning? Water and earth. The root draws its sap and moisture from the soil and forces it up with all its might so that the tree grows big and strong and tall.

What is the cause of this? God's omnipotence and the Word which the eternal, almighty Creator spoke: 'Let the waters bring forth abundantly the moving creature that hath life, and fowl that may fly in the open firmament of heaven. And the earth bring forth the living creature after his kind, cattle and creeping thing and beasts of his kind'. It is the Word and Omnipotence of God that brings it all about.

Sermons from the year 1544.   W.A. 49. 436 f.

We know that the whole creation groaneth and travail-eth in pain together until now. ROMANS viii. 22.

The radiant sun, the loveliest of the creatures, gives only a little of its service to the saints. While it shines on one saint it must shine on thousands and thousands of rogues, and it must give them light in spite of all their godlessness and evil, and so it must permit its loveliest and purest service to the most unworthy, the wickedest and loosest knaves.

It is our Lord God's good creature, and would much rather serve devout people; but the noble creature must bear it and serve the evil world unwillingly. Yet it hopes that that service shall at long last have an end, and does it in obedience to God who has thus ordained it, that He may be known as a merciful God and Father, who (as Christ teaches) 'maketh His sun to rise on the evil and on the good' (Matthew v. 45). For this reason the noble sun serves vanity and renders its good service in vain. But in His own time our Lord and God will find out those who have abused the noble sun and His other creatures, and He will reward the creatures abundantly. Thus the good St. Paul shows the holy cross in all creation, in that heaven and earth and all the creatures therein suffer with us and bear the dear treasured cross. Therefore we must not weep and moan so piteously when we fall on evil days, but must patiently wait for the redemption of the body and for the glory which shall be revealed in us; the more so as we know that the whole creation groans with anxious longing as a woman in travail, and sighs for the manifestation of the sons of God, for then the whole creation will also be re-deemed. It will no longer be subject to vanity, to serve vanity, but it will serve only the children of God, and that willingly and joyfully.

Sermons from the year 1535.   W.A. 41. 307 ff.

The earth is full of the goodness of the Lord.
                              PSALM xxxiii. 5.

God's wonderful works which happen daily are lightly esteemed, not because they are of no import but because they happen so constantly and without interruption. Man is used to the miracle that God rules the world and upholds all creation, and because things daily run their appointed course, it seems insignificant, and no man thinks it worth his while to meditate upon it and to regard it as God's wonderful work, and yet it is a greater wonder than that Christ fed five thousand men with five loaves and made wine from water.

I often heard my father say, that he had heard from his parents, my grandparents, that there are on earth many more people eating than there could be sheaves gathered together from all the fields on earth in a year. Reckon up, and you will find that more loaves are eaten in a year than corn is cut and gathered. Where does all the bread come from? Must you not acknowledge that it is the wonderful work of God, who blesses and multiplies the corn in the fields, and in the barns, the flour in the bin and the bread on the table? But there are few who think of it and notice that those are the wonderful works of God.

Sermons from the year 1544.   W.A. 49. 435 f.

Fifth Week after Epiphany

GOD IS GLORIFIED IN HISTORY

Sunday: MATTHEW xiii. 24–30

But when the blade was sprung up, and brought forth fruit, then appeared the tares also. MATTHEW xiii. 26.

With human power we cannot weed them out, neither can we change them, for they are often cleverer than we. They soon make friends and gather a crowd around themselves, and in this they have the devil, the prince of this world, who has sown them among the wheat, on their side.

Further, they know well how to adorn their cause, pretending to great wisdom and saintliness, and thus they gain great respect among the crowd, just as the large and beautiful thistles which stand with their brown crowns among the wheat, growing taller and looking more majestic than the wheat itself. They have nice green leaves and beautiful large brown crowns; they grow and bloom and flower riotously; they are red, and strong, and beautiful. The precious wheat, on the other hand, has no such beautiful and striking appearance, but looks a pale yellow, so that any man who does not know both would swear on oath that the thistles must be very good and useful plants and flowers. . . .

Thus we cannot eliminate the wicked, because it often happens that some who went astray return. Therefore, if we should set ourselves to root out the tares entirely we should not be able to uproot them without peril to those who may still return. Hence we must bear with them, but not in such a manner that they rule over us, just as we cannot altogether avoid sin, but must not let it become our master. . . . Therefore we must practise God's commandments and call the Lord's Prayer to our aid, until we can fully lay hold on Christ, the Lord, until He has become the joy of our heart.

Sermons from the year 1546. W.A. 51. 184 f.

But while men slept, his enemy came and sowed tares among the wheat, and went his way.

MATTHEW xiii. 25.

The meaning of the Parable is that no Christian, especially no preacher, should grow disheartened or despondent because he cannot bring it about that there are only saints in his church. For the devil does not stand aloof, he throws his seeds in and this is first noticed when they burst forth and shoot up. Thus it happened with the apostles Paul and John, and others. Where they hoped to have devout Christians and faithful labourers in the Gospel, they got the most wicked rogues and the bitterest foes. And thus it happens with us. Those we think godly and righteous do us the greatest harm and cause us the greatest difficulties because we sleep and fear no evil.

And this is the only comfort, that Christ Himself warns us that it will happen thus. For this reason St. John comforts himself in face of such difficulties in his epistle, saying: 'they went out from us, but they are not of us'. For it is the way of the world, that, what should be best turns out worst. Angels become devils. One of the Apostles betrayed Christ. Christians become heretics. Out of the people of God came the wicked men who nailed Christ to the cross.

So it happens still. Therefore we must not be alarmed and must not faint in our ministry when we see tares shoot up amongst the wheat. Rather we must confidently go on and admonish our people, that no man be led astray.

Sermons from the year 1544.   W.A. 52. 132 f.

Know ye not that the unrighteous shall not inherit the kingdom of God?   1 CORINTHIANS vi. 9.

We ought to know that there are two kingdoms. The first is the kingdom of the devil, whom our Lord calls, in the Gospel (John xvi. 11) the prince or king of this world. That is called the kingdom of sin and disobedience. To the saints it is a wretched prison.

We are all in this kingdom until the Kingdom of God comes, and yet not all in the same way. The saints fight against their sins daily, and firmly resist the lusts of the flesh, the enticements of the world, and the suggestions of the devil. For however devout we are, evil desire always seeks to master us. In this way the Kingdom of God fights unceasingly with the kingdom of the devil. And the saints are kept and saved because they fight against the kingdom of the devil within themselves, in order that the Kingdom of God may be increased.

The other kingdom is the Kingdom of God, the realm of righteousness and truth, of which Christ says (Matthew vi. 33): 'Seek ye first the kingdom of God and His righteousness'. But what is God's righteousness? It is when there is no longer any sin in us, and all our members and powers are subject to God, and used in His service so that we can say with St. Paul (Galatians ii. 20): 'I live, yet not I, but Christ liveth in me'. That happens when no sin reigns over us, but Jesus Christ alone with His grace. Therefore God's Kingdom is nothing but peace, order, humility, purity, love, and every kind of virtue, and there is no anger, hatred, bitterness, uncleanness and the like.

Therefore let each examine himself, what his inclinations are, and he will find out to which kingdom he belongs.

Exposition of the Lord's Prayer for   W.A. 2. 96 f.
simple lay-folk.

*And they sought to take him: but no man laid hands
on him, because his hour was not yet come.*

JOHN vii. 30.

No man laid hands on Him. Who is His protector? Who
stands in the way? No one. The text says: His hour was not
yet come. Listen, nothing but an hour. That is a poor and
weak protector. It does not say that He had at His side so
many thousand horses and some thirty thousand infantrymen
to protect Him. One short hour is all the armour which was
given to Him, all that stands between Him and the cross. That
hour was not yet come, and whilst it tarried, all that His foes
planned against Him came to nought.

For so accurately has God measured and appointed all
things that He holds in His hands all thoughts and deeds, that
nothing can come to pass until the hour is come which is
ordained by Him.

Thus has God ordained that each thing in the world shall
have its time and hour; one whole, free hour He has appointed
to each thing. The whole world is the enemy of that hour and
fights against it. The devil throws and shoots at the poor little
hour-glass, but in vain, for all depends upon that hour; until
it is come and the sands have run out, the devil and the world
can do nothing.

To sum up: whatever a man may set his mind on, it shall
not come to pass, or rather it shall come to nought, if it is not
commanded and ordained by God; or if it do come to pass it
will do ten times as much harm. It is all gathered up in one
hour. Our planning will not bring it about, God must ordain
the hour.

This is a glorious comfort.

Sermons on John vi–viii.   W.A. 33. 404 ff.

Thy will be done in earth, as it is in heaven.
MATTHEW vi. 10.

People say: 'Yes, certainly, God has given us a free will'. To this I reply: 'To be sure, He has given us a *free* will; why then will you not let it remain free but make it your *own* will?' If you do with it what you will, it is not a free will. It is your own will. But God has given neither you nor any man your own will, for your own will comes from the devil and from Adam. They made the free will which they received from God into their own will. For a free will desires nothing of its own. It only cares for the will of God, and so it remains free, cleaving and clinging to nothing.

Hence you see that in this prayer God commands us to pray against ourselves, and so teaches us that we have no greater enemy than ourselves. For our will is the greatest power within us, and we must pray against it: my Father, suffer me not to have my will. Oppose my will and break it. Come what may, only let Thy will and not mine be done. For so it is in heaven; self-will is not found there. Let it be the same here on earth. Such a prayer, if it is offered, hurts our nature, for self-will is the deepest and mightiest evil in the world, and there is nothing which we love more than our own will.

Exposition of the Lord's Prayer for   W.A. 2. 104 f.
simple lay-folk.

*Out of the mouth of babes and sucklings hast thou
ordained strength because of thine enemies, that thou
mightest still the enemy and the avenger.*

PSALM viii. 2.

Why does Christ found such a kingdom? Why does He
not send the heavenly Spirits and Princes, Gabriel, Michael,
and other angels, who could offer strong resistance to the
enemy and break his power? For the enemy and avenger is
a strong and powerful spirit. He is the god and prince of this
world, having a strong and everlasting kingdom, and many
other spirits under him, each of which is stronger than all the
people on earth.

Answer: The Lord, our Master, does not will to use
Gabriel or Michael for this purpose, but wills rather to ordain
strength out of the mouth of babes and sucklings. For
because the enemy's wickedness is great and his wrath fierce,
it pleases the Maker to despise this wicked, vain, and furious
spirit and to mock him. Therefore, because He wills to ordain
such strength He lowers Himself so much, is made man, and
even makes Himself subject to all men; as it is written in
Psalm xxii: 'I am a worm and no man; a reproach of man
and despised of people'. He goes about in poverty as He
Himself says in Matthew viii. With such a weak body and
mean appearance He attacks the enemy, allows Himself to
be crucified and slain, and through His cross and death He
overcomes the enemy and avenger.

Thus our Lord God lays aside the great and mighty power
of the angels in heaven and takes the most unlearned, simple,
and weak people on earth and sets them over against the
wisdom and power of the devil and the world. Such are the
works of God. For He is a God who quickens the dead, and
calls that which is not, and it is. It is God's nature that He
shows His divine Majesty and power through weakness.
That is the way in which the Lord, our God, founds His
Kingdom. It is carried on in weakness, but out of that weakness strength shall come.

Sermons from the year 1537.   W.A. 45. 218 ff.

THOU COMMANDEST HIM, AND DOST NEVER COME TOO LATE

He arose, and rebuked the winds and the sea; and there was a great calm. MATTHEW viii. 26.

Thus we should come to know our Lord and Saviour, and to believe that He is the Lord who can control the roaring winds and raging waves of the devil, and stay their power, if He wills. In this we should take comfort and consolation against all the might of the wicked and scornful enemies of the poor Church, that for all their storming against this little ship they will not prevail. The reason: because Christ, the Lord, Who has for more than five thousand years calmed and stilled those winds and waves, still knows how to command and stay them. For five thousand years they have failed and have not succeeded, and in the future, even in the last hour, they will still fail and not succeed in their designs. This Man who is lying here in the ship and is asleep, will through our prayer wake up when the hour is come and will reveal Himself and show that He can command the winds and the waves, and then everything which has fought and stormed against the ship must come to nought.

Sermons from the year 1546.   W.A. 51. 155.

Sixth Week after Epiphany

THE GLORY OF CHRIST

Sunday: MATTHEW xvii. 1–9

This is my beloved Son, in whom I am well pleased;
hear ye him. MATTHEW xvii. 5.

Therefore beware of those thoughts which ignore the Word, wanting to tear and sunder Christ from God. For He has not commanded thee to fly up to heaven to stare at what He does there, with His angels, but this is His command: 'This is my beloved Son; hear ye him.' In Him I have come down to you, so that you can see Me, and hear Me, and touch Me. There and nowhere else shall all find Me, who desire Me and long to be free from their sins and saved. On this word we should immediately seize, and say: Here God Himself speaks. I will follow Him and listen to no other word or preaching, and neither learn nor know anything else about God. For in this Person (says St. Paul) dwells the fulness of the Godhead, and apart from Him there is no God that I can meet or draw near to. And where this man's word is heard or His work seen, the word and work of God are truly heard and seen.

Exposition of John xiv.   W.A. 45. 520 f.

Him hath God the Father sealed.   JOHN vi. 27.

An emphasis is given to this word, as though it means: His father is no rogue or wicked man. I will tell you who he is: He is God; He is the Father who is called God; and the Father has set His eyes upon the Son, and has made all things subject unto Him, that we should eat His flesh and drink His blood, and be sustained by them; else we must all perish. The Father has sealed and set before us Christ the Son alone, and He has laid His whole will and grace on Christ and on no other.

Since God has thus sealed Him with His seal—and He has but one seal—unto Him alone He has given the Holy Ghost, in order that all mankind should turn to Him alone, and all the Scripture points to Him, that He alone has the letter and the seal; for He is the image and the firstborn, begotten, given, and sent that He alone may help us, as God Himself spoke from heaven: 'This is my beloved Son in whom I am well pleased; hear ye him.' God the Father set His seal upon Him: therefore we should accept Him alone, and hearken to none but Him.

Sermons on John vi–viii.   W.A. 33. 79 f.

What he hath seen and heard, that he testifieth.
JOHN iii. 32.

What should Christ do, and of what use is the Messiah? What kind of Messiah is He? Is there nothing else for Him to do? Is He just burst into history? What does He do? He testifies. If He walks in such weakness and holds on His kingship no more firmly than that He testifies, is there nothing else that He can do but preach and talk? If He is no soldier, possesses no land (not even the width of His palm) and no people, what does He do? Preach. Yes, such a Messiah are we bidden to accept.

How if it be God's will that the Messiah should not come like a Cæsar? Such an honour He will not grant unto them, that He should come arrayed with power like theirs. But that He comes so unadorned and does nothing but preach, that is unspeakable wisdom and strength, yes, the treasure of wisdom and knowledge, for whosoever believes in Him shall live eternally. But who sees this? You are not meant to see it. His reign and His preaching are a testimony. It is a preaching which testifies to things which no man can hear, see, or read in books of the law or anywhere else in the world. To witness means to speak of what the hearer has not seen. A judge does not judge what he sees. He must hear witnesses. But here He must preach and witness to something which men do not see, and that is how the Lord Christ is a witness to the Father in heaven, high uplifted above all men. He shall do nothing but preach, and His preaching shall be His testimony to the Father, how He is inclined, how He desires to make men blessed and to redeem them from their sins, and from the power of death and the devil. That is His testimony. He suffers Himself to be made man, to die, and to rise again from the dead, and says, 'Thy testimony consists in these things'. And if you believe in these works and testimony, you believe in the testimony of God.

Exposition of John iii. w.a. 47. 177 f.

I am not ashamed of the gospel of Christ: for it is the
power of God unto salvation to every one that believeth.
ROMANS i. 16.

Christ has no money or purse, nor any worldly kingdom, for He has given all such things to the kings and princes. One thing, however, He has kept to Himself which is the work of neither man nor angel, namely, that He is a victor over sin, death, the devil, and hell, and is able to save and uphold in the midst of death all those who believe in Him through His Word.

Amen! We have cast in our lot with that man, the Lord Christ, the Son of God, and He will certainly not desert us. Our life and soul are bound to Him; where He abides there shall we too abide. Apart from Him I know of nothing wherewith to defy the world. Therefore, if Christ lives, He knows that we do and suffer everything for His sake, as regards preaching, teaching, and writing. As the world knows and we know too, if we venture on Him, He will help us. Yet all things must be broken. Things cannot remain as they are.

Table-Talk.   w.A. Tischreden 6. 73.

*He hath put all things under his feet, and gave him
to be the head over all things to the church.*
                                        EPHESIANS i. 22.

Our greatest honour, glory, and praise is that we have
Christ, the Son of God, flesh of our flesh, yet born without
sin, seated at the right hand of God the Father, a Lord over
all creatures in heaven, on earth, and in hell. But whosoever
wants Him as his Lord, will have the devil as his foe and
enemy.

Of what concern is the whole world to God, or would ten
or more worlds be? He has set up Christ, as it is written in
the second psalm (verse 6). Even if men refuse to accept Him,
He has enthroned Him so firmly that He will never let Him
be overthrown, or cast down from His seat. If the world dares
to attempt that, He throws everything into a heap; for once
with a glorious voice resounding from heaven He gave the
command 'Hear ye Him'.

Table-Talk.   W.A. Tischreden i. 469.

These words spake Jesus, and he lifted up his eyes to heaven, and said, Father, the hour is come; glorify thy Son, that thy Son also may glorify thee.

JOHN xvii. 1.

With these words He indicates how it fares with Him, and what is the sorrow that drives Him to such a prayer. The time is drawing nigh (He says) that I must die the meanest death, and it will darken all My purest light, and swallow up My honour and My Name. Until that hour He had done great things, had preached with wonderful words, done wonderful works, and given proof of His mighty power, so that all the world should praise and honour and adore Him exceedingly. Then adversity befalls Him, He is covered with disgrace and shame, and must hang on the awful tree between two murderers, and die as if He were the wickedest rogue this earth has ever borne, for no murderer has been treated with so much shame and spite.

That really is casting out the faithful, wondrous man into utter darkness. And, behold, this is in Christ's mind when He says that His hour is near or is come, for He prays with such earnestness as if in that moment He were hanging on the cross; as if He spake: Now I am shrouded in shame and death, now I lie in deepest darkness. Yet it is now the time when Thou shalt bring me forth, and lift Me up, and bring Me to honour, for My light is gone out, and the world is trampling Me under foot.

And how did such glorification come to pass? In no other way than that the Father raised Him again from death, threw the devil under His feet, and made Him King and Lord over all creation.

Sermons on John xvi–xx.   W.A. 28. 79 f.

Let this mind be in you, which was also in Christ Jesus. PHILIPPIANS ii. 5.

Brethren, ye should have in yourselves the mind which was also in Christ Jesus, who being in the form of God, did not exalt Himself in order to be like the Father, but of His own will impoverished Himself and took upon Himself the likeness and form of a servant, that in every way and habit He was found to be a man, and like a man, even in that He died in obedience to His Father's will. Mark, dear friends of Christ, what an impressively deep word that is. We should all be the same. For He does not say an evil man, but a man in whom is found the likeness of God, that is, power, honour, justice, wisdom, saintliness, chastity, a man who has never done any evil, and who is filled with virtue. Yet in His humanity, He wished to be like us, not like God, not like Lucifer who wanted to seize the image of God, nor like the proud and haughty who look down upon their neighbours, as though they can scarcely recognise them. Christ did not act thus. He laid aside the form of God and was found in the form of man, in the flesh of sin, although He did no sin; and could not sin. And that is why He became a fool, a mockery, and a derision before the people, He, who carried all our calamities, and in Him may be found all the marks of our poverty and wretchedness. And He did all this that we might freely follow Him.

Sermons from the year 1518.   W.A. I. 268 f.

From Epiphany to Lent

Septuagesima

BEING CALLED AND BEING CHOSEN

Sunday: MATTHEW xx. 1–16

*So the last shall be first, and the first last: for many
be called, but few chosen.* MATTHEW xx. 16.

Because this Gospel speaks of those who think themselves
first before God, it aims high and strikes the most excellent
people, indeed, it frightens the greatest saints. And that is
why Christ holds it up even before the Apostles. For it sometimes happens that a man who appears weak and poor, and
despised before the world, . . . yet secretly within his heart
well pleased with himself, so that he thinks himself the first
before God; and even for this reason is he the last. On the
other hand, there may be a man so fearful and fainthearted,
that despite his gold, honour, . . . he thinks himself the least
before God; and even for this reason is he the first.

It is also well known that the greatest saints have been
moved with fear in this connection, and that many holding
high spiritual office have fallen.

Behold, how Saul fell! How God let David fall! How
Peter had to fall, and likewise some disciples of Paul!

Hence this is the essence of this Gospel: no man is so high
nor can he rise so high, that he need no longer fear that he
may be made the lowest. And again: no man has fallen so low,
nor can he fall so low, that there is no hope of him becoming
the highest, for herein all merit is set at nought, and God's
mercy alone is praised, and it is firmly decreed that 'the
last shall be first and the first last'. In that He says, 'the first
shall be last', He takes away all your pride. . . . But in
that He says, 'the last shall be first', He takes from you all
despair. . . .

Sermons from the year 1525. W.A. 17. II. 139 f.

GOD HAS DEALT TO EVERY MAN THE MEASURE OF FAITH

For I say, through the grace given unto me, to every man that is among you, not to think of himself more highly than he ought to think; but to think soberly, according as God hath dealt to every man the measure of faith. ROMANS xii. 3.

He often does through little saints what He does not do through great saints. When He was twelve years old He hid Himself from His Mother, and let her go about in search of Him. He appeared to Mary Magdalene on Easter Day before He revealed Himself to His Mother and the Apostles. He spoke more kindly to the Samaritan woman and to the woman taken in adultery than He ever spoke to His Own Mother. While Peter fell and betrayed Him, the thief on the cross was full of faith.

With such-like wonders He shows us that He will not have us know the measure of grace He gives to His saints, and that we shall not judge according to the person. He gives His gifts freely, as He pleases, and not as we think. He even says concerning Himself: whosoever believes in Him shall do greater works than He did Himself. And all this is said in order that no man exalt himself above another and place one saint higher than another, but we regard them all as equal in His grace, however different they may be as regards the gifts He bestows. Through St. Stephen He wills to do what He does not do through St. Peter, and again through Peter what He does not do through His Mother; so that He alone is the One who does everything according to His will, without respect of persons.

God may give to a great saint small faith and to a small saint great faith, in order that the one shall always esteem the other higher than himself.

Sermons from the year 1525.   W.A. 17. II. 77 f.

Ye have not chosen me, but I have chosen you.

JOHN xv. 16.

This cuts off and condemns at a stroke all the presumption of spurious saints, who want to do and deserve so much, even to reconciling God and making Him their friend. For what do they do but make the choice and seek to be first, in that their merits precede and God's grace toddles on behind? It is not He who chooses us, but we seek Him and make Him our friend, that we may glory in that He has received much good from us. That is what all the world does in seeking to merit God's grace by previous works. But the Gospel says 'Ye have not chosen Me'. That is, you are My friends not because of what you do, but because of what I do. If it were because of what you do, I should have to regard your merit, but it is because of Me and through Me, because I draw you to Me and give you all that I possess, so that your glory is in nothing but My grace and love, and not your own nor all the world's work or merit. For I have not let Myself be found by you; rather have I had to seek you and bring you to Myself, when you were afar off, without knowledge of God, and were held in the grip of error and condemnation like the rest. But now I am come, and I have called you out of the darkness, before you prayed or did anything about it. Thus you are My friends in that you have received all good from Me, and know that you have received it all for nothing and out of sheer grace.

Exposition of John xv. W.A. 45. 697 f.

Thine they were, and thou gavest them me.
JOHN xvii. 6.

No man on earth can help but fear and tremble and desire to escape if he thinks of God. As soon as he hears God mentioned, he is quiet and subdued. I do not speak of wild people, but of those whose heart is pierced, who feel their sin. (It is only to such we preach.) For the conscience is awake, feeling and knowing that God is hostile to sinners and will condemn them, and that they cannot escape nor flee from His wrath. Therefore their conscience flinches and trembles and quakes, faints and grows pale and chilled as before lightning and thunder. Therefore Christ must deal mightily with such fear and graft into the heart such sweet and kind and comforting words that those grievous, bitter, and horrible thoughts are removed, and must present the Father in as sweet a way as ever a heart could wish. Therefore let us heartily receive these words, and let them sink into our hearts, as the only comfort and salvation of our souls.

If you cleave to your Lord Christ, you are certainly one of those whom God has chosen from the beginning to be His own. Otherwise you would not come to Him, nor listen to such a revelation and accept it.

Therefore let those be troubled who have not the Gospel and do not want to listen to Christ. But you may know that there is no greater comfort on earth than that which He Himself reveals and gives you here, namely, that you are God's own beloved child because His Word pleases you and your heart is graciously inclined towards Him. For if Christ is kind and gracious to you and comforts you, God the Father Himself comforts you. For He revealed Himself in this way so that you would not need to search and wonder what He may have decided concerning you; rather you may know from His Word all that concerns His will and your salvation.

Sermons on John xvi–xx.   W.A. 28. 120 ff.

Holding faith, and a good conscience.   1 TIMOTHY i. 19.

If we reflect upon the diversity of sins which remain in the saints in this life, we must not enquire into the secret election, or Providence, or predestination, as it is called, for such reflection causes nothing but doubt. Is it certainty or is it despair? If you are chosen, no fall can harm you; you are always in grace and cannot perish. If you are not chosen, nothing can help you. Such words are dreadful, and it is a sin to lead the heart to such thoughts. The Gospel points us straight to the plain Word of God, wherein God has revealed His will, and through which He wills to work and to be known. It is plain that God's Word punishes sins and reveals diversity of sins and points to our Saviour Jesus Christ. We should look at this plain word of God and judge according to it whether we are in grace.

For where there is the faith whereby we are made righteous there must be a pure conscience. It is quite impossible for these two things to live side by side—faith which trusts in God, and an evil will or, as it is called, a bad conscience. Faith in God and prayer to Him are delicate things, and a little wound of conscience can drive out faith and prayer, as every advanced Christian must often experience.

But where there is faith and a pure conscience, there the Holy Spirit certainly dwells. Yet such a trust is not based on our good conscience or worthiness, but on Christ alone. Hence we conclude that we are in grace for Christ's sake because of His promise, and true prayer can be offered; as St. John says, 'if our heart condemneth us not, we may confidently pray to God, and whatsoever we ask we shall receive from Him'.

Questions with regard to sin in   E.A. 55. 161 ff.
  believers, in co-operation with
  Melanchthon and Bugenhagen.

Say to them that are of a fearful heart, Be strong,
fear not.   ISAIAH XXXV. 4.

If a man is anxiously afraid that he is not among those who
are chosen, or if he is tempted concerning his election, he
should give thanks and rejoice that he is anxious, because he
may confidently know that God cannot lie, and He said, 'the
sacrifices of God are a broken spirit', that is to say, a spirit
despairing of it. 'A broken and a contrite heart, O God, thou
wilt not despise' (Psalm li. 17). That he is 'broken' he knows.
Therefore he should throw himself with all his heart on to
the truthfulness of God who gave His Promise, and he should
turn himself away from what he knows of the wrath of God,
and he will be chosen and saved.

Commentary on Romans.   323.

But without faith it is impossible to please him.
HEBREWS xi. 6.

Even if it could be done, I should not wish to be given a free will or have anything left in my own hand with which to strive for salvation, not only because I do not know how I should stand against the bribes and evil onslaughts of the devil, but even if there were no danger, no temptation and no devil, all my labour would be uncertain, like one beating the air. And if I lived and worked till the Last Day, my conscience could never be certain how much I ought to do, that God should count it sufficient. For whatever work I did on earth, there would remain that little doubt in the conscience whether God were well-pleased, or if perhaps He demanded something more, as experience shows in all who would be saved through their works, and as I myself have come to know through many a hurtful experience. But since God has taken my salvation out of my free will, and has set it in His free will, and has promised to uphold me, not through my own life and work, but through His grace and mercy, I am certain that He is faithful and will not lie to me. Further, He is so strong and powerful that no devil or adversity can do anything against Him or tear me away from Him. Thus we are certain that we are well pleasing to God, not through the merit of our works, but through the mercy and loving-kindness of His grace which He has promised to us, and if we stumble or do less than we ought, He, with fatherly love, will pardon us and make us better. This is the glory of all Christians in God, their Lord.

On the enslaved will. 334 f.

Sexagesima

WHAT HAPPENS TO THE DIVINE WORD

Sunday: LUKE viii. 5–15

That on the good ground are they, which in an honest and good heart, having heard the word, keep it, and bring forth fruit with patience. LUKE viii. 15.

He says, 'in an honest and good heart'. As a field which is a large level piece of land, with no thorns, or thistles, so pure and wide, and open is the heart that is free from anxiety and greed about temporal food, and the Word of God finds room in it.

Thus we may see that it is no marvel, that there are so few true Christians, for not all the seed falls on good ground; but only a fourth part, and that those should not be trusted who boast of being Christians and praise the teaching of the Gospel. Christ Himself here cries and says: 'He that hath ears to hear, let him hear'; as if He meant to say, O, how few true Christians there are. Indeed, one cannot trust all who are called Christians and who listen to the Gospel. Much more is needed.

Why should we be troubled that many are full of disdain? Is it not ordained that many are called and few are chosen? For the sake of the good soil, which brings forth fruit with patience, some of the seed must needs fall by the wayside, some upon the rocky places and some among thorns. We do know certainly that the Word of God does not remain fruitless, but that it always finds some good ground, as He says here, that some of the sower's seed fell upon good ground. For where the Gospel is, there are Christians: 'My Word shall not return unto me void'.

Sermons from the year 1525.   W.A. 17. II. 156 f.

If any man will do his will, he shall know of the doctrine, whether it be of God, or whether I speak of myself. JOHN vii. 17.

This is the Father's will that we should listen to what the man Jesus says, and give ear to His Word. You are not to try to be clever in connection with His Word, to master it or to argue about it, but simply to hear it. Then the Holy Spirit will come and dispose your heart so that you will believe and say from the bottom of your heart concerning the preaching of the divine Word: 'That is God's word and is the pure truth' and you will risk your life upon it. But if you yourself want to be heard, and to obliterate the Word of Christ with your own reason, if you attempt to subject the Word to your own ideas, kneading false teaching into it, probing, and prying how to understand, to measure, and to distort it so that His Word must sound as you want it to do, and if you ponder it as though you were in doubt about it, wanting to judge it according to your own mind, that is not listening to it, or being a disciple, but being a master.

In that way one can never reach an understanding so as to be able to say: This is the Word of God. Therefore, lock up your reason, tread your wisdom under foot, and do not let them grope about, or feel, or think, in matters that concern your salvation, but simply and solely listen to what the Son of God says, to what is His Word, and stop there. Hearken, hearken! is the command. That is truly and honestly doing our Lord God's will, and He has promised that whosoever hearkens to the Son will receive the Holy Ghost, to enlighten and kindle him so that he will rightly understand that it is the Word of God. God will change him into a man after His own heart. That He will really do.

Sermons on John vi–viii. W.A. 33. 362 f.

At that time Jesus answered and said, I thank thee,
O Father, Lord of heaven and earth, because thou
hast hid these things from the wise and prudent, and
hast revealed them unto babes. MATTHEW xi. 25.

I beg and I admonish faithfully all devout Christians that
they be not offended or stumble over the simple stories related in the Bible, nor doubt them. However poor they may
appear, they are certainly the words, history, and judgements
of the high divine Majesty, Power, and Wisdom. For this is
the book which makes all wise and clever people fools, and
can only be understood by simple people, as Christ says
(Matthew xi. 25). Therefore let go your own thoughts and
feelings and esteem this book as the best and purest treasure,
as a mine full of great wealth, which can never be exhausted
or sufficiently excavated. Thus you will find the divine wisdom which God presents in the Bible in a manner so simple
that it damps the pride of clever people and brings it to
nought. In this book you find the swaddling clothes and the
manger in which Christ lies, and to which the angel directs
the shepherds. Those swaddling clothes are shabby and poor,
yet precious is the treasure wrapped in them, for it is Christ.

Table-Talk.   W.A. Tischreden 6. 16.

Those by the way side are they that hear; then cometh
the devil, and taketh away the word out of their hearts,
lest they should believe and be saved. LUKE viii. 12.

This is the true black, or rather the white appearance of the devil. For he is a bright and brilliant devil, who does not tempt us with gross sins but with unbelief. For when he has our faith he has won. Man must have God's Word and cleave to it by faith. As soon as he allows himself to be sundered from the Word he is lost and there is no help for him.

Therefore mark how the devil works, for he attacks nothing but faith. Pagans, the unbelieving, the non-Christians he does not tempt. They cling to him like scales to a fish. But when he sees those who have the Word of God, faith, and the Holy Ghost, he cannot get at them. He well knows that he can never win the victory over them, though they may stumble. He well perceives that even if one falls into gross sin, he is not lost thereby, for he can always rise again. Therefore he realises that he must try a different method and take away their greatest good. If he can prevail upon the soul and make her doubt whether it is the Word of God, the game is won. For God can work all things for good, however often we may stumble, only if we abide by the pure, true Word of God, which says: this is right and this is wrong. The devil knows this, hence he first sneaks in at this point. Once faith is torn away, no man can of himself resist the devil. He inevitably falls into all kinds of vice.

Exposition of Genesis iii.   W.A. 24. 86.

Behold, the days come, saith the Lord God, that I will
send a famine in the land, not a famine of bread, nor
a thirst for water, but of hearing the words of the
Lord: And they shall wander from sea to sea, and
from the north even to the east, they shall run to and
fro to seek the word of the Lord, and shall not find it.
AMOS viii. 11–12.

God's wrath is never greater than when He is silent and
does not speak to us, but leaves us to follow our own mind
and will, and do as we please.

O, dear Lord God, punish us with pestilence and with any
foul diseases rather than by Thy silence. God speaks: 'I have
stretched out My hand and cried, "Come hither and hearken!"
But you answer: "No, we will not!" I send My servants unto
you, the Prophets Isaiah, Jeremiah, and others, and I say to
you: "Hearken unto them!" "Yes", you say, "we will strike
them dead!" "There, you have My Son." "Yes, we will
crucify Him!" '

We still act in the same way, as can easily be seen. We are
weary and tired of the Word of God. We do not want to hear
devout and faithful teachers who chastise us, and preach to
us the pure and unadulterated Word of God, who keep a
careful watch, earnestly condemning false teaching and faithfully warning us against it. Therefore God will surely
chastise us.

O, heavenly Father, keep us for ever by this radiant sun,
and do not let us fall from Thy Word and stumble into false
teaching.

Table-Talk. W.A. Tischreden 5. 237 f.

*He that rejecteth me, and receiveth not my words, hath
one that judgeth him: the word that I have spoken,
the same shall judge him in the last day.* JOHN xii. 48.

The dear Lord sees what poor and wretched people we are.
Unless we have the treasure of the holy Gospel, one error
always tumbles over another.

And again, when we have the Gospel a far more dreadful
calamity occurs, namely, that every man despises it, and the
few accept it for their betterment. Hence we are thoroughly
poor and wretched people. If God withhold His Word from
us, we cannot live without it, without suffering detriment to
our souls. On the other hand, if He grants it, nobody wants
it. Hence there is nothing better than that the Lord God
should hasten the Last Day, to smite everything into a heap,
for the ungrateful world will not be helped either by grace
or punishment.

Therefore He admonishes us again and appoints another
day, saying: 'Today, if you will hear His voice, harden not
your hearts'. Behold, every day is 'Today!' and God calls
and appeals to us not to miss the opportunity.

And it is right for us to thank God most deeply for such
grace, that He comes so near to us, abides with us in our
homes, at our table, at our bedside and wherever we want
Him, offering and presenting us all His help, and all things
which we may ask of Him. Yes, we ought to treasure and
honour this dear guest because He stays with us.

Sermon on Ephesians v. 15–21.   W.A. 22. 329.

*Wherefore now do ye transgress the commandment of
the Lord? But it shall not prosper.* NUMBERS xiv. 41.

I consider that Germany has never before heard so much
of God's Word as now. There is no trace of it in history. But
if we let it pass by without thanks and honour, I am afraid
that we shall have to suffer plague and grimmer darkness. My
dear Germans, buy while the mart is at your door; gather in
while the sun is shining and the weather good, make use of
God's Word of Grace while it is there. For know this, that
the Word of God's grace is like a sweeping downpour, which
never returns to where it has already been. It has visited the
Jews; but it has gone. Now they have nothing. Paul brought
it to Greece; from there it has also gone. Now they have the
Turks. Rome and the Latin lands have had their visitation;
but it has gone. Now they have the Pope. And you Germans
must not think that you will have it for ever, for it will not
stay where there is ingratitude and contempt. Therefore, let
all take hold and keep hold who can. Lazy hands must have
an evil year.

To the Councillors of all German cities,   E.A. 22. 175 f.
*that they should establish and main-
tain Christian Schools, 1520.*

Quinquagesima

TAKE UP THY CROSS AND FOLLOW ME

Sunday : Luke xviii. 31–34

Then he took unto him the twelve, and said unto them, Behold, we go up to Jerusalem, and all things that are written by the prophets concerning the Son of Man shall be accomplished. Luke xviii. 31.

The right way to reach a true knowledge of Christ's sufferings is to perceive and understand not only what He suffered, but how it was His heart and will to suffer. For whoever looks upon Christ's sufferings without seeing His heart and will therein must be filled with fear rather than joy, but if we can truly see His heart and will in it, it gives true comfort, trust, and joy in Christ.

Such will to suffer He reveals here in the Gospel, when He declares that He will go up to Jerusalem in order to be crucified, as if He spake, Behold My heart, and see that I will endure My suffering freely and gladly in obedience to My Father's will, so that you must not be afraid nor terrified when you behold My sufferings and think that I bear them unwillingly, that I am compelled to endure them and am forsaken, and that the Jews have power to do this to Me.

But the disciples did not understand His meaning and the Word was hidden from them. This shows that reason, flesh, and blood cannot grasp nor understand that the Gospel should tell us how that the Son of Man must be crucified. Much less can they perceive that such should be His will and that He did it joyfully. It is such a great and wonderful thing that the Son of Man is crucified willingly and joyfully in order that the Scriptures should be fulfilled, that is, for our good. It is and it remains a mystery.

Sermons from the year 1525.   W.A. 17. II. 173 f.

> *Rejoice, inasmuch as ye are partakers of Christ's sufferings.*   I PETER iv. 13.

Illness, poverty, pain, and the like must not be called a cross; they are not worthy of that name. But if a man suffer persecution for his faith, that may rightly be called a cross. But how can it be found? Not in cloisters, but in the Gospel and in the true understanding of it. This is finding the cross: to know your own self, or to know the cross. Where do you find that? In your heart. Unless you find it there the finding of it outwardly is of no avail. 'Whosoever willeth to come to me, let him take up his cross and follow me.' You must come to the point when you say, 'My Lord and my God, would that I were worthy of it'. You must be as joyful about it as were the dear saints.

The honour of the cross must be inwardly, within the heart, that is, that I give thanks unto God that I must suffer, and that must spring from a joyful will towards the cross or death.

Is it not a wonder to be possessed of a ready will towards death, while everyone dreads it? Thus is the cross sanctified.

Sermons from the year 1527.   W.A. 17. II. 425 f.

Whosoever doth not bear his cross, and come after me,
cannot be my disciple. LUKE xiv. 27.

Although we must not count our suffering and cross for
merit, or regard it as a means to win salvation, we must follow
Christ in His suffering in order that we may be made like Him.
For God has ordained that we shall not only believe in Christ
crucified, but that we shall suffer and be crucified with Him;
as He clearly shows in many places in the Gospels.

Therefore each Christian must bear a part of the holy
cross, and it cannot be otherwise. As St. Paul says (Colossians
i. 24): 'I fill up that which is behind of the afflictions of Christ
in my flesh'. As if he would say: His whole Christian company is not yet complete. We, too, must follow after, that
nothing of the suffering of Christ fail to reach fruition, but
all be gathered up into one. Therefore each Christian should
consider that his own cross will surely come.

But it must be a cross that really presses and hurts, such as
great risk to honour and possessions, body and life. Such
suffering does really hurt, and if it did not hurt, it would not
be suffering.

But if you know this, it is all the lighter and easier, and you
can comfort yourself, saying: If I will be a Christian, I must
bear the colours. The dear Lord Christ issues no other garment for His Court. Suffering has to be.

Sermon on suffering and the Cross. W.A. 32. 29.

Blessed is the man whom thou chastenest, O Lord,
and teachest him out of thy law. PSALM xciv. 12.

It is highly necessary that we should suffer, not only that
God may thereby prove His honour, might, and strength
against the devil, but also because the great and precious
treasure which we have, if it were given unto us without such
suffering and affliction would make us snore in our security.
And we can see—unfortunately it is a general thing—that
many abuse the Holy Gospel, behaving as if they were freed
from all obligations through the Gospel and that there is
nothing more they need do, or give or suffer. This is a sin and
a shame.

The only way our God can check such evil is through the
cross. He must so discipline us that our faith increases and
grows stronger, and we thus draw the Saviour all the deeper
into our soul. For we can no more grow strong without
suffering and temptation than we can without eating and
drinking.

Therefore since it is better that we should be given a cross
than that we should be spared a cross, no man must falter and
take fright at it. Have you not a good, strong promise wherein
to take comfort? Nor can the Gospel advance except through
us as we suffer willingly and bear our cross.

Sermon on suffering and the Cross. W.A. 32. 37 f.

Nevertheless I am continually with thee.

PSALM lxxiii. 23.

If for the sake of God's Word hardship, sorrow, and persecution come to us, all which follow in the train of the holy cross, the following thoughts should, with God's help, comfort and console us, and should make us determine to be of good cheer, full of courage and confidence, and lead us to surrender the cause trustfully into God's gracious and fatherly will.

First, that our cause is in the hands of Him who says so clearly, 'No man shall pluck them from My hand'. It would not be wise to take our cause into our own hands, for we could and should lose it by our loose ways. Likewise all the comfortable words are true and do not lie, which say, 'God is our refuge and strength'. Has any man who puts his trust in God ever been put to shame? All who trust in God will be saved, and again: 'Thou Lord hast not forsaken them that seek Thee'. Thus it is really true that God gave His only-begotten Son for our salvation. If God gave His own Son for us, how could He ever bring Himself to desert us in small things?

God is much stronger, mightier, and more powerful than the devil. Thus says St. John: 'Greater is He that is in you than he that is in the world'. If we fall, Christ, the Almighty King of this world, must suffer with us, and even if His cause should fall, we should wish rather to fall with Christ than to stand with the highest power on earth.

Comforting words.   W.A. 48. 327 f.

All that will live godly in Christ Jesus shall suffer persecution.   2 TIMOTHY iii. 12.

But we teach that no man should impose upon himself a cross or suffering of his choosing; but if the cross comes to us we should suffer and endure it patiently. We also say that we merit nothing by our suffering. It is sufficient that we know that our suffering is well-pleasing to God, that through it we may be made Christ-like. Thus we see that precisely those who teach so much about a cross and suffering and praise it so highly, know least of Christ and His cross, because they claim their own suffering to be meritorious. My friend, such is not the meaning. Neither is any man constrained or forced to it. If you will not suffer without thought of merit, then leave suffering alone and at the same time deny Christ. This you surely know, that if you will not suffer, you cannot be a servant of Christ. So you may choose which you like of the two: whether you suffer or you deny Christ.

Finally, the suffering of Christians is nobler and finer than the suffering of all other people, for since Christ plunged Himself into suffering He thereby sanctified the suffering of all His Christians. Hence, now, through the sufferings of Christ the sufferings of all His saints are made into a holy thing, because they are anointed with the sufferings of Christ. And that is why we must receive all suffering as a holy thing, for it truly is a holy thing.

Sermon on suffering and the Cross.   W.A. 32. 30 ff.

Peace I leave with you, my peace I give unto you; not as the world giveth, give I unto you. Let not your heart be troubled, neither let it be afraid. JOHN xiv. 27.

Thus we perceive the office of the Holy Ghost, that He is given only to those who are sunk in suffering and misery. For this is the meaning of the words which He speaks: think not that the peace which I give you is like what the world gives. The world calls it peace when the suffering is cut off and sundered from a man, as, for example, when a man is poor he thinks that he has much bitterness because of poverty, and he ponders how to get rid of poverty, thinking that if he can get rid of that, his person will now be able to live in peace and wealth. Again, if a man is about to die, he thinks, if I could but throw off death I should live and have peace. But that is not the peace which Christ gives. Rather He allows the evil which is laid upon a man to lie upon him still and to continue oppressing him, and He does not take it away, but He useth another device: He changes the man and sunders the person from the evil, and not the evil from the person.

And this is how it is done: you are held in the grip of suffering. He turns you away from it and gives you such courage that you would think you were sitting in a rose-garden. Thus there is life in the midst of dying, and peace and joy in the midst of adversity, and that is why it is such a peace as, as St. Paul says to the Philippians (iv. 7), surpasses all understanding.

Sermons from the year 1523.   W.A. 12. 576 f.

Lent

Invocavit

TRIAL AND TEMPTATION

Sunday: MATTHEW iv. 1–11

*For we have not a high priest which cannot be touched
with the feeling of our infirmities; but was in all points
tempted like as we are, yet without sin.*

HEBREWS iv. 15.

When the devil tempts me, my heart is comforted and my
faith is strengthened, because I know Him who for my sake
has overcome the devil, and that He comes to me to be my
help and my comfort. Thus faith overcomes the devil. Therefore, first, God teaches me faith, that I may know that for my
sake Christ has overcome the devil. Then, since I now know
that the devil has no power over me but is overcome by faith,
I must be ready to be tempted. The purpose of this is that
my faith may be strengthened, and that my neighbour may
be given an example by my victory over temptation, and
may be comforted.

And mark this: whenever faith begins, temptation soon
follows. The Holy Ghost does not leave·you to rest in quietness, but soon He throws you into temptation. Why? In order
that your faith may be confirmed, for otherwise the devil
would blow us about like chaff. But if God comes and hangs
a weight on us, making us weighty and heavy, then it is
manifest to the devil and to all mankind that the power of
God is at work. Thus God manifests His glory and majesty
in our weakness, therefore He casts us out into the desert,
that is, He casts us down, so that we are deserted of all
creatures and can see no help. We even think that God Himself has utterly forsaken us. For as He acts towards Christ,
even so does He act towards us. It does not run smoothly.
Our heart must faint within us.

Sermons from the year 1523.   W.A. 11. 22 f.

*And because thou wast acceptable to God, it was
necessary that temptation should prove thee.*

TOBIT xi. 15. (approx.)

Since God Himself has called our life a temptation, and
since it is ordained that we should be afflicted in body, possessions, and honour, and suffer unrighteousness, we should
meet such things joyfully, and receive them wisely, saying:
yes, such is the way of life, what shall I do about it? It is a
temptation and it remains a temptation, and it has no other
meaning. So help me God, it shall not move me nor cast me
down.

No man may be lifted up above temptation. But we can
guard ourselves and seek counsel in prayer, calling for the
help of God. Thus you may read in the book of the Elders,
that a young brother wanted to be rid of his thoughts. Said
the Elder, Dear brother, you cannot hinder the birds in the
air from flying over your head; but you can prevent them from
building a nest in your hair. In that self-same manner (as St.
Augustine says) we cannot guard ourselves against temptation and stumbling; but with prayer and with the help of
God we can prevent them overcoming us.

And why does God suffer man to be thus tempted to sin?
Answer: That man may learn to know God and himself. To
know himself, that he can do nothing but sin and do evil.
To know God, that God's grace is mightier than all creatures.
And thus man learns to despise himself, and to laud and praise
the grace of God.

Exposition of the Lord's Prayer for   W.A. 2. 124 ff.
simple lay-folk.

Then saith Jesus unto him, Get thee hence, Satan:
for it is written, Thou shalt worship the Lord thy
God, and him only shalt thou serve. MATTHEW iv. 10.

This is the twofold armour with which the devil is slain
and at which he is afraid: to hearken unceasingly to the Word
of God, to instruct oneself in it, and to be comforted and
strengthened by it. Then, when temptation and struggle come
upon us, to lift up our hearts to that self-same Word, and cry
to God, invoking Him for help. Hence one of the two things
is always present, continuing as an eternal conversation
between God and the soul. Either He speaks to us and we
are still, listening to God, or He listens to us as we speak to
Him, praying for what we need.

Whatever way it may be, the devil cannot endure it, and
he cannot hold his own against it. Therefore Christians must
be girt with both, so that their hearts may be everlastingly
turned towards God, keeping His Word and with unceasing
sighs eternally praying: 'Our Father'. This perseverance a
Christian will be taught by temptation and calamity with
which he is constantly oppressed by the devil, the world, and
the flesh, so that he must ever keep his head up, watching for
the assault of the enemy who neither sleeps for a moment
nor takes his ease.

Sermons from the year 1539.   W.A. 47. 758.

*The sorrows of death compassed me, and the pains of
hell gat hold upon me: I found trouble and sorrow.
Then called I upon the name of the Lord: O Lord,
I beseech thee, deliver my soul.* PSALM cxvi. 3–4.

When God has given us true faith, so that we walk in firm
trust, having no doubt that He, through Christ, is gracious
unto us, then we are in paradise. But before we do anything
wrong, all that may be changed and God may allow our heart
to faint, so that we think it is His will to snatch the Saviour
from our heart. Then is Christ so veiled that we can have no
comfort in Him, and the devil pours into our hearts the most
terrible thoughts about Him, so that our conscience feels it
has lost Him, and is cast down and disquieted as if there were
nothing but God's wrath towards us, which we by our sins
have well deserved.

Yea, even if we know of no open sins, yet the devil has
the power to make sin out of what is no sin, and thus he
frightens our heart and makes us anxious so that we are tormented by such questions as: Who knows whether God will
have you and give Christ to you?

This is the direst and deepest temptation and suffering with
which God now and again attacks and tests even His greatest
saints, so that the heart feels that God has taken His grace
away from us; that He no longer wills to be our God, and
whithersoever man turns he sees nothing but wrath and
terror. Yet is not every soul sorely tempted, nor does any
man know what it is like unless he has experienced it. Only
the strongest spirits could endure such blows.

Sermons from the year 1525.   W.A. 17. II. 20 f.

Thanks be to God, which giveth us the victory through our Lord Jesus Christ. 1 CORINTHIANS XV. 57.

Here shall a Christian learn how to grasp and use the Gospel message, when the time of battle is come and the Law attacks and accuses him, and his own conscience tells him: this wrong you have done, and you are a sinner, and what you deserve is death, and so on, that at such a time he may with true confidence reply: Alas, I am a sinner and I have well deserved death. You are right, but condemn and kill me on that account you shall not. There is One who will hinder you, who is called my Lord Christ, whom you have accused and murdered, although He was innocent. But do you not know how you were burnt and bruised by Him, thus losing all your rights over me and all other Christians? For He bore sin and death, not for His own sake, but for me. Therefore, I grant you no right over me, rather I have a right over you, because you attack me although I am innocent, you who were before conquered and condemned by Him, so that you should leave me in peace. For I am no longer merely a child of man; I have become the child of God; for I have been baptised in His blood and His victory, and arrayed in all the riches of His bounty.

Behold, in such manner must all Christians arm themselves with the victory of Christ and repel the devil with it.

Sermons from the year 1532.   W.A. 36. 693 f.

Looking unto Jesus, the author and finisher of our faith; who for the joy that was set before him endured the cross, despising the shame. HEBREWS xii. 2.

In all temptations we should keep our gaze fixed on the image of Christ, and keep close to it. For Christ goes on, however much it hurts, and He is full of courage. Therefore we must pray that He will also give us His courage and spirit, that we too may learn to be strong in the midst of weakness and to overcome in the days of affliction. In this way Christ comes to us not as an image. He implants in us all His courage, so that we too can endure. Therefore, whatever may come upon us, however much shame and blame, people will see that Christ, our prince, perceives and overcomes it triumphantly. Therefore we must beseech Him for courage that, in the midst of besetting adversities, we may be made strong and be given power to overcome death.

In this self-same way Paul sets Christ before us in all his Epistles: first, as an example, which we are to follow, then as He gives us the spirit and the courage which He Himself possesses. And this is the true Christian teaching.

Similarly, no one knows how to use the Passion of Christ, and no one rightly experiences it unless he has endured adversities and been brought near to Christ, and has suffered and come through because he received from Christ the power to endure. In this spirit one must come right to the centre and learn how to use Christ.

Sermons from the year 1522.   W.A. 10. III. 77.

And she said, Truth, Lord: yet the dogs eat of the crumbs which fall from their masters' table. Then Jesus answered and said unto her, O woman, great is thy faith: be it unto thee even as thou wilt.

MATTHEW XV. 27–28.

Is not this masterly? She catches Christ by means of His own words. He compares her to a dog, which she admits and she asks no more than that He let her be like a dog as He Himself judges: Whither could He turn? He was caught. No dog is denied the breadcrumbs under the table. They are its rightful share. Therefore He takes heed of her and submits to her will, so that she is no longer a dog but is become a child of Israel.

And this was written in order that we might be comforted and that it may be made manifest to us all how deeply God hides His grace from us, and that we should not judge Him according to our feeling and thinking about Him but in accordance with His Word. For here you see that Christ, although He showed Himself hard, pronounced no final judgement by saying 'No' to her; but all His answers, though they sound like 'No', are yet not 'No' but are indefinite.

Therewith is shown how our heart should stand firm in the midst of temptations, for as hard as we feel Him, so Christ feigns to be. Our heart hears and understands nothing but 'No' and yet it is not 'No'. Therefore sweep your heart clean of such feelings and trust firmly in God's Word and grasp from above or from underneath the 'No' the deeply hidden 'Yes' and hold on to it as this woman did and keep a firm belief in God's justice. Then you have won and caught Him with His own words.

Sermons from the year 1525.   W.A. 17. II. 203.

Reminiscere

HE WAS OBEDIENT UNTO DEATH

Sunday: PHILIPPIANS ii. 5–11

My meat is to do the will of him that sent me, and to finish his work. JOHN iv. 34.

The will of God which Christ came to do can be nothing else but Christ's own obedience, as Paul says: 'He was obedient for us'. By that will we are all sanctified: 'Through the obedience of the one shall the many be made righteous' (Romans v).

'He humbled Himself, becoming obedient even unto death.'

But all this He did, not because we have merited it or are worthy of it (for who is the man to be worthy of such a service from such a person?), but because He obeyed His Father. By this saying St. Paul with one word flings open the gates of heaven, thus letting us behold the unspeakable, gracious will and love of the Father's heart towards us, so that we feel how from the beginning of time Christ's sacrifice for us has been well-pleasing unto God.

What heart should not melt with joy at this? Who should not love, and laud, and thank? Who should not joyfully become the servant of all the world, and even less than nothing, when he perceives that God holds him to be so dear and precious to Him, and that He proves and pours out His Fatherly will so abundantly in His own Son's obedience?

Sermons from the year 1525.   W.A. 17. II. 244.

Thy will be done.   MATTHEW xxvi. 42.

Who is the man to keep this holy command to let go all things and seek his will in nothing? Therefore learn here how important and necessary it is, and with what earnestness of heart this prayer must be prayed, and what a mighty thing it is that our will be slain, and solely God's Will be done. And thus you must confess yourself a sinner, powerless to do the will of God, and then must pray for help and grace that God forgive you for what is lacking and help you to do what is required. For our will must perish, if God's Will is to be done; for they are set against each other. Notice that when Christ our Lord prayed in the garden, that His heavenly Father would take the cup from Him, He prayed even then: 'Not my will, but thy will be done'. If even Christ's Will, which was always truly good, and the best that ever was, had to cease, that His Father's Will should be done, how shall we poor and wretched worms glory in our will, which is always tainted with evil and always deserves to be impeded?

Exposition of the Lord's Prayer for   W.A. 2. 102.
    simple lay-folk.

This is the confidence that we have in him, that, if we
ask anything according to his will, he heareth us.
I JOHN V. 14.

The affliction which caused the Lord in this instance to
pray was a temporal, physical affliction. Now in all things
which concern the body we ought to give our will to God,
for, as St. Paul says, we know not how to pray. Thus it is
often most needful for us that God should leave us under
the cross and overwhelmed by calamities. And as God alone
knows what is good and needful, it behoves us to place His
will before our will and to prove our obedience in patience.

But where the eternal and not the temporal good is concerned, namely, that God keeps us by His Word, sanctifies
us, forgives our sins, and bestows upon us the Holy Ghost
and eternal life, there God's will is certain and manifest. He
wills that all men be saved. He wills that all men shall see and
acknowledge their sins and that they all, through Christ, shall
believe in the forgiveness of sins. Therefore, in such a case it
is not necessary to say 'Not my will, but Thine be done'.
We ought to know and believe that God delights to do such
things, and that He will undoubtedly do them. For, behold,
here we have His Word before our eyes which reveals His
will in such things.

Sermons for the year 1545.   W.A. 52. 741 f.

[He] make you perfect in every good work to do his will,
working in you that which is wellpleasing in his sight,
through Jesus Christ; to whom be glory for ever and
ever. Amen.   HEBREWS xiii. 21.

Even if you desired to convert the whole world to God,
to raise the dead, to lead yourself and all other men to heaven,
and work great miracles, you should think none of these
things unless you have put God's will first and submitted your
own will to do good to Him, saying, 'Dear God, these things
appear to me to be good; if they please Thee, may they be
done; if they do not please Thee, may they remain undone'.

And even such a truly good will God often breaks down
in His saints, lest through the good appearance the false and
wicked good will should enter and in order that we should
learn that our will, however good, is yet unmeasurably lower
than the will of God.

Thus, our good will is obstructed in order that it may be
made better, for God certainly obstructs a good will only to
make it better. And it is made better, when it is subject and
obedient to the will of God (through which it was obstructed)
until it has become utterly free and abandoned, and knows
nothing but that it waits upon the will of God. Behold, that
is what is called true obedience.

Exposition of the Lord's Prayer for   W.A. 2. 103 f.
simple lay-folk.

*Though he were a Son, yet learned he obedience by
the things which he suffered; and being made perfect,
he became the author of eternal salvation unto all
them that obey him.* HEBREWS v. 8–9.

Christ so loved us that for pure love He came down from
heaven. It was the Father's will that He should love us sinners, and likewise is it the Father's will that we, beholding
the manhood of Christ, should love Him. Yet we must remember that He did all this by command, and in accordance
with the most high good pleasure. Otherwise it is a terrifying
thing to meditate upon Christ. For the Father's is the power
and the Son's is the wisdom, and the Holy Ghost's is the love.
To these we can never attain, but we must fall into despair
before them.

But we know that Christ has come down from heaven
to love sinners, out of obedience to His Father; and when
we meditate on that there grows up in us boldness of access,
and a firm hope in Christ, for we perceive that Christ is the
true charter, the golden book wherein we read, and learn to
see Him obedient to the Father's will.

Thus our conscience is no longer wretched, because in
Christ it is quickened and fortified.

And this tastes sweet to a devout soul, and it gives through
the Son, Jesus Christ, all glory, laud, and praise to the Father.
Thus God has only the best, which He imparts to us, feeding
us, upholding us, and waiting upon us, through His Son
Jesus Christ. And thus our heart is changed, so that we follow
Christ.

And this is why Christ loves sinners; for His Father has
commanded Him so to do.

Lenten sermon from the year 1518.   W.A. I. 274 f.

> *Thinkest thou that I cannot now pray to my Father,*
> *and he shall presently give me more than twelve*
> *legions of angels? But how then shall the scriptures*
> *be fulfilled, that thus it must be?*
>
> MATTHEW xxvi. 53–54.

One angel would have been enough to defend Christ against the power of the Jews. And Christ said that He might have had twelve legions of angels, that is, more than seventy thousand angels. One angel would have sufficed to defend Christ even against the whole world.

But Christ says: 'Put up again thy sword into its place. How should the Scriptures be fulfilled?' As if He said, the Scriptures will not be fulfilled except I suffer. But the Scriptures must be fulfilled, therefore these things must all come to pass. This is the reason why Christ suffered. He did not suffer because He was compelled to do so, or because God could not find any other way to manifest His honour and glory; but that God should be found truthful in keeping His Word, which He hath spoken through the Prophets. It was God's will to act according to His good pleasure. He could have acted otherwise, but that was not His will.

Sermons from the year 1534.   W.A. 37. 324 f.

Christ also suffered for us, leaving us an example, that
ye should follow his steps.   I PETER ii. 21.

When your heart is confirmed in Christ and is opposed
to sin out of love, not out of fear of punishment, then the
suffering of Christ should become an example for your whole
life, and you should regard suffering in a different manner.
If pain or illness beset you, think of how little this is compared with the nails and the crown of thorns of Christ. If
you have to do or leave something which you do not wish
to do or leave, think of how Christ was caught and bound
and led hither and thither. If pride tempts you, behold, your
Lord was mocked and despised with the thieves. If lust and
unchastity kindle you, think of how bitterly Christ's tender
flesh was scourged, pierced, and lashed. If hate and envy
tempt you, or if you seek revenge, think of how Christ, with
uncountable tears and sighs, has prayed for you and all His
enemies, He who might well have taken revenge. And if
affliction or any other adversity, physical or spiritual, grieve
you, fortify your heart, saying: 'Why, then, should I not suffer
some small woe when My Lord in the garden sweated blood,
with fear and anguish? 'A wretched and slothful servant
would be the man who lies comfortably in his bed, while his
master struggles with the pains of death'

Meditation on the holy suffering of Christ.   W.A. 2. 141.

Oculi

THE SON OF MAN IS COME TO SERVE

Sunday: JOHN xiii. 1–5

Jesus knowing that the Father had given all things into his hands, . . . took a towel, . . . and began to wash the disciples' feet, . . . JOHN xiii. 3–5.

These are truly great words by which St. John desires to indicate what thoughts were in the mind of the Lord Jesus before He rose and washed their feet. He did not think of His sufferings, neither was His mind heavy with the sorrow which followed soon after He had washed their feet. He thought about His glory which He shared with His Father from eternity, to which, having fulfilled His human life, He was to return, to remain therein for evermore. Those were lofty thoughts which might well have so drawn Him out of the world, that He might not have thought of any man at all.

But just then, when He was meditating on eternal glory, He rose from supper, laid aside His garments, took a towel, girded Himself with it, poured water into a vessel . . .

See how His thoughts and His work agree. His thoughts are: I am God and Lord over all things; in less than a day the devil will have done his worst. Then he and all My enemies will lie at My feet and leave My Christians in peace. But what is His work? He, the greatest of Lords, does what slaves and servants do. He washes His disciples' feet.

In this manner He sought to give us an example, that, as He laid aside His glory and forgot it, and never abused it for His own pride, power, and splendour, but used it for the good of His servants, we should do the same. We should never exalt ourselves because of our gifts, never abuse them as an occasion of pride, but serve our neighbour with them to the very limit of our power.

Sermon on Maundy Thursday, 1544.　　　　W.A. 52. 218 f.

Even as the Son of man came not to be ministered unto, but to minister, and to give his life a ransom for many.   MATTHEW xx. 28.

Look at this picture and love it. There is no greater bondage or form of service than that the Son of God should be the servant and should bear the sin of every man, however poor and wretched or despised. What an amazing thing it would be if some great king's son should go into a beggar's hut to nurse him in his illness, wash off his filth and do all the things which otherwise the beggar would have to do. All the world would gape with open mouths, noses, ears, and eyes, and could never think and talk enough about it. Would that not be a wonderful humility?

Therefore would it be well to sing, talk, and preach of this for evermore, and on our part to love and praise God for so gracious a gift. But, behold, what does it mean? The Son of God becomes my servant and humbles Himself so much that He carries even my afflictions and my sin; yea, the whole world's sin and death He takes upon Himself, saying to me: You are no longer a sinner, but I, I Myself step into your place. You have not sinned; I have. The whole world lies in sin, but you are not in sin, but I am. All your sin shall be upon Me, and not on you.

No man can comprehend it. In the life hereafter we shall have a knowledge of the love of God and gaze upon it in eternal blessedness.

Exposition of John i.   W.A. 46. 680 f.

Being in the form of God, he thought it not robbery to be equal with God: but made himself of no reputation, and took upon him the form of a servant, and was made in the likeness of men, being found in fashion as a man. PHILIPPIANS ii. 6–8.

First we need a Saviour who can save us from the god and prince of this world, the devil, and likewise from sin and death, that is, a Saviour who is eternal God, through whom all that believe in Him are justified and blessed. For if He is no more and no higher than Moses, Elias, Isaiah, or John the Baptist, He is not our Redeemer. But if He, as the Son of God, sheds His blood for us in order to redeem us and cleanse us from sin, and if we believe it and hold it under the devil's nose whenever he frightens and plagues us with our sin, the devil will soon be beaten so that he must give way and leave us in peace.

Then we need a Saviour who is also our brother, of our flesh and blood, made in all things like us, yet without sin, as we are taught to say and sing as little children, so that I can say with a joyful heart: I believe in Jesus Christ, the only begotten Son of God, who sits at the right hand of the Father and intercedes for me, who is also my flesh and blood, yes, my Brother. Because for us men and for our salvation He came down from heaven and was made Man and died for our sin.

Exposition of John i.   W.A. 46. 556 f.

*Who gave himself for our sins, that he might deliver
us from this present evil world, according to the will
of God and our Father.*   GALATIANS i. 4.

Friend, take these words : 'who gave Himself . . .' to heart,
and meditate upon them with earnest zeal. Then you will
come to see that the word 'sin' comprises the eternal wrath
of God and all Satan's hellish might and power. For, that he
inflicts so much misery and woe on earth that our lives are
not for a moment safe from him, and we must be unceasingly prepared for many dire afflictions, all this is because of
sin. Therefore it is not so trifling a matter as blind and confident reason dreams.

Therefore this passage ends most emphatically, saying that
all men are in the bondage of sin, or (as St. Paul says elsewhere) 'they are sold under sin' (Romans vii. 14). Further,
that sin is a powerful and cruel master and tyrant over all
mankind in the whole earth, and that no man can resist it,
however wise, high, learned, and mighty he may be. Yes,
even if all men under the sky would unite, even with all their
power, they could not overcome this tyrant, but would all
have to submit, and be slain and devoured by him. Jesus
Christ alone is the hero who can thwart that cruel, unconquerable foe. But it costs our Lord very dearly, for He must
lose His life in doing it.

Commentary on Galatians.   W.A. 40. I. 82 ff.

*Who hath delivered us from the power of darkness,
and hath translated us into the kingdom of his dear
Son: in whom we have redemption through his blood,
even the forgiveness of sins.*   COLOSSIANS i. 13–14.

Because sin was under an eternal, unchangeable condemnation (for God cannot and will not be gracious to sin, wherefore His wrath remains eternal and irrevocable against it), this
redemption could not take place unless something precious
and valuable should compensate for sin, taking the wrath
upon itself and paying the price, so taking away sin and
blotting it out utterly. No creature could do this, nor was
there any other way to help except that God's own Son
should come to our aid and be made Man, should draw the
Eternal wrath upon Himself and give His own life and blood
as a sacrifice.

This He has done, in His great and immeasurable mercy
and love towards us. He gave Himself and bore the condemnation of eternal wrath and death. This costly sacrifice
is so dear and precious to God because it is the deed of His
own beloved Son, who is one with Him in Godhead and
Majesty, that He is reconciled through it and forgives the
sins and receives in grace all that believe in His Son.

For this reason alone we enjoy the fruits and merits of the
dear redeeming deed, won and given to us out of unfathomable and unspeakable love, and thus we have nothing of our
own to boast about, but we can only give thanks and praise
Him who gave such a price to redeem us lost and condemned
sinners.

Exposition of Colossians i. 3–14.   W.A. 22. 389.

And Moses made a serpent of brass, and put it upon
a pole, and it came to pass, that if a serpent had bitten
any man, when he beheld the serpent of brass, he lived.
NUMBERS xxi. 9.

Similarly, you must think only of Christ's death, and you will find life. Look not on the sin which is in the sinner, or in your own conscience, or in those who remain in their sins and are damned. You would surely follow them and be overcome. You must turn your thoughts away and not look upon sin except in the image of grace. Form this image in your mind with all your strength and keep it before your eyes.

The image of grace is nothing other than Christ crucified, and all His dear saints. How is that to be understood? That Christ on the cross takes away your sin and carries it for you and destroys it. That is grace and mercy. Believe firmly in it, have it before your eyes and do not doubt it. That is to behold the image of grace and to form it in yourself.

Lo! The wonder: Sin is no longer sin. It is bound and consumed in Christ. Thus Christ is the image of life and of grace, and over against the picture of death He is our bliss and beatitude.

Sermon on preparing to die.   W.A. 2. 689 f.

Remember the word that I said unto you, The servant is not greater than his lord. If they have persecuted me, they will also persecute you. JOHN XV. 20.

These words should be engraved (as we have said) into the hearts of all the servants of Christ, and should move them to do and suffer joyfully whatsoever is ordained for them. For the Lord Christ has done so much for them that they must think: since my Lord, although He was under no obligation, has served me, why should not I, in my turn, serve Him? He was pure and without sin, and yet He cast Himself so low and shed His blood for me and died to blot out my sin. Should not I then suffer a little for Him, to please Him? Whoever considers this must have a heart of stone if it does not move him. For when the Lord goes ahead, surely, His servant follows.

Therefore St. Peter says: 'Thereunto are ye called'. Whereunto? To suffer injustice as Christ did, as if he meant to say: If you would follow Christ, do not argue and complain when you suffer injustice, but accept the suffering with patience and forbearance because Christ, although He was without sin, suffered everything.

You should praise God and give thanks to Him that you are worthy to be made like Christ, and not complain or be impatient when people do you hurt.

Exposition of 1 Peter.   W.A. 12. 339 f.

Laetare

CHRIST'S SACRIFICE

Sunday: ROMANS V. 1–11

God commendeth his love toward us, in that, while we were yet sinners, Christ died for us. ROMANS V. 8.

He sacrifices Himself on the cross, becomes a sinner and a curse; and yet He alone is the blessed seed through whom all the world shall be blessed, that is, redeemed from sin and death. And that He hangs on the cross between two male-factors, being counted equal to them, and that He dies there a shameful death, all this He does for the benefit of the whole human race, to redeem it from the eternal curse. Thus He is both the greatest and the only sinner on earth, for He bears all the world's sin, and the only righteous and holy One; for no man can be made righteous and holy before God save through Him alone.

And whosoever believes that his sin and the sin of the world is laid on our dear Lord, who was baptised and nailed to the cross for it, and shed His precious blood in order that He, the only sin-bearer, should thus cleanse us from sin, and make us holy and blessed, that man receives forgiveness of sins, and eternal life; and Christ's baptism, cross and blood become his own.

Sermons from the year 1540.   W.A. 49. 121.

Who in the days of his flesh, when he had offered up
prayers and supplications with strong crying and
tears unto him that was able to save him from death,
and was heard in that he feared.   HEBREWS V. 7.

Merciful Father, why does my Lord Christ Jesus shrink?
Why does the Son of God shrink? What is His agony? He
asks that the cup be taken from Him. What kind of cup is it?
It is the bitter death upon the cross. But why should He suffer
death? He is without sin, He is holy and just. It is for the sin
of the world which God has laid upon Him. That presses
upon Him, and alarms Him.

And is it not true that if God has laid my sin upon Him
(for St. John called Him the Lamb of God which takes away
the sin of the world) I am free and rid of my sin? Why then
should I accuse myself and my Lord Christ Jesus? I am a
sinner. Alas, it is true. Sin frightens me. That, alas, I feel
deeply and my heart ever faints within me. I fear before God
and His severe judgement. And yet, of what shall I accuse
myself, and of what shall I accuse my Lord Christ Jesus?
There, on the Mount of Olives, He shivers and shakes and is
in such dread and alarm that He sweats blood. And my intolerable sin brings Him to this, my sin which He has taken
upon Himself and which is so hard to carry. Therefore I will
let it lie there and confidently hope that, whenever I come
before God and His judgement, He will find no sin in me.

Behold! The Mount of Olives is a comfort to you, that
you may be certain, that Christ has taken your sin upon Himself, and paid the price for it. If, then, your sins are laid on
Christ, be content. They lie in the right place, where they
belong.

Sermons from the year 1545.   W.A. 52. 738.

Surely he hath borne our griefs, and carried our sorrows. ISAIAH liii. 4.

These are clear and powerful words. The sufferings of this king are our griefs and sorrows. He carries the burden which ought to be ours for ever. The stripes and bruises which we have merited, namely, that we should suffer thirst and hunger, and die eternally, all this is laid on Him. His suffering avails for me, and for you, and for us all; for it was undertaken for our good. But we esteemed Him to be the one who was afflicted and smitten of God.

And that is true. For Moses himself says, 'Cursed be the man that hangeth on the tree'. That is why He was railed at as one condemned and cursed. He cannot even help Himself, how then can He heal others? But they did not see properly. For lo, He is carrying our sorrows. According to the outward appearance He seems to be cursed, but according to the spirit He carries my sorrows and yours, and the sorrows of us all. 'The chastisement of our peace was upon Him, and with His stripes we are healed'. He is chastised, we are in peace. I and you, and all men have called forth God's wrath; He has atoned, that we, redeemed from sin, may rest in peace. He must suffer, we are set free.

We ought not so shamefully to forget such great love and mercy.

Sermons from the year 1531.   W.A. 34. I. 264 f.

I am a worm and no man; a reproach of men, and despised of the people.   PSALM xxii. 6.

St. Paul, too, speaks about it (Philippians ii.). He says that Christ, though being in the form of God, emptied Himself, that is, that He made no use of His divine power, neither did He turn His eyes towards an almighty strength, but He laid it aside while He suffered. During this emptiness and humility the devil tempted Him with all his hellish power. The Man, and Son of Man, stands there and bears the sin of the world. And as He was not sustained by divine comfort and strength, the devil bit his teeth into the innocent lamb and tried to devour it. So must the just and guiltless man tremble and shrink like a poor wretched sinner and in his tender guiltless heart feel the bitterness of God's wrath and judgement upon sin, and taste for us eternal death and condemnation. In short, He must suffer everything which a condemned sinner has deserved and should suffer eternally.

Thereby is won for us the bliss of heaven, eternal life and salvation, as Isaiah says, chapter liii: 'He shall see of the travail of his soul and shall be satisfied'. His body and soul, he says, travail in heavy suffering; but He did this for our great good and as a great joy to Himself. For He overcomes His enemies and wins the victory, and by His knowledge justifies many.

Sermons from the year 1537.   W.A. 45. 240 f.

But he was wounded for our transgressions, he was bruised for our iniquities; the chastisement of our peace was upon him; and with his stripes we are healed.

ISAIAH liii. 5.

Accept this, and take comfort from it, believing that it was done for your sake, and for your good. For here you hear it, not once, or twice, but many times: what He suffers, He suffers innocently.

Why does God allow this? Why does God ordain it and bring it to pass? In order that you should be comforted by it. He did not suffer for His own sake. He suffered for your sake and for the whole world's sake. That is why it is so full of contradiction. He is the Son of God, entirely holy and without sin, and therefore He should have no part in death nor the curse. We are sinners, under God's curse and wrath, and therefore we should bear death and condemnation. But God reverses it; He who has no sin, in whom there is nothing but grace, must be made the curse and bear the chastisement, and through Him we are in a state of grace, and the children of God. Therefore we should hold fast to this comfort and especially treasure this testimony of Christ's innocence. For our guilt and sin were the occasion of what Christ innocently suffered. And that is why we can take comfort against sin and every ill, through His innocence. For such innocence is a sure and certain testimony, that we enjoy the fruit of His sufferings, and that our devoted Lord and gracious Redeemer has suffered for us and paid our debt.

Sermons from the year 1545.   W.A. 52. 786 f.

*Now once in the end of the world hath he appeared to
put away sin by the sacrifice of himself.*
HEBREWS ix. 26.

Such knowledge and trust make a joyful heart, which can
surely and truthfully say, I know of no sin, for they are laid
on Christ. Now, they cannot lie at the same time on Him
and on us. Therefore no man can say that he has atoned for
sin by his own righteousness. To expiate and abolish sin
belongs to Christ alone. And Christ is neither your nor my
nor any man's doing; neither are His body and blood, which
He sacrificed for our sin, but He is true God and Man, who
carries the sin of all the world. He drowns and chokes it by
His baptism and cross, and causes it to be preached to you
that He gave His body for you and shed His blood for the
forgiveness of your sins. If you believe it, your sins are forgiven, you are holy and righteous and you receive the Holy
Ghost, so that from now on you can withstand sin. And even
if in your weakness sin overtake you, it will not be counted
against you as long as you remain in faith.

That is what the forgiveness of sins means.

Sermon on the Friday after Easter,   W.A. 49. 125.
1540.

> *Stand fast therefore in the liberty wherewith Christ*
> *hath made us free, and be not entangled again with*
> *the yoke of bondage.*   GALATIANS V. I.

Christ has not freed us from human duties, but from eternal wrath. Where? In the conscience. That is the limit of our freedom, and it must go no further. For Christ has set us spiritually free, that is, He has set us free in the sense that our conscience is free and joyful and no longer fears the coming wrath of God. That is true freedom, and no man can value it high enough. For who can express what a great thing it is that a man is certain that God is no longer angry with him and will never be angry again, but for the sake of Christ is now, and ever will be, a gracious and merciful Father. Truly, it is a wonderful freedom above all understanding, that God's high Majesty is gracious unto us.

And from this there follows another freedom, that we, through Christ, are set free from the law, sin, death, hell, and the power of the devil. For, as the wrath of God can no longer frighten us, because Christ has set us free from it, so the law and sin can no longer accuse or condemn us.

The Prophet Joel,   E.A. op. lat. 25. 288 f.
  with Commentary.

Judica

A HIGH PRIEST FOR EVER

Sunday: HEBREWS ix. 11–15

Thou art a priest for ever after the order of Melchisedec. HEBREWS v. 6.

Priest is a strong and lovely word. There is no lovelier or sweeter name on earth. It is much better to hear that Christ is called 'Priest', than Lord, or any other name. Priesthood is a spiritual power which means no other than that the priest steps forth, and takes all the iniquities of the people upon himself as though they were his very own. He intercedes with God for them and receives from Him the Word with which he can comfort and help the people. It is lovelier and more comforting than 'Father' and 'Mother', for this name brings us everything else. For by being a priest He makes God our Father and Himself our Lord. When I believe in His priesthood, then I know that His work is none other than to be seated in heaven as our Mediator, and that He makes intercession for us, before the Father, without ceasing, and all the time speaks on our behalf. This is the highest comfort which can be given to any man, and no sweeter sermon can be preached to our hearts.

He offered Himself once for all, so that He is Himself both Priest and Sacrifice, and the Altar is the Cross. No more precious sacrifice could He offer to God than that He gave Himself to be slain and consumed in the fire of love. That is the true sacrifice.

Exposition of Genesis xiv.   W.A. 24. 280.

How much more shall the blood of Christ, who through the eternal Spirit offered himself without spot to God, purge your conscience from dead works to serve the living God? HEBREWS ix. 14.

He refers to two kinds of priesthood. The old priesthood was of the body, with bodily adornments, house, offering, forgiveness, and all that belongs to it. The new priesthood is spiritual, with spiritual adornments, house, offering, and all that belongs to it! For Christ did not go about wearing precious stones and gold and silk when He fulfilled His priesthood and sacrificed Himself upon the cross, but in godly love, wisdom, patience, obedience, and all the virtues, which no one saw but God, and such as the Spirit enlightened; for that is spiritual adornment.

Therefore, although the body and blood of Christ were seen like any other bodily thing, it was not in the same way seen that they were an offering and that He sacrificed them. It was not as when Aaron made offerings, where there were not only the calf, the ram, the bird, the bread, and other material things, but the people clearly saw that he made it an offering and that it was a sacrifice. But Christ offered Himself, within His heart, before God, and this no one saw or noticed; therefore His bodily flesh and blood are a spiritual offering.

Similarly, the tabernacle, or house, and Churches of Christ are spiritual. They are in heaven, or in the presence of God. For on the cross He hung not in a temple but in the presence of God, where He still is. Again, the altar is in a spiritual sense the cross, for anyone could see the wood but no one knew that it was the altar of Christ. Thus His prayer, the shedding of His blood, His incense, were all spiritual, for it all took place through His Spirit. And in accordance with that the fruit and the benefit of His sacrifice and ministry (which is the forgiveness of sins and our justification) were spiritual.

Sermons from the year 1525.   W.A. 17. II. 227 f.

The Lord hath laid on him the iniquity of us all.
ISAIAH liii. 6.

This High Priest is both priest and offering, for He offers His body and life upon the cross. It looks very unpriestly that He hangs there on the cross, stripped and naked, bruised and covered with blood, having a crown of thorns pressed down upon His head. And yet, He is the true priest and bishop who offers Himself and out of His great love gives His own body to be consumed, as through fire, for the redemption of all the world. The old priesthood was endowed with great splendour, but about this High Priest there is no splendour. His altar is the cross and the gallows. That is a shameful, ghastly, and unusual altar. And that is why He is in the eyes of the world such a mean, disdained high priest. He has such an offensive and dishonourable altar and is such a sacrifice as makes people shudder.

There, then, we have this High Priest, Jesus Christ, with His altar and offering, most shamefully treated by the Jews and soldiers. And yet He carries on His shoulders the sin of us all. There we lie, you and I and all men, from the first man Adam until the end of the world.

Sermon for Good Friday, 1534.   W.A. 37. 353 f.

*Christ hath redeemed us from the curse of the law,
being made a curse for us: for it is written, Cursed is
every one that hangeth on a tree.*   GALATIANS iii. 13.

Who, then, will take offence at the cross? Who will think
such a death shameful? Who will not give thanks to God that
His Son hangs on the tree and takes upon Himself the curse
which because of our sin belongs to us? There He hangs like
a cursed man, who is hateful to God, whom God allows to
fall into shame, distress, and anguish. All this takes place (says
St. Paul) for me and for you in order that we may attain to
salvation. Learn this difference so that you do not judge by
what your eyes see, but in accordance with what the Word
of God tells you. From the outward appearance the death of
our Lord Christ is a shameful death, and as God Himself calls
such a death, a cursed death. The tree on which He dies is
damned and accursed. But why? Because the sin of us all
hangs on it. The tree is accursed, and the man that hangs on
it is accursed. The cause of His hanging on it is also accursed.
For upon sin there follows the curse, and the more sin lies
upon the Lord the greater is the curse. But it is a death for
our salvation, which takes away the curse from us and wins
for us the blessing of God.

Sermons from the year 1545.   W.A. 52. 807.

But now I go my way to him that sent me. JOHN xvi. 5.

This word 'I go unto the Father' comprises the whole work of our redemption and salvation for which God's Son was sent down from heaven, and which He has done for us and goes on doing until the end of time; namely, His suffering death and resurrection, and His whole kingdom in the Church. For this going to the Father means nothing else than that He gives Himself as a sacrifice through the shedding of His blood and through His dying in order to pay for our sin. And after that through His resurrection He overcomes sin, death, and hell, and brings them under His power, and as the living One seats Himself at the right hand of the Father, where He reigns unseen over all things in heaven and on earth. From thence He gathers His Church and causes it to grow, and as an eternal Mediator and High Priest He represents and intercedes before the Father, for those who believe, because they are still beset by weakness and sin. Further, He gives the power and the strength of the Holy Ghost, in order that sin, death, and devil may be overcome.

Behold, this then is the Christian's justification before God, that Christ goes to the Father, that is, He suffers for us and rises again, and so reconciles us to the Father, so that for His sake we receive forgiveness of sins and grace. There is nothing of our work or merit, but it is all because of His going to the Father, which He did for our sake. That means another man's righteousness (for which we have done and merited nothing and never could merit anything) is given to us and made our own, so that it is our righteousness through which we become well-pleasing to God and His heirs and His dear children.

Sermon on John xvi. 5–15.   W.A. 21. 363.

By his own blood he entered in once into the holy
place, having obtained eternal redemption for us.
HEBREWS ix. 12.

Through His kingdom and reign He protects us from all
evil in all things, but through His priesthood He protects us
from all sins and from the wrath of God. He steps into our
place, offering Himself in order that He may reconcile God
to us, so that through Him we can put our trust in God, and
our consciences need not fear His wrath nor stand in dread
of His judgement, as St. Paul says (Romans v.–2): 'Through
Him we have our peace with God and our access by faith to
His grace'.

And that He makes us confident towards God and at peace
in our own consciences, so that God is not against us and
we are not against ourselves, is a far greater thing than that
He takes away all harm which the creatures might do to us.
For guilt is much greater than pain, and sin than death. For
it is sin which brings death, and without sin there would be
no death, or death would do us no harm.

It is a mighty defiance that a man can set this High Priest
over against his sin, over against his bad conscience, over
against God's terrible wrath and judgement, and in sure faith
can confess, Thou art a High Priest for ever.

Sermons from the year 1522.   W.A. 10. I (i). 717 ff.

For such an high priest became us, who is holy, harm-less, undefiled, separate from sinners, and made higher than the heavens; who needeth not daily, as those high priests, to offer up sacrifice, first for his own sins, and then for the people's: for this he did once, when he offered up himself. HEBREWS vii. 26–27.

The sacrifice of Christ, which was offered once, avails for ever, and we are blessed because we believe in it. If any-one sets up anything alongside this sacrifice, it is sacrilege. Christ is Himself the sacrifice which He offered in His death, to cleanse us from sin eternally. Therefore, where His suffering is ended and the offering is perfected, His honour begins. On the cross His honour falls to the ground along with His good repute and His mighty deeds. Men begin to doubt whether when He helped people, He did it in the power of God or of the devil. There, at that moment, His own con-science fails and the might of death prevails over Him. Therefore, if it is to be a sacrifice, His own blood must be taken; the little lamb must be stabbed; the sacrifice costs blood. Yet the struggle of Christ endures but a while. And Christ cries out with priestly voice: 'My Father, though they have wrought this against Me, pardon them, and forgive'.

And what does Christ do after that? He sits at the judge-ment-seat of God. When all the world has deserted Him and thinks He is finished, He begins His eternal reign, and repre-sents us before the Father, interceding for us, when we are accused of sin. Judgement is spoken over us; the alarmed con-science feels God's anger at sin. There is then no help for us save in the sacrifice of Christ, who prays to the Father for us, saying, 'My Father, the sinner is weak, and is gripped by great anxieties. Give him to Me, I have atoned for him. He trusts in my eternal sacrifice'.

But whoever turns away from this sacrifice, looking else-where, can never find any help.

Sermon on Hebrews vii.

W.A. 45. 398.

Palm Sunday

THE CRUCIFIED CHRIST

Sunday: MATTHEW xxi. 1–9

*Pilate therefore said unto him, Art thou a king then ?
Jesus answered, Thou sayest that I am a king. To
this end was I born, and for this cause came I into
the world, that I should bear witness unto the truth.
Every one that is of the truth heareth my voice.*

JOHN xviii. 37.

See how Christ the King abandons possessions, body, and
life, and learn from this that His Kingdom is not of this world.
To enjoy the Christian faith here on earth does not mean to
have all things to the full and lack nothing. Look at your King,
the Lord Jesus, how does He fare? Of what does He boast?
What comfort has He in life? How highly is He praised? Is
it not true, that He has nothing but suffering, scorn, and disdain and dies in shame? One little thing He has with which
to rule, and that applies only in the case of a few people. It
is His testimony to the truth, the holy Gospel. Through this
He pours the Holy Spirit into the hearts of men, forgives sin
and bestows the hope of eternal life. But all these things
remain in faith and in the Word. They are not seen. They
are not handled. They exist in hope.

Any man who knows the way of this King and His Kingdom willingly bears the cross, for he not only knows that
Christ, the eternal King, fared in the same way, and is thus
himself willing and ready to suffer because a servant should
not fare better than his Lord, but also he takes comfort in
the knowledge that the life hereafter is full of joy and splendour, even though suffering must be endured on earth. That
makes Christians joyful even in the midst of sorrows and
trials.

Sermons from the year 1545.   W.A. 52. 768.

Godly sorrow worketh repentance to salvation not to be repented of; but the sorrow of the world worketh death. 2 CORINTHIANS vii. 10.

Judas has a heavier load on his back than Peter. Therefore he falls into despair, thinking there is no help or consolation for ever, and thus, for woe and sorrow, he went away and hanged himself, poor man! But why? Because he had been slothful in hearing the Word of God. He despised it and never bettered himself by it. Thus, when he needed consolation and had the Word no longer, it was impossible for him to find help.

Peter also weeps bitterly. He is anxious and worried because of his sins, but he had been more diligent in listening to the word of his Lord Christ, and had engraved it on his mind. Therefore now, in the hour of his need, he seizes upon it and holds fast to it, comforts himself with it, and hopes that God will be gracious to him. That is the one true help in such a need, and the hapless Judas lacked it. But that Peter held firmly to the Word and grace of God, the Lord Himself testifies when He says, Luke xxii. 32 f.: 'I made supplication for thee, that thy faith fail not'.

Therefore learn here what is true repentance. Peter weeps bitterly; that is the beginning of repentance, that the heart acknowledges sin and is grieved for it, that it has no love for it or desire to continue in it, but is saddened that it has not kept God's Will and has fallen into sin. But we cannot do that of ourselves; the Lord must look upon us as He looked upon Peter.

Sermons from the year 1545. W.A. 52. 768.

And they that had laid hold on Jesus led him away
to Caiaphas the high priest, where the scribes and the
elders were assembled.   MATTHEW XXVI. 57.

Thus our dear Lord Christ Jesus suffered, not secretly at
the hands of those who had no authority, but publicly and
at the hands of those holding public authority, so that we
should not take offence when we see that both spiritual and
worldly authority are against God. Christ suffered, as we
testify in the Christian Creed when we say, I believe in Jesus
Christ who suffered under Pontius Pilate. In all ages, and
still today, Christians and true martyrs are put to death by
public authority, both spiritual and worldly.

No prophet has ever been treacherously murdered, but
they have all been put to death by those in true official power.
All blood which is shed in the name of Christ is shed by those
who are kings, princes, judges, or counsellors in worldly
jurisdiction, or bishops and preachers and the like, in spiritual
jurisdiction. Prophets die by the judgement of man.

But what will happen when once the tide turns? Then will
God do what will grieve them, and leave undone what they
desire. They stormed against God and would not let Him
remain, although He would have let them remain. Because
they would not let God remain, they must perish.

Sermons from the year 1534.   W.A. 37. 322 f.

*Jesus turning unto them said, Daughters of Jeru-
salem, weep not for me, but weep for yourselves, and
for your children.* LUKE xxiii. 28.

He suffers for our sake. For this reason it grieves the Lord,
that His suffering should make us weep. He wants us to be
happy, to praise God and give thanks for His grace, and to
glorify Him and bear our witness, for it is through His
Passion that we received God's grace, and were freed from
sin, and death, and became God's dear children. But we are
as slow to the one as to the other, for by nature we are contrary. When we should weep over our sins, we laugh; when
we should laugh and our hearts be joyful because Christ,
through His death, has won eternal life for us, we weep. For
either we have no regard for such joy, because our hearts are
bewitched by the merriment of this world, or we weep,
lament, and pine as if Christ had never died, never paid for
our sin, never stilled the wrath of God, and never redeemed
us from death.

Therefore prayer is needed for both: first, that God through
the Holy Ghost may touch our hearts, that He may make us
loathe sin, may draw us away from it, and take away our trust
in ourselves. Then, that He may kindle in our hearts His
comfort in the midst of sin, and give us a firm confidence in
our Lord's sacrifice and satisfaction.

Sermons from the year 1545.   W.A. 52. 798 ff.

My soul is exceeding sorrowful, even unto death.
                                    MATTHEW xxvi. 38.

Our dear Lord Christ stands here for our sake, as a poor sinful man. The divine Nature constrains Itself, and the comfort and assurance which till now have belonged to Christ have deserted Him. So the tempter, the devil, is able to draw closer to Him, and to assault Him harder than before. That is why He speaks here as a man in the midst of the struggle, wrestling with death, seeking comfort from His disciples, whom till now He had comforted. He trembled and quaked and His heart was filled with sadness, for He despaired of life and felt death, and saw that He must die. That is why He laments before His disciples. Such great fear and anguish break upon Him that He turns to His disciples, although they are so much weaker than Himself.

No man has words to tell the sufferings of our dear Lord Jesus in the garden. It is above all human thought and understanding, what had befallen that divine and godly Man.

More deeply has this Man been distressed than any man on earth. More sorely has He dreaded death than any man. And this was done for our sake.

Sermons from the year 1534.   W.A. 37. 326.

HOW TO RECEIVE THE SACRAMENTS

*As often as ye eat this bread, and drink this cup, ye do
show the Lord's death till he come. But let a man
examine himself, and so let him eat of that bread,
and drink of that cup.* 1 CORINTHIANS xi. 26, 28.

Anyone who wishes to receive the Holy Sacrament must
offer to God Almighty an empty, single, and hungry soul.

Therefore it is most fitting when the soul is least fit, which
means, when the soul feels altogether wretched, poor, and
devoid of grace, it is most receptive for God's grace and least
fitted to receive it.

But then the soul must endeavour to come to the Sacrament with perfect faith, or with all the faith possible, and
most firmly believing that she will receive grace. For a man
receives as much as he believes he will receive. Therefore
faith alone is the best and highest preparation.

Your hungry heart must build upon these words and you
must trust in the promise of the divine truth, and in this
spirit go to the Sacrament, imploring God and saying, Lord,
it is true that I am not worthy that Thou shouldst come
under my roof, yet I am needy, and eager for Thy help and
grace, that I too may be made godly. Thus I come with no
plea but that I have heard sweet words, namely, that Thou
dost invite me to Thy table. Dear Lord, Thy Word is true,
I do not doubt it. In that faith I eat and I drink with Thee.
May it be done to me according to Thy Will and Words.
Amen.

That is to come worthily to the Sacrament.

Sermon on the worthy reception of the　　　W.A. 7. 694 f.
　holy and true Body of Christ.

Good Friday

He said unto Jesus, Lord, remember me when thou comest into thy kingdom. And Jesus said unto him, Verily I say unto thee, Today shalt thou be with me in paradise. LUKE xxiii. 42–43.

As comfort came in the garden from an angel, so here on the cross it came from a murderer who hung beside Him. He is a wonderful God who allows His Son to be comforted by a murderer. The robber must have seen through the veil of Christ's body, through shame, disdain, and suffering. Otherwise he could not have believed and testified that Christ was Lord of a mighty kingdom. Thus, then, Christ had passed through hell, and comfort begins to reach Him through the robber. God does not allow His Church to perish. Therefore it is well said, that the faith which had died in Peter rose again in the robber. For this word must stand: 'Be Thou Lord amongst Thine enemies'. Then Christ thinks, After all, I have a gracious God who has prepared for Me a kingdom, and He permits the sinner to enjoy the fruit of My sufferings. Therefore He says to him: 'Today shalt thou be with me in paradise'. The robber, perceiving his guilt and Christ's innocence, thinks: Christ's innocence will help me. And he sees right into the heart of Christ, as though through a solid wall. The malefactor is one of us, and we are like him; therefore let us cry unto Christ and He will say unto us: 'Yes, Amen!' As He did to the robber.

Comment on Luke xxiii. 42–43.   W.A. 45. 371.

CHRIST DIES

When Jesus therefore had received the vinegar, he said, It is finished: and he bowed his head, and gave up the ghost. JOHN xix. 30.

Here He reminds Himself of the divine Will that He had to suffer thus. He can think of nothing else that remains to be done, for all that was written in Holy Writ was finished. Therefore He gives Himself up to God, saying (Psalm xxxi. 5): 'Into thine hand I commend my spirit'. That is Christ's farewell, which He speaks for our sake, so that we may perceive the Father's heart. For what Christ suffered in the body we ought to have suffered in the soul before the eyes of God, and the severity which God here manifests in His Son, we deserved. And if God were to act justly He would do the same to us. Therefore we should repent; then forgiveness of sins follows, so that as God saved His Son Christ, our pattern, from death and the devil, He will save us too. That is our comfort and our salvation. Because we perceive this in Christ we should not turn away from God but should remember the words about Christ which say: 'Rule thou in the midst of thine enemies', and no suffering will be too hard for us. If we are burdened with sins, let us carry them to Christ, He has nailed them to the cross, and will forgive us, and subdue death and the devil. Thus we are made partakers even of the death of Christ.

Comment on John xix. 30.   W.A. 45. 372.

HE DESCENDED INTO HELL

And having spoiled principalities and powers, he made a shew of them openly, triumphing over them in it. COLOSSIANS ii. 15.

There are two ways of speaking of our Lord's descent into hell. First, simply, with childlike and simple words and pictures. This is the best and the surest way. On the other hand, one may talk about it critically, what it was in itself, how it could have happened that Christ descended into hell and yet His body was lying in the grave until the third day. But what is the good of long and keen disputes about it? Our thinking will never fathom it. I must let it remain in faith and in the Word, for my words and thoughts will never reach it.

Therefore my faithful counsel is that you let it remain at those simple words and childlike pictures and do not let yourself be troubled by those keen and clever spirits who think about it without any picture, and seek to fathom it with their clever reason.

When I say that Christ is Lord over the devil and hell, and that the devil has no power and might over Him and over those who belong to Him, that is spoken without the use of pictures and flowery speech. If I can believe it and understand it in such a way of speaking, that is good. If I portray it with flowers and images, and if I make a flag with which Christ broke into hell, so that those who cannot grasp it without images may likewise understand, grasp, and believe, that, too, is good. Thus, in whatever way we may comprehend it, whether with the help of outward pictures or without, both are right and good, so long as this Article remains firm and unshaken, which says that our Lord Jesus Christ descended into hell, broke it to pieces, overcame the devil and redeemed those who were held prisoner by him.

Sermon on Easter Day, 1532.   W.A. 36. 159.

HIS REST WILL BE FULL OF GLORY

Now in the place where he was crucified there was a garden; and in the garden a new sepulchre, wherein was never man yet laid. There laid they Jesus therefore because of the Jews' preparation day; for the sepulchre was nigh at hand. JOHN xix. 41–42.

It is a good ministry that they take care of the body of Jesus and do not fear Pilate's power. They go and close the tomb: Christ is at rest, God must work. Thus the burial takes place.

Our Lord God approves when we honour the dead and do not cast them out like dogs. For if a soul has passed away by the Word of God, the body must rise again; for we do not live by bread alone, but by every Word of God. This is the ground of the resurrection.

Yet we must remember that all the women, and even the Apostles, doubted the words of Christ, and no one believed that He would rise from the dead, as the two said when they were on the way to Emmaus. For if they had had any hope, they would not have embalmed Him and laid Him in a grave. And if it had been the doing of man, God would not have been the doer of it, and this day would not have been called in the Scriptures the great day. This is a much greater Article than the first, that God created heaven and earth, for no one can be saved unless he believes that God raised Christ from the dead. Such faith is no human work, but is wrought by God, as St. Paul and the Scriptures say in many places.

And the saying about His rule must be fulfilled.

Comment on John xix. 38 ff.   W.A. 45. 375 f.

Easter

CHRIST IS RISEN

Easter Sunday: MATTHEW xxviii. 1–10

*Death is swallowed up in victory. O death, where is
thy sting? O grave, where is thy victory? . . .
thanks be to God, which giveth us the victory through
our Lord Jesus Christ.* 1 CORINTHIANS xv. 54–57.

This is a strange and unprecedented message, such as
reason cannot comprehend. It must be accepted in faith. The
message is that Christ is alive and yet dead, and dead in such
a way that in Him death itself has had to die, and lose all its
power. . . .

And as the Lord Christ has conquered death, He has also
conquered sin. For in His own Person He is pure and just;
but because He takes upon Himself the sins of others He
becomes a sinner. That is why sin can assault Him. And He,
the Lord Christ, is very ready to be thus assaulted and nailed
to the cross in order that He may die, as if He had Himself
sinned and brought His death upon Himself. But there, hidden
under the sin of others, His holiness is so great that death
cannot overcome Him. Thus sin, like death, attacked the
wrong man, and so grew weak and died in His body.

And likewise the devil wanted to prove his power over
Christ, and uses all his might against Him, trying to bring
Him down. But He meets with a higher power which he cannot overcome. And all this has been wrought in order that
our Lord Christ might glory because by being cast down
He was lifted up on high, and these three mighty foes, sin,
the devil, and death, must low lie under His feet. This great
victory we celebrate today. Now all power consists in this,
that we take it well to heart and firmly believe in it.

Sermon for Easter Day, 1544. W.A. 52. 249 f.

Easter Monday

HE IS NOT HERE

And the angel answered and said unto the women,
Fear not ye: . . . he is risen, . . .

MATTHEW xxviii. 5–6.

The dear angels preach very well, for they have good reason so to do. The substance of their preaching is this: You seek Jesus in the tomb. But He is become a different man. You believe that He was crucified, but we will tell you where He is now. 'He is risen from the dead and is not here.' You will not find Him in this life. On earth, which is the realm of death, you must not seek Christ. Different eyes, fingers, or feet are needed to see Christ, to take hold of Him or to walk towards Him. I will show you (he says) the place where He lay, but He is no longer there. His name is now 'He is not here', as St. Paul writes to the Colossians (iii. 1–3): 'If ye then be risen with Christ, seek those things which are above'...

Christ is not here. Hence a Christian must not be here. Therefore no man can tie down Christ or a Christian with certain special rules. It says, 'He is not here'. He has left the husks down here, such as earthly justice, piety, wisdom, the Law, and whatever else belongs to earth; of all those He has stripped Himself entirely. You must not seek Him in the things which appear upon the earth. They are nothing but husks, and husks are never used a second time. Therefore, no man, in so far as he is a Christian, can be caught in them, but, as Christ is above all things, so is a Christian above all things. Christ has in Himself overcome all things and left them behind. And in that we believe this, we too are called 'Not here', even as He is. As St. Paul says, 'Set your affection not on things on the earth'. What a wonderful saying it is. Your life is hid, not in a chest, for there it might be found, but in Him who is nowhere. Our life shall be above all human wisdom, justice, and piety. As long as you abide in yourself, you are not devout, which means that our life is hidden high above our eyes, . . . and high above all that we can feel.

Sermons from the year 1530.   W.A. 32. 49 f.

Christ was delivered for our offences, and was raised again for our justification. ROMANS iv. 25.

When I look at my sins, they slay me. Therefore I must look upon Christ, who drew my sins upon Himself and has become a blessing. Now they lie no longer on my conscience but on Christ, and they seek to slay Him. Let us see, then, how they get on with Him. They cast Him down and kill Him. O, Lord God, where is now my Christ and my Redeemer? Then God comes and brings Christ forth and makes Him alive, and not only alive, but He sets Him in heaven and lets Him rule over all things. Now where is sin? It is on the gibbet. And when I hold on to this and believe it I have a joyful conscience, like Christ, for I am without sin. Now I dare death, the devil, sin, and hell to do me harm. Inasmuch as I am a descendant of Adam they can harm me; I must shortly die. But now that Christ has laid upon Himself my sin, and has died for it, and been slain for it, they can do me no harm, for Christ is too strong for them. They cannot hold Him. He breaks forth and smites them to the ground, and ascends into heaven, binds and fetters sin and sorrow, and rules over them eternally. Therefore I have a good conscience, I am joyful and blessed, and fear those tyrants no longer, for Christ has taken my sin away from me and laid it on Himself. But they cannot remain on Him.

On the fruit and power of the resurrection of Christ. W.A. 10. I (ii). 221.

If Christ be not raised, your faith is vain; ye are yet in your sins. 1 CORINTHIANS xv. 17.

Firmly believe that Christ has taken upon Himself your sin and death. For that is how the virtue of the resurrection is given to me and to you and to all mankind who believe in Christ. For if I do not make use of it in this way I do my Lord Christ great injustice, for I let His triumph and victory remain barren. It should not remain barren, for He wills that it shall bear great fruit, namely, that in all affliction, sin, and fear, I should see nothing but Christ triumphant rising from the dead.

Whoever can picture this victory in his heart, is already saved. But whoever has no Good Friday and Easter Day, has no good day in the year, that is, whoever does not believe that Jesus suffered and rose for him is without hope. For we are called Christians because we can look to Christ and say, Dear Lord, Thou hast taken upon Thee my sin and hast become Martin, Peter, and Paul, and has trodden my sin underfoot and consumed it! There I look for my sin as Thou hast directed me. On Good Friday I still see my sin before my eyes, but on Easter Day a new man has been born. His hand has been made new and sin is seen no more. All this Thou hast given to me freely, and hast said that Thou hast overcome my devil, my sin, and my death.

Sermons from the year 1530.   W.A. 32. 44.

Jesus saith unto her, Touch me not; for I am not yet ascended to my Father: but go to my brethren, and say unto them, I ascend unto my Father, and your Father, and to my God, and your God. JOHN XX. 17.

And if Christ is our brother, I should like to know what we could lack? For as it applies with brothers in the flesh, so it applies here. Brothers in the flesh possess common goods. They have *one* father, *one* inheritance, which does not decrease by sharing, as other inheritances do. Rather it grows more and more because it is a spiritual inheritance.

And what is Christ's inheritance? His is life and death, sin and grace, and all things which are in heaven and on earth, eternal truth, might, wisdom, and justice. He rules over all things, over hunger and thirst, over joy and sorrow, over all things which can be conceived, whether in heaven or on earth, and not only spiritual things but material things as well. In a word, He holds everything in His hand, whether it be temporal or eternal. And when I believe in Him, I, along with Him, have a share in them all, and not in one thing or merely a part of the whole. Like Him, I rule as lord over all things, such as eternal righteousness, eternal wisdom, and eternal power.

On the fruit and power of the   W.A. 10. I (ii). 214 f.
resurrection of Christ.

Then the same day at evening, being the first day of the week, when the doors were shut where the disciples were assembled for fear of the Jews, came Jesus and stood in the midst, and saith unto them, Peace be unto you. JOHN XX. 19.

What did the disciples fear? They feared death. Yes, they were in the midst of death. But whence came that fear of death? From sin; for if they had not sinned they would not have been afraid. Death could not have harmed them, for the sting of death, with which it slays, is sin. Yet they lacked, as we all lack, the right knowledge of God. For if they had known God to be God, they would have been confident and without fear. But one who does not believe in God must be afraid of death. Such a man can never have a glad and sure conscience.

Whenever a man in such fear cries unto God, God cannot refrain from helping him. Just as Christ did not stay long outside, away from His frightened disciples, but soon was there comforting them and saying: 'Peace be unto you', 'I am come, be of good cheer and fear not', so it is still. When we are afraid, God lifts us up and causes the Gospel to be preached to us, and thus restores to us a glad and sure conscience.

Where Christ is, yea, surely, the Father and the Holy Ghost surely come; then there is pure grace and no law; pure mercy and no sin; pure life and no death; pure heaven and no hell; and there I take comfort in the works of Christ as if I had done them myself.

Sermon for the first Sunday after   W.A. 10. I (ii). 234 ff.
Easter, 1526.

*For if we believe that Jesus died and rose again, even
so them also which sleep in Jesus will God bring with
him.* 1 THESSALONIANS iv. 14.

As in His resurrection He has taken all things with Him,
so that both heaven and earth, sun and moon, and all creatures
must rise with Him and be made new, even so will He bring
us with Him. The same God who raised Christ from the
dead will quicken again our mortal bodies, and with us all
creatures, which are now subject unto vanity, and which with
earnest expectation await our glorification, and desire to be
set free from this transient existence and to be made glorious.
For us more than half of our resurrection is already accomplished, because our heart and head are already above, and
only the smallest part remains to be done, namely, that the
body be buried in order that it too may be made new.

No one will deny that the corpse of a dead man is a
wretched thing. But I possess an understanding higher than
the eyes can see, or the senses perceive, which faith teaches
me. For there stands the text saying: 'He is risen', He is no
longer in the grave and buried under the earth, but He is
risen from the dead, and this not for His own sake but for
our sake, that His resurrection be made ours so that we too
may rise in Him, and not remain in the grave and in death,
but that our bodies may celebrate with Him an everlasting
Easter Day.

Sermons from the year 1532.   W.A. 36. 161 f.

Quasimodogeniti

REBORN

Sunday: 1 JOHN v. 15

Blessed be the God and Father of our Lord Jesus Christ, which according to his abundant mercy hath begotten us again unto a lively hope by the resurrection of Jesus Christ from the dead. 1 PETER i. 3.

How, or by what means has such rebirth come to pass? He says, Through the resurrection of Jesus Christ from the dead; as if he would say, God the Father has begotten us again, not of corruptible seed but of incorruptible seed, that is, of the Word of truth, which is a power of God which re-creates and quickens and saves all who believe in it. What sort of a Word is that? It is the Word of Jesus Christ which is preached unto us, namely, that He died for your sin and for the sin of the whole world, and rose again on the third day, that through His resurrection He might win for us justification, life, and blessedness. Whoever believes in this message, namely, that Christ died and is risen for his sake, with him the resurrection has proved its power. He is reborn through it, which means that He is created anew after the image of God, He receives the Holy Ghost and knows the gracious will of God, and has such a heart, mind, courage, will, and thoughts as no hypocrite ever had or any man who believes in salvation through his own works. For he knows that no works of the law and no righteousness of his own, but Christ alone in His suffering and resurrection, can make him just and blessed.

This is rightly called apostolic preaching.

Exposition of 1. Peter.   E.A. 52. 11.

> *Jesus answered, Verily, verily, I say unto thee, Except a man be born of water and of the Spirit, he cannot enter into the kingdom of God.* JOHN iii. 5.

Do not think that you will enter the Kingdom of God unless you are first born anew of water and of the Spirit. That is a strong and hard saying, that we must be born anew. It means that we must come out of the birth of sin to the birth of justification; else we shall never enter the kingdom of heaven. Upon this birth or justification good works must follow.

Of these things the Lord Christ speaks much with Nicodemus, but Nicodemus cannot understand, nor can they be understood unless a man has experience of them and has been born of the Spirit.

Exposition of John iii.   W.A. 47. 10.

Of his own will begat he us with the word of truth,
that we should be a kind of firstfruits of his creatures.

JAMES i. 18.

The first thing and greatest thing which He has done for us from above is that He has begotten us and made us His children and heirs, so that we have become and are called 'children born of God'. How, or by what means, did that happen? Through the Word of Truth.

Thus have we become firstborn of His creation, which is a new-begun creature and work of God. Thus He separates His new creation from the world and human creatures.

God has made for Himself a new creature which is so called because it is made by Him and is His work without any human help and skill. In virtue of this a Christian is called a new creature of God, which He Himself alone makes, above and besides all other creatures and works, yet in such a way that in this temporal life there is made but a beginning, and He works daily at it until it is perfected, when it will be a godly creature, pure and bright like the sun, without any sin and frailty, and all on fire with godly love.

Sermons from the year 1536.   W.A. 41. 585 ff.

He that believeth on the Son hath everlasting life.

JOHN iii. 36.

We should preach on these words for a hundred thousand years, and proclaim them again and again. In fact, we can never preach enough about them, for Christ promises eternal life immediately to him who believes. He does not say, he who believes will receive eternal life, but immediately you believe in Me you *have* eternal life already. He does not speak of some future gift, but of a present grace, namely, if you can believe in Me you are already saved and you have already received the gift of eternal life.

I receive eternal life in advance. Unless I receive it here on earth I shall not win it hereafter. Here in this mortal body I must obtain it and attain to it. How then is it attained? God makes the beginning and becomes your Master, preaching to you. He works the beginning of eternal life in that He preaches to you the oral and outward word. He then gives the heart which receives the Word and believes it. Such is the beginning. And those selfsame words which you hear and believe lead you to Jesus Christ alone; you cannot go further. If you can believe in Him and cleave to Him, you are redeemed from physical and spiritual death, and you already have eternal life.

Sermons on John vi–viii.   W.A. 33. 160 f.

Purify your souls in obeying the truth through the
Spirit . . . being born again, not of corruptible seed,
but of incorruptible, by the word of God, which liveth
and abideth for ever. I PETER i. 22–23.

You are not what you were before. You are new men.
That has not come about through works, but through a new
birth. For you cannot make the new man, but he must grow,
or be born. As a joiner cannot make a tree, but it must grow
itself out of the earth.

The Apostle means here, inasmuch as you are now new
creatures should you not now bear yourselves differently, and
lead a new life? As you used to live in hate you must now
walk in love, doing the opposite in all things.

How then does that happen? In this way: God lets the
Word, that is the Gospel, go forth and lets the seed fall into
the hearts of men. Wherever that takes root in the heart the
Holy Ghost is at work making a new man, who really does
become another man, with other thoughts and words and
works. Thus you are wholly transformed. All things from
which you previously have fled you now seek, and what you
previously sought you now flee. For in this way you begin
to be all on fire with godly love, and you become a different
man, completely reborn, and everything that is you is
changed. Now you are as eager to be chaste as you were
before to be unchaste, and the same applies to all your desires
and inclinations.

Sermons from the year 1522.   W.A. IO. III. 88.

According to his mercy he saved us, by the washing of regeneration, and renewing of the Holy Ghost.

TITUS iii. 5.

He calls the washing a regeneration, a renewing in the Holy Ghost, in order that the greatness and the might of grace may be perfectly expressed. So great is this thing, that no creature can do it, but the Holy Ghost alone. Ah! how much dost thou, St. Paul, spurn the free will, the good works and the great merits of the proud saints! How high you place our blessedness, and yet you bring it so near to us, even within us. How purely and clearly you preach grace. Therefore, however you may work to renew a man and change him, it is only possible through the washing of the regeneration of the Holy Ghost.

Behold, this is preaching freely and fully of the grace of God. No patching with works avails, only the complete changing of the nature. Those who truly believe must suffer much affliction and must die, in order that grace may demonstrate its nature and its presence.

God's grace is a great, strong, mighty, and active thing. It upholds, leads, drives, draws, changes, and works all things in a man and is really felt and experienced. It remains hidden, but its works are manifest. Works and words point to where it is, just as the fruit and the leaves show the kind and nature of the tree.

Sermons from the year 1522.   W.A. 10. I (i). 116 ff.

Whatsoever is born of God overcometh the world.
                                    1 JOHN V. 4.

With these words he admonishes the Christians that those
who believe should remember that they should give proof of
the power and practice of their faith in life and deed. For he
wrote this epistle mainly in order to punish the false Christians, who like to listen when we teach that we are saved
through Christ alone, and that our works and deeds merit
no salvation, and then think when they have heard it that
they, too, are now Christians and that they need not work or
join in the fight. They do not perceive that through and out
of such faith new men should be born, who overcome the
world and the devil.

These words here spoken do not mean that you are born
of God and yet remain in the old, dead, worldly nature, and
live on in sins, to the delight of the devil just as you were
before, but that you resist the devil and all his works. Thus,
if you do not overcome the world, but are overcome by it,
you may well glory in your faith and in Christ, but your own
deeds witness against you, that you are not a child of God.

Sermon on 1 John v. 4–12.   W.A. 21. 280.

THE GOOD SHEPHERD

Sunday: JOHN X

I am the good shepherd. JOHN X. 14.

These are comforting words, which set before our eyes a gracious picture of our Lord Jesus Christ, and teach us what sort of a Person He is, what sort of work He does, and how He is disposed towards men.

And if you ask me whether Christ is saintly, I answer without hesitation 'Yes', and I place Him like a shield before my own saintliness, and I trust in Him with my whole heart. For I was baptised in Him and have received in the Gospel a letter and seal, that I am His dear lamb, and that He is my good shepherd, who seeks His lost lamb and deals with me in no legalistic way. He demands nothing of me, neither does He drive me on; He does not threaten, neither does He frighten me, but He shows me His sweet grace, and lowers Himself to me, even beneath me, and takes me upon Himself, so that I now lie on His back and am carried by Him. Why then should I be afraid at the quaking and thundering of Moses or even of the devil? I am under the protection of the Man who has given me His saintliness and all that He has, who supports me and upholds me that I cannot be lost so long as I remain His lamb and do not doubt Him or wilfully fall away from Him.

Sermons from the year 1532.   W.A. 36. 296.

When he hath found it, he layeth it on his shoulders,
rejoicing.   LUKE XV. 5.

There is scarcely any more precious illustration in the
whole Gospel than when the Lord Christ compares Himself
to a shepherd carrying back to the flock, on His shoulders,
the sheep which was lost. He is still carrying to this day.

Therefore the sum of the Gospel is this: the kingdom of
Christ is a kingdom of grace and mercy, in which there is
never anything but carrying. Christ bears our griefs and
infirmities. He takes our sins upon Himself and is patient
when we fall. We always rest on His shoulders, and He never
tires of carrying us, which should be the greatest comfort to
us when we are tempted to sin. Preachers in this kingdom
should comfort the consciences, and deal kindly with them,
and feed them with the Gospel. They should carry the weak,
heal the sick, and know just how to minister the Word to
each man according to his need.

Sermon on Luke x. 23–27.   W.A. 10. I (ii). 366.

*All we like sheep have gone astray; we have turned
every one to his own way; and the Lord hath laid on
him the iniquity of us all.* ISAIAH liii. 6.

My friend, if we can nourish ourselves, rule ourselves, keep
ourselves from error, through our own merit attain grace and
forgiveness of sins, all Holy Writ must be a lie, for it testifies
of us that we are lost, scattered, wounded, weak, and defenceless sheep. Then we need no Christ as a shepherd to seek for
us, gather us together, lead us, bind up our wounds, care for
us, and strengthen us against the devil. In that case He gave
His life for us in vain, for, if we can obtain all this by our own
strength and devotion, we do not need Christ's help.

But this passage says the very opposite, namely, that you
are a lost sheep and you cannot, of yourself, find the way to
the shepherd. Of yourself you can go astray, and unless
Christ, your shepherd, sought you and fetched you back, you
would simply fall a prey to the wolf. But now He comes,
seeks you, finds you, and brings you back to His flock, that
is, through the Word and the Sacraments back into the
Christian Church, gives His life for you, keeps you henceforth in the right way, that you fall into no error. There you
hear nothing about your own strength, good works, and
merits, except that your strength, good works, and merits
mean going astray, being defenceless and lost. Christ works,
merits, and manifests His strength in this alone; He seeks,
upholds, and leads you. He wins life for you through His
death. He alone is strong enough to protect you so that you
do not perish, and are not snatched out of His hand (John x.).
Towards all this you can do nothing but lend your ears, listen,
and receive with gratitude this unspeakable treasure and learn
easily to recognise your shepherd's voice and to shun the
voice of the stranger.

Exposition of Psalm xxiii.   W.A. 51. 275 f.

But he that is an hireling, and not the shepherd, whose own the sheep are not, seeth the wolf coming, and leaveth the sheep, and fleeth; and the wolf catcheth them, and scattereth the sheep. JOHN X. 12.

There are many, alas, all too many, who are called shepherds, and who dare to take upon themselves to govern souls, to feed them, and to direct them. But I am the only one who is called the Good Shepherd. Apart from Me the shepherds are not good. All the others are merciless and cruel, because they leave the poor sheep to the jaws of the wolf. But you should learn to know Me, as your dear, faithful, saintly, kind, gracious, and comforting shepherd, towards whom your hearts should be joyful and full of trust because through Me you are redeemed from all your burdens, fears, sorrows, and dangers. He will not and cannot suffer you to be lost. This I prove (He says) in that I lay down My life for the sheep.

Therefore hold on to Me with a cheerful heart, and let no other man rule over your conscience, but hearken unto Me who speak such comforting words to you, and show you in very deed that it is not My will to force you on, plague and burden you, like Moses, and others, but with lovingkindness to lead you and direct you, protect you and help you.

Exposition of John x. 12–16.   W.A. 21. 331.

Ye were as sheep going astray; but are now returned unto the Shepherd and Bishop of your souls.

1 PETER ii. 25.

If we want to grow in confidence and to be strengthened and comforted, we must learn to recognise the voice of our shepherd, and to ignore all other voices, which lead us into error, chasing us and driving us hither and thither, and we must listen to and comprehend this article alone which sets Christ before us more kindly and helpfully than any man could paint Him. Hence we can say with full confidence, 'My Lord Jesus Christ is the one and only shepherd, and I am, alas, the lost sheep which has gone astray. I languish in fear and fright, and would so like to be saintly, and to have a gracious God, and peace in my conscience. Then I hear that He longs as sorrowfully for me as I for Him. My soul is anxious and troubled about how I can come to Him for help. And, behold, He is anxious and troubled and only wants to bring me back to Himself.

Behold, if we could so portray our Lord and imprint His heart on our heart, with His overflowing longing, concern, and desire for us, it would be impossible for us to be afraid of Him. Rather we should joyfully run towards Him, and stay with Him and listen to no other word nor master.

Sermons from the year 1532.   W.A. 36. 292.

*I am the good shepherd, and know my sheep, and am
known of mine. As the Father knoweth me, even so
know I the Father: and I lay down my life for the
sheep.* JOHN X. 14–15.

Who is it that knows and recognises the sheep while they
are so deeply covered up and buried with shame, suffering,
death, disgrace, and scandal, that they do not even know
themselves? Certainly, none but Christ alone, and He speaks
to them these comforting words that in spite of all the things
which lead the world and our own flesh and blood astray,
He will know His lambs and will not forget them or desert
them, although at times He seems to do.

And that He may implant this knowledge the firmer in
our hearts, He uses a parable, saying: 'As my Father knoweth
me'. And that is indeed a penetrating knowledge, that God
the Father knows His dear only begotten Son while He lies
in a manger, the child of a wretched beggar, yes, not only
unknown, but even disdained and cast out by His own people, yes, and while He hangs most shamefully and ignomini-
ously in the air, bare and naked, between two murderers, as
the most wicked blasphemer and stirrer-up of the people,
accursed of God and all the world, so that He was moved to
cry in great distress: 'My God, my God, why hast thou
forsaken me?'

And yet He says here: 'My Father knoweth me' (even in
such shame, and suffering, and disgrace) as His beloved Son,
sent forth by Him to be made the sacrifice and to surrender
My soul to save and to redeem My sheep. And in the same
way I know the Father and know that He will not forget Me
or forsake Me, but that through shame, and cross, and death,
He will lead Me to life and to eternal glory.

Likewise My lambs, when they are in sorrow, shame, distress, and death, will learn to know Me as their precious and
faithful Saviour, who has suffered like themselves, and have
even sacrificed My life for them. And they will trust in Me
and look to Me for help . . .

Exposition of John x. 12–16.   W.A. 21. 335 f.

He saith to him again the second time, Simon, son of
Jonas, lovest thou me? He saith unto him, Yea,
Lord; thou knowest that I love thee. He saith unto
him, Feed my sheep.   JOHN xxi. 16.

Lord God, are we so blind that we do not take such great
love to heart? Who could have discovered that God lowers
Himself to such a depth that He looks on all the deeds which
we do to the poor as if they had been done to Him? Thus the
world is full of God. In every lane you meet Christ. You
find Him at your door. Do not stand gaping into heaven, saying, if only I could see our Lord God, how eager I should be
to render Him every service possible. You are a liar, says St.
John in his first epistle (iv. 20), if you say you love God, and
hate your neighbour whom you see suffering before your
eyes. Listen, wretched man, do you wish to serve God? You
have Him in your house, in the persons of your servants and
your children. Teach them to fear God, to love Him, and to
trust in Him alone. Go and comfort your sad, sick neighbours, help them with your possessions, wisdom, and skill.
Behold, I will be very close to you in every poor brother
who needs your help and teaching. There am I, right in the
midst. Whether you help little or much, you do it unto Me.
A cup of cold water will not be given in vain; you will
receive fruit a thousandfold, not because of the work which
you have done, but because of the promise which I have
given.

Sermons from the year 1526.   W.A. 20. 514 f.

Jubilate

THE HEART SHALL REJOICE IN THE HOLY GHOST

Sunday: JOHN xvi. 16–23

*Ye now therefore have sorrow; but I will see you again,
and your heart shall rejoice, and your joy no man
taketh from you.* JOHN xvi. 22.

The one thing needful is that we trust in our Lord Jesus
Christ and believe in His Word, which means that when we
are cast down under sorrow and temptation, it is but for a
little while, so that we may find comfort in our suffering. For
it is impossible for a man to attain to happiness, unless he
has previously suffered pain and sorrow.

But, behold, what comfort! The Lord informs His disciples
what joy awaits them. He says, 'I will see you again'. This
came to pass on holy Easter Day when they saw Him again
in a new and everlasting life. Similarly Christ also sees us, and
our hearts see that for our sake He has overcome sin, death,
and the devil that we too through Him should live eternally.
That is everlasting and eternal joy, which overcomes all sorrow, and shall never be taken from us. Therefore we must
not lose patience nor be fainthearted under the cross. For
Christ is risen and is seated at the right hand of the Father,
that He may shield us from the devil and from all misery, and
make us blessed for evermore. May our faithful God and
Father grant us this through His Son our Redeemer, Jesus
Christ. Amen.

Sermon on John xvi. 16–23.   W.A. 52. 288 f.

*Verily, verily, I say unto you, That ye shall weep and
lament, but the world shall rejoice; and ye shall be
sorrowful, but your sorrow shall be turned into joy.*
                                        JOHN xvi. 20.

There are many kinds of sorrow on earth, but the deepest
of all sorrows is when the heart loses Christ, and He is no
longer seen, and there is no hope of comfort from Him. Only
a few are so sorely tempted. All comfort has gone, all joy is
ended, there is no help from heaven or sun or moon, from
angel or any creature. There is even no help from God. But
the world rejoices.

Behold, such joy Christ here gives to the world, and on the
other hand, deep sorrow to His Christians. And yet at the
same time, He paints the world as a place of horror and a
child of the devil, for it has no greater joy than to see Christ
perish and His Christians shamefully condemned and lost.

And that is why Christ tells us here, You have heard both
how the world will rejoice and how you will be sorrowful.
Therefore hear it and remember it so that when sorrows
abound you may have patience and receive true comfort
from such sufferings. I must tempt you thus and let you taste
what it means to have lost your Saviour and to have died in
your hearts, so that you may be given a little knowledge of
this mystery. Otherwise you cannot be given a knowledge
of My nature. It is too high for you to understand aright,
this lofty work, that the Son of God returns to His Father,
that is, He dies for you and rises again, that He may bring
you likewise into heaven.

Sermon on John xvi. 16 ff.   W.A. 49. 258 ff.

*A woman when she is in travail hath sorrow, because
her hour is come; but as soon as she is delivered of the
child, she remembereth no more the anguish, for joy
that a man is born into the world.* JOHN xvi. 21.

We must look carefully at this parable. For it is the same
in all temptations as it is here, and most of all in the anguish
of death. Behold, how God deals with a woman when she is
in travail. She is left by all lying helpless in her pain. No one
can help her. The whole creation cannot save her from this
hour. It stands alone in the power of God. The midwife and
others who are with her can give her some comfort, but they
cannot save her from her travail. She must pass through it
and risk her life in it. She may die, or she may recover, with
the child. She is right in the travail of death, completely surrounded by death.

It is the same with us when our conscience is alarmed or
when we are in anguish of death. There is no comfort.
Reason cannot help, or any creature, or anything we have
done. You think that God and all creatures have abandoned
you, and even that God and all creatures have turned against
you. Then you must be still and cleave to God alone. He
must deliver you, and nothing else can, whether in heaven or
on earth. And He will help you when He thinks it right and
good: as He helps the woman, giving her something that
makes her so happy that she forgets her pains; and whereas
before she was filled with death and anguish she is now full
of joy and life. So it is with us. When we are beset with
temptation, or when we are struggling with death, God alone
can gladden our hearts, and give us peace and joy where there
was nothing but fear and sorrow.

Sermon on the third Sunday after   W.A. 22. 429.
Easter.

These things have I spoken unto you, that my joy might remain in you, and that your joy might be full.
JOHN XV. 11.

To this end we must cleave to the Word with our whole heart and find strength in His precious promise that He will be with us in union with the Father, shielding us so that no calamity shall harm us and no power of the world or the devil shall oppress us or snatch us from His hands. Thus we always find joy and comfort, growing happier and happier, letting no suffering or opposition dismay us or make us despair. It is a lovely thing to bear all suffering for the love of Jesus. There is no other joy for a Christian on earth, which is perfect. For if you had all the world's happiness gathered up in one heap, it would not help you at all against sorrow and calamity, for the world's joy is based only on uncertain temporal goods, honour, lust, and so forth, and it cannot last longer than they do, but it withers and perishes when a slight chill wind blows on it and it suffers a small discomfort. But this is a joy without end (as it is grounded in the Eternal), and in the midst of outward calamity it stands and grows, so that with a joyful heart we can despise the world's happiness and lightly give it up.

Sermons on John xvi–xx.   W.A. 28. 156 f.

The fruit of the Spirit is . . . joy. GALATIANS v. 22.

By this we should learn that God does not want people to be sad and that He hates sad thoughts and sayings, and doctrines which oppress us. He makes our hearts joyful. For He did not send His Son to make us sad, but to make us glad. That is why the prophets and apostles and the Lord Christ Himself admonishes us and even commands us at all times to be joyful and of good cheer (as in Zechariah ix. 9), 'Rejoice greatly, O daughter of Zion; shout, O daughter of Jerusalem', and many times in the Psalms, 'Let us rejoice in the Lord', and St. Paul in Philippians (iv. 4), 'Rejoice in the Lord alway'; and Christ (Luke x. 20), 'Rejoice, because your names are written in heaven'. Where there is this joy of the Spirit there is a dear joy in the heart through faith in Christ, and we know of a certainty that He is our Saviour and High Priest, and this joy is seen in the things we say and do.

Commentary on the Prophet Jonah.   E.A. op. lat. 26. 50.

*I will shew him how great things he must suffer for
my name's sake.* ACTS ix. 16.

If you would be a joint-heir with your Lord Jesus Christ,
but will not suffer with Him and be His brother and be made
like Him, He will certainly not accept you as His brother and
joint-heir at the Last Day, but He will ask you where your
crown of thorns, your cross, your nails, and scourging are;
whether you too have been an abomination to the world, as
He and all His members have been from the beginning of the
world. And if you cannot give proof of this, He will not be
able to accept you as His brother. In a word, we must suffer
with Him, and must all be made like the Son of God, or else
we cannot be exalted to His glory.

The marks, nails, crown of thorns, and scourgings I must
bear, and so must all Christians, and not just painted on the
wall, but stamped in our flesh and blood.

Here St. Paul admonishes every Christian to bear the
marks of Christ our Lord. And He comforts them that they
should not be afraid even if all human suffering should be
laid upon them, as now for some years has been the lot of
our brethren. But it will become even worse when the hour
of our foe and the might of the darkness comes. But let it be.
We must suffer or we shall not come to the glory. But they
will see what it will profit them to have murdered us.

Sermons from the year 1535.   W.A. 41. 304 f.

Ask, and ye shall receive, that your joy may be full.
JOHN xvi. 24.

Joy cannot be perfect till we see the Name of God perfectly hallowed. But that will not be done in this life, but in the life to come, where there will be perfect joy and no sorrow at all. In this life we can have it only in part, a little drop, in faith, which is the beginning or foretaste of it, laying hold on the consolation that Christ has redeemed us and that we, through Him, have entered the Kingdom of God. But we are weak and slow to follow Him and claim His power. We will not follow and cannot remain pure in faith and life, for we fall again and again and are weighed down by sadness and a heavy conscience, so that our joy cannot be pure, or there is so little joy that we can scarcely feel it.

Therefore this passage must be added which calls for prayer for help and strength that we may at last be given a pure, whole, and perfect joy. You must not seek it in yourself or within this world, for its joy is impure and in the end death takes it all away. But seek it in prayer, says Christ, asking in My Name that for which I came into the world and called you and ordained you may come to pass, that God's Name and Kingdom and Will may be glorified in all the world, and that the opposition which the world, the flesh, and the devil wage without ceasing may be hindered and brought to an end.

Exposition of John xvi.   W.A. 46. 91 f.

Cantate

THE CHURCH'S SONG OF PRAISE

Sunday: JOHN xvi. 5–15

And when he is come, he will reprove the world of sin, and of righteousness, and of judgement: of sin, because they believe not in me. JOHN xvi. 8–9.

Every man is in danger because of his own deeds, and if a man is lost it is because of his own guilt. Not because he is a descendant of Adam, or because of his former unbelief, is he a sinner deserving damnation, but because he refuses to accept this Saviour, Christ, who abolishes our sin and condemnation. But if I do not believe, sin and condemnation must remain upon me, because I do not lay hold of Him who alone can save me from them. Indeed, the sin and condemnation become twice as great and heavy because I will not accept the redemption wrought through this precious Saviour, nor believe in Him who seeks to help me.

Thus our salvation or our condemnation both depend on whether we will or will not believe in Christ. Unbelief retains all sin, so that it cannot find forgiveness, while faith destroys all sin. Therefore, apart from such faith, all things are sinful and remain sinful, even the most noble living and the best works which a man can do, for though they are in themselves praiseworthy and even commanded by God, they are corrupted by unbelief and therefore cannot please, while all the works and ways of a Christian please Him because they are done in faith. To sum up, apart from Christ all is lost and condemned; with Christ all is good and blessed, so that even sin (which remains still in flesh and blood born of Adam) cannot bring us to harm and condemnation.

Exposition of John xvi. W.A. 46. 41 f.

HE WILL REPROVE THE WORLD IN RESPECT OF RIGHTEOUSNESS

And when he is come, he will reprove the world of sin,
and of righteousness, and of judgement ... of righteous-
ness, because I go to my Father, and ye see me no more.
JOHN xvi. 8, 10.

Christians should know of no other righteousness with
which to stand before God and be justified and to receive the
forgiveness of sins and eternal life, than this going of Christ
to His Father, which means that He took upon Himself our
sin and for our sakes suffered death upon the cross and was
buried and descended into hell. But He did not remain under
sin and death and in hell, but passed through them in His
Resurrection and Ascension, and now He is seated at the right
hand of the Father, a mighty Lord over all creatures.

And this righteousness is hidden not only from the world
and reason, but also from the saints. For it is not a thought,
word, or deed within ourselves, but it is right outside us and
above us. It is this going of Christ to His Father, and this is
not within the range of our eyes or senses, so that we can
neither see it nor feel it. It can be perceived only through
faith in the Word which is preached about it, that He Himself
is our righteousness, so that we do not glory in ourselves
but in Christ the Lord alone.

Exposition of John xvi.   w.a. 46. 43 f.

HE WILL REPROVE THE WORLD IN RESPECT OF JUDGEMENT

*When he is come, he will reprove the world of sin, and
of righteousness, and of judgement . . . of judgement,
because the prince of this world is judged.*

JOHN xvi. 8, 11.

Thus this judgement proceeds from the authority and power
of our Lord Jesus Christ sitting at the right hand of the
Father, and the judgement is publicly preached, that the prince
of this world and all that belongs to him is already condemned and has no power against Christ. The devil must let
Him be Lord and must lie for ever under His feet and suffer
the bruising of his head.

Although the world goes on in its usual way, despising the
judgement already passed on the devil and all his members,
scoffing at it because they cannot see it before their eyes,
Christ goes on, meekly suffering to be disdained yet mani-
festing to the devil and the world that He is the Lord who
can break the devil's wrath and raging, cast down His enemies,
and make them all into a footstool for His feet. But this none
but the Christians believe, and they hold that the Word of
their Lord is true. They know His power and His kingdom
and are comforted by their Lord and King. The children of
the world will have no other reward than what they seek with
their lord, the devil. Because of their raging against the
Christians, they will be cast down into the deepest abyss of
hell and perish in eternal darkness.

Exposition of John xvi. 5–15.   W.A. 21. 371 f.

*O sing unto the Lord a new song; for he hath done
marvellous things: his right hand, and his holy arm,
hath gotten him the victory.*   PSALM xcviii. 1.

This is the new song about the new kingdom, new
creatures, new men, born not of the law or of works but of
God and the Spirit, who themselves are miracles and who
work miracles in Jesus Christ our Lord.

And because the Holy Ghost commands us all to sing, it
is certain that he also commands us to believe in the miracles
which have been wrought and proclaimed for our sake.
Therefore doubt and unbelief are here condemned, when they
say, 'How can I be sure that God, by His authority or His
arm (that is through His Son) has wrought such victories
and miracles for my sake?' Listen (says the Spirit): for you,
for you, for you it was done. You, you, you should sing,
and give thanks and be happy. That is My wish and will.

Sayings from the Old Testament.   W.A. 48. 56.

*David the son of Jesse said, and the man who was
raised up on high, the anointed of the God of Jacob,
and the sweet psalmist of Israel, said, The Spirit of
the Lord spake by me, and his word was in my
tongue.* 2 SAMUEL xxiii. 1–2.

Faith knows no rest, or ease. It goes out, speaks and
preaches, and for very joy it begins to compose sweet and
lovely Psalms. It sings joyful and merry songs in order to
praise God joyfully and give thanks to Him, and to move
men and teach them. But it not only thinks of the sweetness
and loveliness of the Psalms as regards the grammar and
music, how neatly and skilfully the words are arranged, and
how sweet and lovely the chanting and the music sounds,
that is of beautiful wording and notation, but of the lovely
theology and spiritual meaning of the Psalms. Yet the music
helps as a wonderful creation and gift of God, especially
where the congregation joins in the singing and their minds
and hearts are in earnest.

He calls His Psalms Israel's Psalms, and does not want to
call them His own, and Himself alone be honoured because
of them. Israel should confirm them and judge and acknowledge them as her own. For a word or psalm needs to be
accepted or rejected by the congregation or the people of
God. Thus do we Christians talk about *our* psalmists.

St. Ambrose wrote many lovely hymns, and they are called
'Church hymns' because the Church accepted them and uses
them as if the members had written them themselves and
they were their hymns. That is why we do not say: thus St.
Ambrose, Gregory, Prudentius, or Sedulius sing, but we say:
so sings the Christian Church. For the singing of Ambrose,
Sedulius, etc., are the hymns of the Christian Church, which
the Church sings in union with them, and when they die,
the Church remains, singing their hymns for ever.

On the last words of David.   W.A. 54. 33 f.

*Let the word of Christ dwell in you richly in all wis-
dom; teaching and admonishing one another in psalms
and hymns and spiritual songs, singing with grace in
your hearts to the Lord.* COLOSSIANS iii. 16.

The Psalms not only present to us the common and simple
speech of the saints but their loftiest thoughts and words in
which they talked earnestly about the highest things with
God Himself. This is the greatest gift of the saints which
their hymns pass on to us, so that we know for certain how
their hearts felt and their mouth spoke to God and man.

For a human heart is like a ship on a wild sea, tossed about
by all the four winds of the world.

And such storms teach us to pray earnestly, to open our
heart and pour forth our inmost thoughts. For when a man
is hemmed in by fear and sorrow he speaks very differently
about trouble than one who is surrounded by joy, and he
who is surrounded by joy speaks very differently of happiness than one who is hemmed in by fear. It does not come
from the heart (people say) when a sad person laughs or a
glad person weeps, that is, the innermost heart is not revealed.

And do not most of the Psalms consist of such earnest
prayer in the midst of storms? And where are lovelier words
of joy to be found than in the Psalms of praise and thanksgiving? There you see into the hearts of the saints, like looking into gay and beautiful gardens, or even heaven. What
sweet and fine and lovely flowers bloom there from all kinds
of lovely, happy thoughts about God and His benefits! And
again, where are sadder and more plaintive words of sorrow
to be found than in the penitential psalms? There we can look
into the hearts of the saints as into death, or even hell. How
dark and black it is there because of the sense of the wrath
of God! Thus, when they speak of fear and hope they use
such vivid words that no painter could make the pictures
clear, and no Cicero or any orator could so depict it.

Preface to the Psalter, 1531.   E.A. 63. 29 f.

> *Sing unto him a new song; play skilfully with a loud noise.* PSALM xxxiii. 3.

Music is one of the loveliest and most glorious gifts of God. Satan hates it because it has great power to dispel temptations and evil thoughts. The devil does not wait on this lady. Music is one of the finest arts. The music makes the words live. It drives away the spirit of sadness, as is seen in the story of Saul, the king.

Music is the best balm for a sad heart, for it restores contentment and quickens and refreshes the heart.

Music is a glorious gift of God, very like to theology. I would not part with my little gifts of music for anything in the world. We ought to teach the young this art, for it makes fine and clever people.

'Sing unto the Lord a new song; sing unto the Lord all the world!' for God has made our hearts and minds joyful through His beloved Son whom He gave for us and for our redemption from sin, death, and the devil. Whosoever earnestly believes this cannot help speaking and singing joyfully about it so that others may hear it and discover the cause. But if a man does not sing and speak about it, that is a sign that he does not believe in it, and has not entered into the new and joyful testament, but is still under the old, dull testament.

Preface to the Hymn Book.   W.A. 35. 477.

Rogate

THE PRAYER OF THE CONGREGATION
Sunday : JAMES V

The effectual fervent prayer of a righteous man availeth much. JAMES v. 16.

No man can conceive the power of prayer except one who has tried it and learned by experience. But it is a great thing that a man faced with a dire calamity may forthwith call upon the Lord. This I know. Whenever I have prayed earnestly about a matter which has concerned me very deeply, it has been richly answered and I have received more than I have asked. Sometimes God has been slow in coming, but He has always come. Lo, what a great thing is the fervent prayer of a true Christian! How it avails with God that a poor man should speak with His High Majesty in heaven and be not afraid of Him, but know that God smiles graciously on him for the sake of Jesus Christ His beloved Son, our Lord and Saviour! The heart and conscience need not turn back and run away. It need not be in doubt because of its unworthiness, and need not be afraid, but may believe with complete certainty that our prayers are always answered when we pray believing in Christ.

Therefore, brethren, pray in your hearts, and at times with words, for (by the will of God) prayer upholds the world. Without it the world would be very different. At home I am not so brave and cheerful, though I am not content that it should be so, but in the Church with the multitude, prayer comes straight from the heart and prevails.

Table-Talk.   w.a. Tischreden. 3. 448.

*When he shall hear the voice of thy cry, he will
answer thee.*   ISAIAH XXX. 19.

You must learn to pray and not sit alone or lie about, hanging your head and shaking it, brooding over your thoughts,
worrying about how you can escape and looking at nothing
but yourself and your sad and painful condition. Get up, you
lazy villain, then fall upon your knees, lift your eyes and
hands towards heaven, take a Psalm or the Lord's Prayer,
and pour out your trouble with tears before God, lamenting
and calling upon Him. Psalm cxlii.: 'I poured out my com-
plaint before him; I shewed before him my trouble', and
Psalm cxli.: 'Let my prayer be set forth before thee as incense', and the lifting up of hands, prayer, and the mentioning
of trouble are sacrifices most pleasing to God. He desires it,
and it is His will, that you should pour out your trouble
before Him, and not let it lie upon yourself, dragging it
about with you and being chafed and tortured by it, so that
in the end you make two, or even ten or a hundred calamities
out of one. He wills that you should be too weak to bear and
overcome such trouble, in order that you may learn to find
strength in Him, and that He may be praised through His
strength in you. Behold, this is how Christians are made!

Exposition of Psalm cxviii.   W.A. 31   95 f.

*Verily, verily, I say unto you, Whatsoever ye shall
ask the Father in my name, he will give it you.*
                                        JOHN xvi. 23.

Therefore, when you desire to pray, kneel down, or stand,
bold and unashamed (inasmuch as you have acknowledged
your sin and desire to be bettered) and speak thus with God:
Lord God, heavenly Father, I pray and will not be denied,
the answer should and must be Yes, and Amen, and nothing
else, otherwise I will not pray or admit that I have prayed—
not that I have a right to it or deserve it. I know and readily
confess that I do not deserve it—on the contrary, for my
many great sins I deserve hell fire and Thy eternal wrath.
Yet I have shown some small obedience in that I have
followed Thy behest and Thy command to pray in the Name
of Thy beloved Son, our Lord Jesus Christ. Trusting in this
consolation of Thy unfathomable grace, and not in my own
righteousness, I kneel or stand before Thee and pray for . . .
etc.

On the other hand, we have been repeatedly taught that
we must not tempt God in prayer, that is, we must not fix a
time, measure, goal, manner, or person, how, when, or by
what means He shall answer us; but must humbly leave all
this to Him who in His divine, incomprehensible wisdom
will do all things well. And we must not doubt that our
prayer is most certainly answered, even if it looks otherwise.

Exhortation to prayer against the Turks.   W.A. 51. 605 f.

*Therefore I say unto you, What things soever ye
desire, when ye pray, believe that ye receive them,
and ye shall have them.*　　MARK xi. 24.

Concerning the little word 'Amen'. The little word 'Amen'
means surely, or truly. Think carefully about it, for it ex-
presses the faith that we should have in all our prayers.
Therefore when a man is about to pray he should test and
examine himself, whether he believes or doubts that he will
be heard. And if he finds that he doubts it, or without any
conviction hazards it as a venture, his prayer is futile. For his
heart is not composed. Therefore God can pour no certainty
into it, just as you cannot give a man something if he does
not keep his hand still. And think how you would like it, if
someone urgently asked you for something and in the end
said, but I do not believe you will give me it—although you
had promised him for certain. You would deem such a prayer
a mockery, and would withdraw all that you had promised.
You might even punish the man. How, then, can it please God
who has promised that He will give us what we ask, when
we give the lie to His promises through our doubt, and in
the very act of praying, act contrary to the prayer, thus
insulting the Truth to whom we pray?

Exposition of the Lord's Prayer for　　　　W.A. 2. 126 f.
　simple lay-folk.

LUKE xxiv. 50–53

*The Lord said unto my Lord, Sit thou at my right
hand, until I make thine enemies thy footstool.*

PSALM CX. 1.

Christ is seated on high awaiting the time when His
enemies shall be made His footstool. That is His proper work.
He does not sleep, but He watches us. He does not ask anyone
to deputise for Him. He does it Himself. When people incline
towards Him, He is present to help. If a man is tempted and
he cries unto Christ, he will be helped. The Last Day is not
yet come, and the flesh and sin and death still remain, but on
the Last Day Christ will deliver up the Kingdom to His
Father. Now He rules in our hearts. He comforts us, makes
us clean, and intercedes for us. On the Last Day all His
Christians will rule in unity with Him, and they will be seated
at the right hand of the Father. Then the last and proper
enemy will be slain. Here on earth is still unstable faith,
anxiety about food, and despair, if ever God shows His displeasure. What is now our comfort? Christ, our Priest, who
has atoned for us and looks upon us and sees our enemies
and reminds the Father that He is our portion. When we feel
this in our conscience, we have a sure access to the Father
in every need. We fail to see this only because our eyes are
not sufficiently penetrating to pierce the clouds and look into
heaven, and be assured that Christ is our Advocate.

Sermon on Hebrews viii.   W.A. 45. 398 f.

> *The Spirit also helpeth our infirmities: for we know
> not what we should pray for as we ought: but the
> Spirit itself maketh intercession for us with groanings
> which cannot be uttered.*   ROMANS viii. 26.

It is not a bad but rather a good sign when our prayers
are answered by events which seem to be the very opposite
to what we have asked, just as it is not a good sign when our
prayers are fulfilled exactly as we desired. The reason and
cause of this is that God's will and wisdom are high above
our will and wisdom. Therefore it may come to pass that when
we pray to God for something and He hears and begins to
answer, that He does it in a way which runs counter to our
ideas, so that it appears to us that He is more angry with us
after our prayers than before, and that there is less hope of
the fulfilment of our desires than before we prayed. God does
all this because it is His way first to destroy what there is in
us before He bestows His gifts.

And when all is hopeless and everything goes against our
prayers and desires those inexpressible groanings begin. Then
the 'Spirit helpeth our infirmities'. For without the help of
the Spirit it would be quite impossible for us to endure this
way God has of answering our prayer and fulfilling our re-
quests. Here the soul is bidden: Be brave! Keep your courage!
Let your heart be strong, and wait upon the Lord.

And whosoever has received the Spirit receives help. For
the work of God must remain hidden and unknown while it
is going on, but it cannot be hidden except in a manner which
is contrary to our thinking and understanding.

Commentary on Romans.   *305.*

*If ye abide in me, and my words abide in you, ye shall
ask what ye will, and it shall be done unto you.*

JOHN XV. 7.

Life apart from Christ is a wretched business. It means
hard work for people and yet nothing accomplished; much
praying, seeking, and knocking, yet nothing gained, found,
or done, for they are not knocking at the right door. For
whatever they do and pray, they do it like any other work,
without faith. They have no comfort or confidence, and even
no conviction that it is well-pleasing to God or that He will
hear them. And that is why they never pray, for, as I have
often said, prayer is the work of faith alone, which none but
a Christian can do. For Christians do not pray trusting in
themselves, but in the Name of the Son of God in which they
were baptised, and they know for certain that such prayer is
well-pleasing to God, for He has commanded them to pray
in the name of Christ and has promised to answer. Other
people who begin to pray in their own name, taking a long
time to prepare themselves until they are right and worthy,
and so gaining merit, do not know this. And if they are asked
whether they are sure that they will be heard, they answer:
I have prayed, but whether I shall be answered, God alone
knows. But what manner of prayer is that when you do not
know what you are doing or what God will say to it?

A Christian, however, does not so rise from prayer, but
as he begins it in response to God's command and promise
he makes it an offering to God in the Name of Christ and
knows that what he has asked will not be denied him, and so
he finds in his experience that he is helped in every time of
need.

Exposition of John xv.   W.A. 45. 681.

Whitsuntide

Exaudi

THE PROMISE OF THE SPIRIT

Sunday: JOHN xv. 26–xvi. 4

*I will pour upon them the spirit of grace and of sup-
plication.* Zechariah xii. 10.

The Spirit should create these two things in all Christians:
first, that their hearts are sure and certain that God is gracious
unto them; then, that they can help others too with their
prayers. The first means that they are reconciled to God and
have everything they need. When they have that, they should
become as gods and saviours of the world, through their
prayers.

For when a Christian begins to know Christ as his Lord
and Saviour, through whom he is redeemed from death
and brought into His Kingdom and inheritance, his heart is
aglow with a flaming love of God and he would gladly help
everyone to the same experience, for he has no greater joy
than that he possesses this treasure, that he knows Christ.
Therefore he goes out and teaches and exhorts other people,
praising and testifying to it before all men, praying and
yearning that they too might attain to such grace. That is a
restless spirit enjoying the highest rest, in the grace and peace
of God, for it cannot be silent or idle, but is always striving
with all its powers to spread the honour and glory of God
among the people, that others too may receive this Spirit
of grace and may then help with the work of prayer.

Exposition of John xiv.   W.A. 45. 540.

I have glorified thee on the earth: I have finished the work which thou gavest me to do. JOHN xvii. 4.

If Christ had not been glorified, the Father's glory could not have come to us, but would have perished with Christ. They are interlocked and interwoven. The glory of the Father and of the Lord Christ is one indivisible glory, so that the Son receives His glory from the Father and the Father is glorified in and through the Son.

And as Christ, our Head, prays, so also must we who cleave to Him pray that He may be glorified in us. For as He fared on earth so must we fare, and for His sake we (because we glorify Him and praise Him with our teaching and living) must submit to shame, condemnation, cursing, and death, so that in our suffering also His Name and holy Word will be persecuted and reviled. But that His honour may remain and to keep His Word, He must help us out, and turn the wheel so that the world must be shown to be wrong, and condemned with all its shame, while we enter into the highest honour and glory. Thus His honour and praise stand out most vividly and spread through the Holy Ghost, and the mouth of Christians, into all the world. This He calls the work which the Father gave Him to do, namely, drawing upon Himself all shame and blame, and suffering and death, for the honour of the Father, and all this for our sake that we might be redeemed and have eternal life.

Sermons on John xvi–xx.   W.A. 28. 108.

*At that day ye shall know that I am in my Father,
and ye in me, and I in you.* JOHN xiv. 20.

This is the first main point and most important article,
that Christ is in the Father, that no one doubts, that what
this Man says and does is and must be said and done in
heaven before all the angels, in the world before all the
tyrants, in hell before all the devils, and in the heart before
all bad consciences and self-willed thoughts. For, if I am
certain that what He says, thinks and wills, the Father also
wills, I can brave all that is angry and evil. For in Christ I
have the Father's heart and will. And if you perceive this
you perceive Christ in the Father and the Father in Christ,
and you see no wrath or death or hell, but pure grace and
mercy, heaven and life.

The other point. After ye know and experience this you
will advance to the knowledge that I am your Saviour, in the
following way: that what you are and what you lack, how
you are condemned sinners held in the grip of death, that is
all in Me, and there it should lie. But whatsoever is in Me
must be pure righteousness, life, and blessedness. Now
through your faith you come to be in Me, with all your sorrow, sin, and death. Although you are sinners yourselves, you
are justified in Me. Although you have death in yourselves,
you have life in Me. Although you are not at peace in yourselves, you have peace in Me; although you are condemned
in yourselves, you are saved and blessed in Me.

Exposition of John xiv.   W.A. 45. 589 f.

> *I pray not for the world, but for them that thou hast
> given me.*   JOHN xvii. 9.

We have been told for whom He prays, namely, for all
those who believe in His Word, and love Him with all their
hearts and cleave firmly to His Word. These may joyfully
rely that they are certainly included in this prayer and will
abide with Christ.

But, on the other hand, that is a terrible thing that He says:
'I pray not for the world'. Let us then take heed that we are
not found amongst those for whom He will not pray. For
nothing can follow but that they will certainly be lost, for
Christ has cast them out from Himself and will not have
anything to do with them. The world should be filled with
fear and petrified with horror at such judgement. But it
merely mocks and laughs, and remains in its grim and stub-
born blindness, feeling so secure that it casts it to the wind
and lets it go in at one ear and out at the other, as if a fool
had said it.

Sermons on John xvi–xx.   W.A. 28. 128 f.

*I will pour upon them the spirit of grace and of sup-
plication.*   ZECHARIAH xii. 10.

For when a Christian begins to know Christ as his Lord
and Saviour, through whom he is redeemed from death and
brought into His kingdom and inheritance, his heart is aglow
with a flaming love of God and he would gladly help everyone to the same experience. For he knows no greater joy
than that he possesses this treasure, that he knows Christ.
Therefore he goes out and teaches and exhorts other people,
praising and testifying to it before all men, praying and yearning that they too might attain to such grace. That is a restless
spirit enjoying the highest rest in the grace and peace of
God, for it cannot be silent or idle, but is always striving
with all its power to spread the honour and glory of God
among the people, that others too may receive this Spirit
of Grace and may then help with the work of prayer. For
where the Spirit of grace is, He quickens our hearts, so that
we can, and may, and must begin to pray.

Exposition of John xiv.   W.A. 45. 540.

I pray not that thou shouldst take them out of the
world, but that thou shouldst keep them from the evil.
Sanctify them through thy truth; thy word is truth.
JOHN xvii. 15, 17.

The whole of Christendom consists of a little group of
people who must bend their back, and suffer, and carry more
grief and anguish, laid on them by the world and the devil,
than all other men. What man, in face of such outward
appearance, could feel, or see, or conclude, that they are right
with God? Certainly not reason, but the Holy Ghost, must
convince people, and He is called the Spirit of truth because
He strengthens and upholds the heart against such appearance
and feelings. Without Him no man would have believed, or
would believe now, that this Jesus Christ is true God, sitting
eternally at the right hand of the Father, He who was thus
shamefully nailed to the cross by His own people, like a thief.
And again, how could we of ourselves tell with certainty
that we (who believe in this Christ crucified), condemned
and cursed, and done to death by all the world, as the devil's
friends and God's foes, are in very truth God's children and
saints, which even we ourselves do not feel, for our heart
tells us something very different because we are still so weak
and sinful? But it is the work and power of the Holy Ghost
which confirms this in our hearts, so that we can believe that
it is true, as the Word tells us, and can live and die in that
belief.

Exposition of John xvi.   W.A. 46. 54.

Peace I leave with you, my peace I give unto you. . . .
Let not your heart be troubled, neither let it be afraid.
                                        JOHN xiv. 27.

This is a very precious, final word, that He does not leave
them cities and castles, or silver and gold, but His peace as
the greatest treasure in heaven and on earth. They are not to
be afraid or to mourn, but are to have true and lovely and
longed-for peace in their hearts. For as far as it rests with
Me, He says, you will have nothing but pure peace and joy.
For My presence and preaching have taught you that I love
you with all My heart, and desire only your good, and My
Father looks upon you most graciously. This is the best gift
I can leave to you. For this is the highest peace, when the
heart is content; as it is said 'the joy of the heart is the greatest
of all joys'; and again, 'the sorrow of the heart is the greatest
of all sorrows'.

Exposition of John xiv.   W.A. 45. 623.

Whitsuntide

THE CHURCH OF THE HOLY SPIRIT

Whitsunday: ACTS ii. 1–13

They were all filled with the Holy Ghost. ACTS ii. 4.

On this holy and joyful feast of Pentecost we give thanks to our Lord God as we celebrate the great unending mercy which He made manifest on earth in that He revealed from heaven to us poor men His holy Word, which is not a plain and common word, but a special and a different Word, compared with the Law of Moses. For this day the Kingdom of Christ began through the Apostles, and was manifested through the Gospel for all the world. Of course, in His Person, Christ possessed His Kingdom from eternity, but today, on Whitsunday, it was made manifest by the Holy Ghost through the Apostles to all the world, and this revelation was accompanied by the great courage, daring, and joy of those wretched fishermen, the Apostles, who had previously denied Christ and deserted Him because their minds were stupid and afraid and in despair.

Today, on this Whitsunday, we celebrate the joyous, blessed, and precious Kingdom of Christ, which is full of joy, and confidence and courage.

Sermon for Whitsunday, 1534.   W.A. 37. 399 f.

*God hath chosen the foolish things of the world to con-
found the wise; and God hath chosen the weak things
of the world to confound the things which are mighty.*
                                        I CORINTHIANS i. 27.

Thus Christ begins His Kingdom through the untaught
laymen and simple fishermen, who had not studied the
Scriptures. It sounds very foolish, that the Christian Church
should have begun with those poor beggars and the scandalous preaching of the crucified Jesus of Nazareth, who was
mocked, defiled, slandered and most shamefully treated,
scourged, and finally as a blasphemer and rioter nailed to the
cross and shamefully done to death, as His title on the cross
proves—'Jesus of Nazareth, the King of the Jews'. Of the
same it is openly preached on Whitsunday that He suffered
wrong and violence, and that those who nailed Him to the
cross and killed Him are devils, and God's enemies, who have
sinned gravely and have provoked the fierce wrath of God.
And through this preaching Christ's Kingdom and the
Christian Church began. This is a daring deed of the Apostles
and disciples, and a great comfort to them that they were
given power to preach such tidings openly on Whitsunday.
Who is so daring that he would preach as they preached?

And in what does that same might and strength consist?
In nothing but the Word and the Spirit. See, what power
Peter has! And, indeed, not Peter only, but all the others as
well! How sure they are of their message, how mightily do
they use the Holy Scriptures, as if they had studied them for
a hundred thousand years and learned them perfectly! I could
not master the Scriptures as well, although I am a doctor of
Divinity and these are fishermen who had not read the Bible.

Thus Christendom began with the word of the poor
fishermen, and with the despised and disdained work of God,
which is called Jesus of Nazareth, nailed to the cross.

Sermon for Whitsunday, 1534.   W.A. 37. 400.

*I will pray the Father, and he shall give you another
Comforter, that he may abide with you for ever.*

JOHN xiv. 16.

Therefore must we learn to know the Holy Spirit and
believe Him to be as Christ describes Him and sets Him
before the eye of the soul, namely, that He is not a Spirit of
wrath and terror but of grace and comfort, and that thus the
whole Godhead shows nothing but comfort. The Father wills
to comfort us, for He gives the Holy Ghost; the Son gives
comfort, for He prays the Father to send Him; and the Holy
Ghost is Himself the Comforter. There is therefore here no
terror, threat, or wrath over Christians, but only gracious
laughter and sweet comfort in heaven and on earth. And
why is that? The reason is (He says) because you have
already enough torturers and hangmen to plague and frighten
you.

This is the right way of teaching about the Holy Ghost,
that He is called a Comforter, and that that is His nature,
character, and ministry. His divine essence or substance we
will not now discuss in any detail. As regards His Godhead,
He is of indivisible divine essence with the Father and the
Son; but to us He is called a Comforter, and a comforter is
one who makes a sad heart glad and joyful towards God and
tells you to be of good cheer for your sins are forgiven, death
is slain, heaven is open, and God smiles upon you. Whoever
could grasp this definition rightly would have already won
the victory and would not find or see anything but sheer
comfort and joy in heaven and on earth.

Exposition of John xiv.   W.A. 45. 562 ff.

RIGHTEOUSNESS AND PEACE AND JOY IN THE HOLY SPIRIT

*The kingdom of God is . . . righteousness, and peace,
and joy in the Holy Ghost.*   ROMANS xiv. 17.

If I am to be made saintly, it is not enough to do good
works outwardly, but I must do them from the bottom of
my heart with love and desire, that I may be fearless, free,
and joyful and stand before God with a good conscience and
complete confidence, knowing how I stand with Him.
Nothing I do can give me this assurance, and no creature,
but Christ alone. Such faith makes me well-pleasing to God,
and Christ fills my heart with the Holy Ghost, who makes
me happy and glad to do anything that is good. In this way
only can I be justified, and in no other; for works make you
the more unhappy the longer you trust in them.

But the more you do this work and the better you know
it, the more does it make your heart joyful, for where there
is such knowledge the Holy Ghost cannot remain outside.
And when He comes He makes the heart joyful, willing, and
gay, so that it freely goes and gladly and with good heart
does all that is well-pleasing to God, and suffers what has to
be suffered, and would gladly die. And the purer and greater
the knowledge, the deeper grows the bliss and joy. Thus the
Lord's command is fulfilled and all is done that should be
done; and thus you are made just.

Sermons from the year 1523.   W.A. 12. 547.

Thou hast crowned him with glory and honour.

PSALM viii. 5.

He talks here about the royal adornment with which Christ, crowned as a king, will be glorious in this world and in the world to come. It is the custom to adorn kings when they are to appear in splendour. Christ, the king, will likewise be adorned not for Himself alone in His natural body, but also for us in His spiritual body, which is the Church. For He gathers His Church through the preaching of the Gospel, and adorneth her with His Holy Spirit. And this adornment is set over against His wretched appearance, of which Isaiah says (chapter liii) that the Son of Man has no form nor comeliness, and few to follow Him, at the time of His suffering. His own people cry over Him: 'Crucify Him, crucify Him!' Even His own disciples desert Him and flee from Him. But after His resurrection He will be gloriously adorned, and a multitude of Christians will follow Him on earth. And that will be the beautiful adornment with which He will be crowned in this world.

Sermons from the year 1537. W.A. 45. 242 f.

Others mocking said, These men are full of new wine.
ACTS ii. 13.

Once, on Whitsunday, Christ gave the Holy Spirit visibly
to the Apostles when there were seen sitting upon each of them
cloven tongues like as of fire, and they spoke in many tongues,
and exorcised devils and healed the sick. But now, and to the
end of the world, He no longer gives the Holy Spirit and His
gifts to His Christians as He did then, but invisibly and
secretly. But as little as our reason believes that Christ has
overcome and taken captive all our foes, death and the devil,
so little does it believe that Christ pours forth gifts among
men. For when the Apostles received the Holy Ghost on
Whitsunday, began to speak with other tongues, went to
Jerusalem and preached, and also in the whole of Judæa,
Samaria, and thereafter in all the world according to the
behest of the Lord, who believed that they were in their right
mind? Indeed, they were told by their own people, the Jews,
that they were full of new wine, and also that they were possessed and full of devils; and by both Jews and Gentiles they
were done to death as blasphemers, deceivers, and rogues.

That is why the world neither sees nor understands the
gifts of the Holy Ghost, but despises and scorns them. In
fact, everything which our Lord does and says does not and
cannot suit the world. They even deem His Word to be
heresy and the devil's teaching. On the other hand, they hold
the devil's work in high esteem, and call it the word of God.
Only the Christians recognise the Word of God and deem
it to be the highest treasure on earth; they only perceive the
dignity and power of His great divine works, although even
they never sufficiently marvel at them and praise them as they
should. For as the Apostles fared, we also fare in our time.

Sermon on the Fruit and Power   E.A. 18. 185 f.
  of the Ascension of our Lord
  Jesus Christ, 1527.

And base things of the world, and things which are
despised, hath God chosen, yea, and things which are
not, to bring to nought things that are: that no flesh
should glory in his presence. I CORINTHIANS i. 28–29.

May God in His mercy save me from a Christian Church
where there are none but saints. I want to be with that little
company, and in that Church where there are faint-hearted
and weak people, the sick, and those who are aware of their
sin, misery, and wretchedness, and feel it, and who cry to God
without ceasing and sigh unto Him for comfort and help;
and believe in the forgiveness of sins and suffer persecution
for the Word's sake. Satan is a cunning rogue. Through his
fanatics he seeks to make the simple-minded believe that the
preaching of the Gospel is useless. The right approach is quite
different. It consists of such things as walking in holy ways,
taking our cross upon us and suffering much persecution.
Through such false appearances of self-chosen sanctity (which
is contrary to the Word of God) many are led astray. Yet our
sanctification and justification is Christ in whom (and not
in ourselves) we are perfect, and therein I find my comfort
and strength in St. Paul's word, that 'Christ Jesus is of God
made unto us wisdom and righteousness, and sanctification,
and redemption'.

Exposition of John i.   W.A. 46. 583.

Trinity Sunday

THE HOLY TRINITY

Sunday: ROMANS xi. 33–36

*Of him, and through him, and to him, are all things:
to whom be glory for ever. Amen.* ROMANS xi. 36.

The other feasts in the year wrap our Lord up in the works
and wonders which He has done. At Christ's nativity we
celebrate that God was made Man, at Easter that He rose
from the dead, at Whitsun that He poured out the Holy
Ghost and instituted the Church, and so forth, so that all
the other feasts of the year speak of our Lord God as He is
seen clothed in some work. But this feast shows us how He
is in Himself, in His divine nature without any wrappings
and works. Here you must soar high above all reason, leaving
all creatures far below, and must swing yourself up and listen
only to what God says of Himself, and of His innermost
being. In no other way can we know this. And there God's
folly and the world's wisdom clash.

Therefore we should not dispute about how it can be that
God the Father, the Son, and the Holy Spirit are One God,
for it is by its very nature beyond all reason, but it should
be enough for us that God speaks thus about Himself and
reveals Himself thus in His Word.

This is a strengthening message, and it should make our
hearts joyful towards God. For we see, that all three Persons,
the whole Godhead, turns Himself to us in order that we poor
wretched men should be helped against sin, death, and the
devil, that we may be brought to justification, the Kingdom
of God, and eternal life.

Sermon on John iii.   W.A. 52. 346.

Who only hath immortality, dwelling in the light which no man can approach unto; whom no man hath seen, nor can see: to whom be honour and power everlasting. Amen. 1 TIMOTHY vi. 16.

This hidden Will should not be investigated but adored, with trembling, as a deep, holy secret of God's High Majesty, which He has reserved to Himself.

Thus we must not search God's nature and His hidden will. For therein we have nothing to do with Him, nor does He desire to have anything to do with us. God is at work in many ways which He does not reveal to us in His Word. Likewise He has many intentions which he has not revealed to us in His Word. Therefore we should behold the Word and leave the unfathomable Will alone, for we have received no command about it. For we must direct ourselves in accordance with His Word and not with His unfathomable Will. It behoves us not to seek the high, great, holy secrets of the Majesty who dwells in a light which no man can approach, as Paul says (1 Timothy vi.). We should cleave unto God who permits us to draw near to Him, and to Him who was made man, Jesus Christ the crucified (as St. Paul says), in whom are hidden all the treasures of God's wisdom. For in Him we have superabundantly received all things which we know and which it behoves us to know.

On the enslaved will. 146–148.

*How unsearchable are his judgements, and his ways
past finding out!* ROMANS xi. 33.

Why, then, do we poor wretched men rack our brains over
the nature of God, while we yet fail to grasp by faith the
rays of the divine promises or comprehend a spark of God's
commands and works, both of which He has confirmed with
words and mighty works?

Of a truth, we ought to teach of God's unsearchable and
unfathomable Will, but to take upon ourselves to understand
it is a very dangerous thing, through which we may stumble
and break our neck. It is my habit to restrain and direct myself by the word which the Lord Christ spoke to Peter—
'What is that to thee? Follow thou me'. For Peter also dis-
puted and brooded over the works of God, asking in what
manner He would deal with another, that is, what might
befall John. And again, how He answered Philip when He
said (John xiv. 8): 'Shew us the Father', what did He reply?
'Believest thou not that I am in the Father and the Father is
in me? He that hath seen me hath seen the Father'. For Philip,
too, was anxious to behold the Majesty and Presence of the
Father. And again, even if we knew all these hidden judgements of God, of what use and benefit could it be to us over
and above the command and promise of God?

Yet over and above all things practise faith in God's promises and in the works of His commandments.

Table-Talk.   W.A. Tischreden. 6. 39 f.

Christ may dwell in your hearts by faith.
EPHESIANS iii. 17.

The Holy Spirit teaches us the knowledge of Christ. He pours Him into the heart, setting it all on fire with love and making it steadfast through faith in Him. Where He dwells, there, please God, is fulness of life, whether the soul be weak or strong.

And that Christ dwells in our hearts means nothing else than to know who He is and what we may hope of Him, and that is, that He is our Saviour through whom we have been brought into that state where we can call God our Father, and receive through Him the Spirit who gives us courage in the face of all calamities. Thus He has made our hearts His abode, and we cannot lay hold on Him in any other way, because He is not a dead thing, but the living God. But how can He be contained in the heart? Not by thoughts, but by living faith alone. He cannot be possessed through works, nor can looking draw Him. Only the heart can hold Him. If, then, your faith is right and sound, you both have and feel Christ in your heart, and know everything that He thinks and does in heaven and on earth, and how He rules through His Word and Spirit, and what is the mind of both those who possess Him and who do not possess Him.

Sermons from the year 1525.   W.A. 17. I. 436.

For ye have not received the spirit of bondage again to fear; but ye have received the Spirit of adoption, whereby we cry, Abba, Father. ROMANS viii. 15.

Here is described the power of Christ's Kingdom and the true work and lofty ministry which is wrought by the Holy Ghost in the faithful, namely, the comfort through which the heart, freed from the fear and terror of sin, is set at rest, and the heartfelt prayer which awaits in faith the answering help of God. Neither of these can be brought about through the Law or one's own sanctity. For in this way a man can never receive certain comfort of God's mercy and love towards him, rather he always remains in fear and anxiety about wrath and condemnation, and because he is in such doubt, he flees from God and cannot call on Him.

Where there is faith in Christ, on the other hand, there the Holy Ghost pours both comfort and childlike confidence into the heart. And the heart no longer doubts God's gracious Will and help, because He has promised both grace and help, fulfilment and comfort, not because of our own worthiness, but because of the merit and the Name of Christ, His Son. Of these two works of the Holy Ghost, comfort and supplication, the prophet also says, that God will begin a new message and work in the Kingdom of Christ when He will pour forth the Spirit of grace and of prayer. It is the same Spirit who assures us that we are children of God, and moves our hearts that we cry to Him with heartfelt supplication.

Exposition of Romans viii. 12–17.   W.A. 22. 137 f.

And if children, then heirs; heirs of God, and joint-heirs of Christ; if so be that we suffer with him, that we may be also glorified together. ROMANS viii. 17.

There you hear the high praise, honour, and glory of Christians. Who can adequately praise and express it? No words can express it, nor can reason grasp it.

But here is found that deep human weakness within us, for if we could believe this and not doubt it, what is there to fear, and who is there to harm us? For, whoever can say to God from the bottom of his heart 'Thou art my beloved Father and I am Thy child', will obviously defy all the devils from hell, and with a joyful heart despise all the world's threatening and boasting. For in this Father he has a Lord before whom all creatures must tremble, and without His will they can do nothing. Thus he possesses such an inheritance and dominion that no creature can harm or hurt him. But he adds this little word 'if so be that we suffer with Him', that we may know, that we must live in such a way on earth that we give proof that we are devout and obedient children, who do not follow the lust of the flesh, but suffer for the Kingdom's sake whatever may befall us, and what hurts the flesh. If we do that, we should and shall find glorious comfort in the words and shall rejoice in the truth of them: 'For as many as are led by the Spirit (that they follow not the flesh) they are the sons of God'.

Exposition of Romans viii. 17.   W.A. 22. 139.

*The Spirit itself beareth witness with our spirit, that
we are the children of God.*   ROMANS viii. 16.

The knowledge that we are children of God and may be
fully assured that we are, is not derived from ourselves, or
from the Law, but it is the witness of the Holy Spirit who
bears witness to it, against the Law and the feeling of our own
unworthiness; and in spite of our weakness He makes us
fully assured of it. And such witness is wrought in such a
way that we are made aware of it and feel the power of the
Holy Spirit which He works within us, through the Word,
and our experience agrees with the Word or the message. For
you can feel it, if you are in sorrow and affliction and you
receive comfort from the Gospel, and are enabled to overcome fear and doubt, so that your heart can firmly believe
that you have a gracious God and that you no longer need
flee from Him, but through such faith you can joyfully call
on Him, and expect help from Him. And where there is such
faith the experience follows that we receive help; as St. Paul
says (Romans v. 4–5),' Tribulation worketh patience, and
patience experience, and experience hope. And hope maketh
not ashamed'.

This is the true inward witness by which you perceive
that the Holy Spirit is working within you.

Exposition of Romans viii. 16.   W.A. 22. 138 f.

Trinity I: St. John Baptist

THE CHURCH OF SANCTIFICATION

First Week after Trinity

WHEREIN TRUE FAITH CONSISTS

Sunday: ACTS iv. 32–35

*Faith is the substance of things hoped for, the evidence
of things not seen.* HEBREWS xi. 1.

This is the noblest and dearest virtue of faith, that it closes
its eyes and simply and joyfully leaves everything in the hands
of God. It does not desire to know why God acts as He does,
and it still holds Him to be the Highest Goodness and
Justice, although to all reason, the senses and experience,
nothing appears but wrath and injustice. That is why faith is
called the proving of things not seen, and even the very
opposite to what is seen. Therefore this is the highest honour
and love towards Gòd and the highest degree of such honour
and love, that in these contrary things you can regard and
praise Him as good and just. Here the natural eye must be
completely plucked out, and there must be nothing but sheer
faith. Otherwise there will be a grim and fearful vexation of
spirit.

Letter to Hans v. Rechenberg, 1522.   W.A. 10. II. 323.

The apostles said unto the Lord, Increase our faith.
                              LUKE xvii. 5.

In this Christian brotherhood no man possesses more than
another. St. Peter and St. Paul have no more than Mary
Magdalene or you or I. To sum up: Taking them all together,
they are brothers, and there is no difference between the persons. Mary, the Mother of the Lord, and John the Baptist,
and the thief on the cross, they all possess the selfsame good
which you and I possess, and all who are baptised and do the
Father's Will. And what have all the saints? They have the
knowledge that their sins are forgiven. They have comfort
and help promised them through Christ in every kind of
need, against sin, death, and the devil. And I have the same,
and you, and all believers have.

But this also is true, that you and I do not believe it so
firmly as John the Baptist and St. Paul; and yet it is the one
and only treasure. It is the same as when two men hold a
glass of wine, one with a trembling, the other with a steady
hand. Or when two men hold a bag of money, one in a weak,
the other in a strong hand. Whether the hand be strong or
weak, as God wills, it neither adds to the contents of the
bag, nor takes away. In the same way there is no other
difference here between the Apostles and me, than that they
hold the treasure firmer. Nevertheless I should and must
know that I possess the same treasure as all holy Prophets,
Apostles, and all saints have possessed.

Sermons from the year 1530.   W.A. 32. 85 f.

There is no searching of his understanding.
ISAIAH xl. 28.

There can be no faith unless all that I believe is hidden and invisible, for what I see I do not need to believe. But nothing can be more deeply hidden than when it seems absurd, and I see and perceive and understand it as the opposite to what faith shows it to me to be. Thus God acts in all His works. When He wills to bring us to life, He puts us to death; when He wills to make us saintly, He smites our conscience and makes us first sinners; when He wills to raise us up into heaven, He casts us first into hell, as the Scriptures say: 'The Lord killeth and maketh alive, He bringeth down to hell and bringeth up' (1 Samuel ii. 6).

Thus God hides His eternal and unspeakable goodness and mercy under eternal wrath, His justice under injustice. And herein is the highest degree of faith: to believe that the God who makes so few souls blessed is nevertheless the most merciful God; to believe that the God whose will it is that some should be condemned is none the less the most just God.

But if by reason we could understand how God is good, merciful and just, when He shows such cruel wrath and injustice, how could faith be necessary? But as reason cannot understand, faith is there, and you can practise faith when such things are preached unto you.

On the enslaved will.   54 f.

The Lord dwelleth in the thick darkness.
1 KINGS viii. 12.

Therefore faith is such a knowledge that, though it is completely and utterly dark, and nothing is visible, it is yet sure and sees, in such utter darkness, that it really holds Christ, just as in former time our Lord God was seated in the midst of darkness on Mount Sinai and in the Temple. Therefore our righteousness, which makes us appear just before God and well-pleasing to Him, is not the love which gives this appearance to faith, but it is the faith itself, and the hidden mystery and the secret knowledge in the heart, that is a trust in what is invisible, which means in Christ invisible and yet really present. But the reason why faith makes us just is that it seizes Christ, the noble and precious treasure, and keeps Him present. But how He is present thought cannot express, for as I have said, it is pure darkness, which means that it is a hidden, high, secret, and unsearchable knowledge. Therefore, where there is such a full trust and genuine confidence of the heart, there, certainly, is Christ within the dark mist and in the faith. That is the right justification, which causes the person to be regarded as righteous and acceptable before God.

Commentary on Galatians.   288 f.

And forgive us our debts, as we forgive our debtors.
                              MATTHEW vi. 12.

I say that God is gracious towards many and He heartily forgives their sins and says nothing to them about it, but deals with them inwardly and outwardly in such a way that they think God is ungracious to them and wills to condemn them for time and eternity. David was such a one when he said (Psalm vi. 1): 'O Lord, chasten me not in thine hot displeasure'. On the other hand, He secretly retains the guilt of some and is hostile to them, and says nothing to them about it, but deals with them in such a way that they think they are His beloved children. Outwardly they fare well, inwardly they are happy, and they feel sure of heaven. They are described in Psalm x. 6: 'I shall not be moved, for I shall never be in adversity'.

Thus from time to time He grants comfort to the conscience and a joyful confidence in His grace, so that the soul may be fortified and may have hope in God even in times when the conscience is full of fear. On the other hand, He sometimes lets a conscience be afraid and troubled, in order that the soul, even in the happy days, may not forget the fear of God.

The first forgiveness is bitter and hard for us, but it is the noblest and the dearest; the other is easier, but not so precious.

Exposition of the Lord's Prayer for   W.A. 2. 116 f.
   simple lay-folk.

Behold, I give unto you power to tread on serpents
and scorpions, and over all the power of the enemy:
and nothing shall by any means hurt you. LUKE x. 19.

God is such a Craftsman that He has the skill to make those
things that would harm and hinder us help and further us.
What would do us to death must serve us unto life; what
would bring us into sin and condemnation must serve to make
hope and faith firmer within us, to make prayer stronger and
more richly answered.

For here is the Craftsman who always brings to pass the
opposite to the purpose and thoughts of the world, and He
uses for good what the world means to be evil. For He is the
God who calls that which is not that it be, who changes all
things and makes all things new. Certainly, when His Christians are trodden under foot, or when their heads are hacked
off, it does not look like honour or glory, joy and blessedness,
and it feels like the exact opposite. But I can call into being,
saith the Lord, what is not, and from a sad and sorrowful
heart I can call forth pure joy. I can say: death and tomb,
be thou life; hell, be heaven and blessedness; poison, be thou
balm and medicine; devil and world, be thou of better service
to My dear Christians than the angels and holy saints. For I
can and will build and tend my vineyard in such a way that
through all kinds of suffering and calamity it shall become
better.

Exposition of John xv.   W.A. 45. 640 f.

I watch, and am as a sparrow alone upon the housetop.
                              PSALM cii. 7.

Let us not sleep like others, but let us watch and be sober, for temporal desires are to the eternal good as the images in a dream are to true pictures. Therefore sleep now is nothing but love and desire for creatures. But to be wakeful is to hold to the eternal good and to seek it and long for it.

But in this the Christian is alone and none is with him. All the others are asleep. And he says: 'On the roof': as if he said: the world is a house where they all lie shut in asleep, but I am outside the house, on the roof, not yet in heaven, and yet no longer on earth. The world is below me and heaven is above. Thus I hover in solitude between the life of the world and the life eternal.

The seven Penitential Psalms.   W.A. I. 198 f.

Second Week after Trinity

WHEREIN TRUE CHARITY CONSISTS

Sunday: 1 JOHN iii. 13–18

The love of God is shed abroad in our hearts by the Holy Ghost which is given unto us. ROMANS v. 5.

Mark here that it says: the love of God. For through it alone do we love God. Here is nothing to be seen or felt, either inwardly or outwardly, which you might love or fear, or on which you might ground your confidence. No, love is caught up high above all things, into the invisible God who surpasses all feeling and all understanding, and is carried right into the innermost darkness; and it has no knowledge of what it loves, although it knows well what it does not love, and it loathes all that is known and felt, and longs only for what it does not yet know.

And this high virtue that is in us is not born of ourselves, as the Apostle says, but we must pray to God for it. From this follows: (1) shed abroad, that is, by no means brought forth or born of us, and (2) through the Holy Ghost, that is, not won through virtue and habit, in the way in which we win moral virtues; (3) in our hearts, that is, into the innermost core and marrow of our heart, not on the surface of the heart merely, like foam on the water; (4) which is given unto us, that is, which we have not merited, nay, rather have we merited the opposite. And that this is really so is confirmed by what follows, namely, that it is really 'given' and not merited. So Christ was slain for the sake of the weak, and by no means for the strong and deserving.

Commentary on Romans. 207 f.

As the Father hath loved me, so have I loved you;
continue ye in my love. JOHN XV. 9.

Such is the devil's desire and delight that he strives for
nothing else but to shatter love among the Christians and to
cause hate and envy. For he well knows that through love
Christendom is built up and sustained.

That is why Christ exhorts us so earnestly that we should
above all things hold fast to love, and mentions both the
Father and Himself as the noblest and most perfect example.
My Father (He means to say) loves Me so dearly that He sets
all His power and might in Me. Now He lets Me suffer, but
all that I do and suffer He takes to Himself as if it were done
unto Him, and He will raise Me out of death into life, and
make Me a Lord over all things, and will glorify His divine
majesty in Me. So (says He) love I *you*. For I do not leave
you in your sins and death, but I give My body and My life
for you, to help you out of them and lay on you My purity,
My sanctity, My dying, and My resurrection, and all things
which I have in My power. Therefore continue ye in My
love towards one another. And though for My sake you are
hard pressed and sorely tempted to fall away from Me, hold
fast and endure; let My love be stronger, greater, and mightier
than the suffering and pain which you feel.

Therefore we should follow this example of Christ and
learn to practise this command among one another, each
according to his ability.

Exposition of John xv.   W.A. 45. 686 f.

We love him, because he first loved us.   1 JOHN iv. 19.

As there is no fire without heat and smoke, so is there no faith without love. For when through faith a man knows how dearly God loves him, he must gain a sweet and loving heart towards God, and this heart cannot stay by itself alone. It must flow forth and freely show its gratitude and love.

But as God does not need our work and has not commanded us to do anything for Him but to praise and thank Him, the Christian makes haste to give himself wholeheartedly to his neighbour, serving and helping him freely with his counsel, for he knows that God showed him His grace freely out of sheer mercy, without any merit, nay, while he was still in sin, while he was God's foe and never gave a thought to God. But now when he sees his neighbour in error or sin he cannot help but show unto him the right way. He leads him to the place where he himself has found comfort and help; he preaches the Gospel to him and leads him to the forgiveness of sins. After that, if he sees him naked, he clothes him; hungry, he feeds him; thirsty, he gives him to drink, and so forth. To sum up, as he would that it should be done to him, so he does to his neighbour. Whatever way he finds he can serve his neighbour, he does it gladly and willingly, before he asks him.

Sermons from the year 1527.   W.A. 17. II. 275 f.

God is love. 1 JOHN iv. 16.

So you see what 'God is love' means. It is so clear that any man must see and grasp it if he will but open his eyes. For the gracious gifts of God stand every day before your eyes whichever way you look: the sun, the moon, and the heavens filled with light; the earth full of leaves, grass, and corn, and many kinds of plants, prepared and given to us for food. Further, father and mother, house and homestead, peace, safety, and security through worldly government, etc. And over and above all this He gave His beloved Son for you and through His Gospel brought Him home to you, to help you in every grief and dire affliction. What more could He have done for you or what more or better could you wish? His love is such a burning fire, I hold, that no human thought could fathom it. The man who does not see or heed it must be as blind as a bat, or as hard as a stone, or dead.

Now since you (says St. John) who desire to be Christian and to know God, see and know that God is nothing but pure love, most richly poured forth and shed abroad upon us, take this to your heart, that you should do the same towards your neighbours. Because it is impossible that any man who feels such fire of God's love should not be at least a little warmed and kindled by it.

Sermons from the year 1532. w.a. 36. 429.

And uphold me with a free spirit.   PSALM li. 12.

That is, with the Holy Spirit, who gives men the desire to serve God freely, not out of painful fear and false love, for all who serve out of fear continue their service no longer than the fear lasts. Indeed they are, as it were, serving Him under compulsion, against their will, and they would cease to serve Him if there were no punishment and no hell. And likewise, those who serve God for the love of prosperity and for reward are not constant; for if they should hear that there is no reward, or when prosperity ceases, they too cease to love God. All these have no joy in God's salvation, neither have they a true spirit or a pure heart, but they love their own selves more than God. But those who serve God out of a good, firm will are steadfast in His service, whether things go well or ill, whether they are sweet or bitter, for they have been made firm by God with a noble, princely, unconstrained free will; for the little word 'free spirit' which stands here means in Hebrew a favourable, unconstrained spirit. All that is done by force does not last; but what is freely willed remains firm.

The seven Penitential Psalms.   W.A. I. 191 f.

If a man love me, he will keep my words. JOHN xiv. 23.

The Church on earth must exist and fight in weakness, poverty, and affliction, fear, death, shame, and blame. Calamity will force you to step out of yourself and not to rely on the counsel, help, and strength of men, but you must have Christ in your heart, so that you hold His Name, Word, and Kingdom higher, dearer, and more precious than all things on earth. To him who does not do this but loves his own honour and power, the world's praise, lust, joy, and friendship more, this word is preached in vain; as Christ, soon after, Himself says: 'He that loveth not me keepeth not my sayings'.

But it does not say to love with words alone. There must be living works and the evidence of love, as the words 'keep my sayings' mean. That is, a love which fights and overcomes. For it is the nature of true love to do all things for the sake of the beloved, and there is nothing too hard for her to suffer and to bear, that she would not do with joy.

If His unspeakable goodness were to go right to our hearts, nothing would be too vexing or too hard for us to suffer or to bear for His sake, that we only abide in His love. This means, then, not only hearing the Word with joy, but holding on to it firmly and winning the victory.

Sermon on John xiv. 23–31. W.A. 21. 453 f.

> *Be kindly affectioned one to another with brotherly love.* ROMANS xii. 10.

No feeble love is demanded here, but a love which comes from the heart, so that our heart bears us witness that the sorrow of others hurts us as much as if it were our own and their prosperity cheers us as much as if it were our own, just as parents are delighted when their children do well and are very troubled when they fall or fail.

And here we learn how far we still are from fulfilling the command which says, 'Thou shalt love thy neighbour as thyself', which means that we should love them so deeply that we should be entirely theirs, with body and soul, with possessions and honour. It is a great thing to love. It is far greater to love like a brother, but the greatest of all is to love as a father loves his child; and this love is called an ardent and untiring love which flows from the heart.

Sermons from the year 1527.   W.A. 17. II. 277 f.

Third Week after Trinity

JUSTIFICATION

Sunday: LUKE xv. 1–10

Be of good cheer; thy sins be forgiven thee.
MATTHEW ix. 2.

These words indicate that in this spiritual kingdom there is, and should be, sheer forgiveness of sins.

Now we must study with diligence what forgiveness of sins means. It is easily said, forgiveness of sins. Ah! if it could be won and done with words! But when it comes to the serious encounter, nothing is known of it. For it is a great thing, which I must believe and grasp with my heart, namely, that all my sins are forgiven and that through this faith I am justified before God. That is a wonderful justice and very different from the justice of the judges and of the wise and prudent people in the world. For they all say that justice is to be found within man's heart and soul as a quality wrought into it. But this Gospel teaches us that Christian righteousness is not a quality within man's heart or soul; but we should learn that we are redeemed and made just through the forgiveness of sins.

Sermon on St. Matthew's Day.　　　　　E.A. 6. 171 ff.

He will reprove the world . . . of righteousness,
because I go to the Father. JOHN xvi. 8, 10.

Such justification is hidden not only from reason and the
world but also from the saints. For it is not a thought, word,
or work in us, but it is quite outside and above us, for it is
Christ's going to the Father, which means His suffering,
Resurrection, and Ascension. And this does not take place
within the range of our senses, so that we might see or feel
it; but we can grasp it through faith alone.

And that is a remarkable justification, that we should be
called just or possess a righteousness which is no work or
thought of ours, and is nothing in us, but is completely outside of us, in Christ, and yet is truly made ours through His
gracious gift and as completely our own as if it had been
attained and merited by our own selves. No reason could
understand this language which gives the name justification
to me where I neither do or suffer anything, neither think,
sense, or feel anything, and there is nothing in me by reason
of which I could be saved and made well-pleasing to God;
but apart from myself and all man's thoughts, works, and
powers, I hold on to Christ (seated on high at the right hand
of the Father), although I cannot see Him.

But faith can grasp it and build upon it and find strength
through it in the midst of temptation.

Exposition of John xvi.   W.A. 46. 44 f.

He will reprove the world . . . of righteousness,
because I go to the Father.   JOHN xvi. 8, 10.

The ground must be kept firm and unshaken, that faith alone, without works, without any merit, reconciles a man to God and sanctifies him, as St. Paul says to the Romans (iii. 21–22): 'But now the righteousness of God without the law is manifest'. This and suchlike sayings we must firmly hold and must rely on them, and not be moved, for they say that forgiveness of sins and justification are granted to faith alone without works.

Consider the parable which Christ gives in Matthew (vii. 17): 'Every good tree bringeth forth good fruit, but a corrupt tree bringeth forth evil fruit'. There, you see, it is not the fruit which makes the tree good, but without and before there is any fruit the tree must be good, or be made good, before it bears good fruit.

Thus it is undoubtedly true that a man must be sanctified without any good works, and before he can do any good works.

Therefore it is convincingly proved that there must be something greater and more precious than all good works, which makes a man saintly and good, before he can do what is good, just as he must be sound in body before he can do sound work. The same great and precious thing is the noble Word of God which in the Gospel preaches and offers us the grace of God in Christ. And whoever hears and believes it is thereby made saintly and just. Therefore it is called a Word of life, of grace, and a Word of forgiveness. But whoever does not hear and believe it cannot be sanctified in any other way.

Sermon on the unrighteous mammon.   W.A. 10. III. 283 f.

*The righteousness of God is by faith of Jesus Christ
unto all and upon all them that believe.* ROMANS iii. 22.

Faith not only leads to the soul being made like the divine
Word, full of grace, free, and blessed, but it unites the soul
with Christ as a bride with her bridegroom. From this marriage it follows (as St. Paul says, Ephesians v. 30) that Christ
and the soul become one body; and in this they have all things
common, be they good or ill, so that what belongs to Christ
now belongs to the believing soul, and what belongs to the
soul now belongs to Christ. Since Christ possesses every
good and blessedness, these now belong to the soul. Since
the soul is burdened with sin and wretchedness, these now
become Christ's.

Here now begins the joyful exchange, and the struggle.
Because Christ is God and Man, and because He has done
no sin, and His pity is invincible, eternal, and almighty, when
He, through the wedding-ring, which is faith, takes upon
Himself the sins of the believing soul as though He had committed them, they must be swallowed up and drowned in
Him. For his invincible righteousness is stronger than all sin.
Thus the soul is cleansed from all sin through her dowry, that
is, because of her faith she is free and unhampered and endowed with the eternal righteousness of Christ, her bridegroom.

On the freedom of a Christian.   W.A. 7. 25 f.

For all have sinned, and come short of the glory of God; being justified freely by his grace through the redemption that is in Christ Jesus. ROMANS iii. 23–24.

However great and heavy sin may be, this article is still greater, higher, and wider, for no man has spoken it out of his own wisdom, or established it, but He who created and upholds heaven and earth. My sin and my saintliness must remain here on earth, for they concern this life and my doings here; but there on high, I have a different treasure, greater than these two, where Christ is seated holding me in His arms, covering me with His wings, and overshadowing me with His mercy.

You say: How can that be, since I feel my sin daily, and my conscience condemns me, and holds up the wrath of God before me? Answer: you should learn that Christian justification, whatever you may think or imagine, is nothing but the forgiveness of sins, which means that it is such a kingdom or sovereignty as deals only with sins and with such overflowing grace as takes away all wrath.

For it is called forgiveness of sins because we are downright sinners before God and there is nothing in us but sin, although we may possess all human righteousness. For where He speaks of sin there must be real and great sin; just as forgiveness is not a joke but something really serious. Therefore when you look at this article you have two things, first, that sin takes away all your sanctity, however devout you may be, on earth; and second, forgiveness brings to nought all sin and wrath, so that your sin cannot cast you into hell nor can your sanctity lift you into heaven.

Therefore, before the world I will be devout and do as much as I can, but before God I will gladly be a sinner, and not be called by any other name, in order that this article may remain true. Otherwise there would be no forgiveness or grace, but it would have to be called a crown of righteousness and of my own deserving. Apart from forgiveness there is and remains nothing but sin which condemns us.

Sermons from the year 1529.   W.A. 29. 573 f.

> *His merciful kindness is great toward us; and the*
> *truth of the Lord endureth for ever. Praise ye the*
> *Lord.* PSALM cxvii. 2.

There is a kingdom of grace which is mightier in us and over us than all wrath, sin, and evil.

You must picture this kingdom in childlike fashion, as though through the Gospel God has built over us, who believe in Him, a great new heaven, which is called the heaven of grace, and it is far greater and more beautiful than the heaven which you can see, and in addition it is certain, imperishable, and eternal.

Whoever lives underneath this heaven can neither sin nor abide in sin; for, it is a heaven of grace, everlasting and eternal. And if a man stumbles or sins, he does not fall out of this heaven, unless he does not wish to remain, but would rather go to hell with the devil, as the unbelievers do. And though sin makes itself felt or death shows its teeth and the devil frightens you, far more grace is here to rule over our sin, and far more life is here to rule over death, and far more of God is here to rule over all the devils, so that sin, death, and the devil are nothing more in this kingdom than black clouds under the lovely sky, which hide it for a while, but are not able to cover and conceal it for ever, but must remain beneath it and suffer it to be above and to remain supreme. In the end they must all pass away.

All this cannot be wrought through works, but through faith alone.

Exposition of Psalm cxvii.   W.A. 31. I. 245.

Christ hath redeemed us from the curse of the law,
being made a curse for us.   GALATIANS iii. 13.

What more could God do? How could a heart restrain
itself from being happy, glad, and obedient in God and Christ?
What work or suffering could befall to which it would not
gladly submit, singing with love and joyful praise to God?
If it fails to do so, faith has certainly broken down. The more
faith there is, the more joy and freedom there is; the less
faith, the less joy. Behold, this is the true Christian salvation
and freedom from the Law and from the judgement of the
Law, that is, from sin and death. Not that there is no Law or
death, but that both death and Law become as if they were
not. The Law does not lead to sin, nor death to doom, but
faith walks through them into everlasting life.

Exposition of Galatians iv. 1–7.   W.A. 10. 1 (i). 367 f.

Fourth Week after Trinity

FORGIVE ONE ANOTHER

Sunday: LUKE vi. 36–43

Be ye therefore merciful, as your Father also is merciful. LUKE vi. 36.

How does God, our heavenly Father, show His mercy? In that He gives us freely out of sheer goodness all that is good for body and soul, for time and eternity. If He should give us according to our merit, He could give us nothing but hell fire and eternal condemnation. Therefore, whatever good and honour He gives us, it is out of sheer mercy. He sees that we are stuck in death, and He has mercy upon us and gives us life. He sees that we are children of hell, and He has mercy upon us and gives us heaven. He sees that we are poor, naked, hungry, and thirsty, and He has mercy upon us and clothes us, feeds us, gives us drink, and satisfies us with all that is good. Thus, all that we have in body and spirit He gives us, out of sheer mercy, and pours out all His goodness upon us. That is why Christ says here: 'Be ye merciful, as your Father also is merciful'.

The mercy of Christians must not seek its own, but must be complete and comprehensive, regarding friend and foe alike, as our Father in heaven does.

And where this mercy is absent, faith also is absent.

Sermons from the year 1522.   W.A. 10. III. 224 f.

The Pharisee stood and prayed thus with himself,
God, I thank thee, that I am not as other men are,
extortioners, unjust, adulterers, or even as this
publican.   Luke xviii. 11.

All commandments are here broken and set at nought, for
he denies God and does no good to his neighbour. Thereby
he has gone to ruin, for he has not fulfilled one letter of the
Law. For if he had said: 'Oh God, we are all sinners. This
poor sinner is also, and so am I, like all other men', he would
then have fulfilled God's first commandment, namely, that
he had given honour and praise to God. And if he had afterwards said: 'Oh God, I see that this man is a sinner, and is
in the jaws of the devil, help him, dear Lord', and had thus
taken him upon his back and carried him before God and
prayed to God for him, he would also have fulfilled the
other commandment, namely, that of Christian love, as St.
Paul says and teaches (Galatians vi. 2): 'Bear ye one another's
burdens, and so fulfil the law of Christ'.

But now he comes along praising himself that he is just,
boasting most gloriously of his supposed good works, of
how he fasts and gives a tenth of all that he has. After that
he is so full of hatred towards his neighbour that, if God
would let him be judge, he would thrust the poor publican
into the deepest depth of hell. Is not that an evil heart and
dreadful to hear about, that I should wish all men to be
doomed while I alone should be praised?

And this has been set before us that we should be on our
guard against it.

Sermons from the year 1522.   w.a. 10. iii. 301 f.

Charity shall cover the multitude of sins. 1 PETER iv. 8.

Learn here to seek your neighbour as a lost sheep, to cover his shame with your honour, and to let your sanctity be a cover for his sins. But now, when people come together they hack one another to pieces, to prove how fiercely they fight against sin. Therefore, you men, whenever you come together, do not hack the people to pieces. And likewise you women, when you come together, cover the shame of others and do not make wounds which you cannot heal. And if you come across two people in a chamber, throw your cloak over both and close the door. Why? Because you would that it should so be done to you.

That is what Christ does. He, too, keeps silent and covers our sin. He, too, could bring shame upon us, and tread us under His feet, but He does not do so. And you must do the same. A virgin must place her crown on a harlot; a saintly wife must give her veil to an adulteress, and all that we have we must make into a cloak to cover sinners. For each man will have his lost sheep to recover, and each woman her piece of silver; and all that is ours must also belong to another.

Sermons from the year 1522.   W.A. 10. III. 220 f.

*For if ye forgive men their trespasses, your heavenly
Father will also forgive you.*   MATTHEW vi. 14.

Think how you would like it if God should do unto you
as you do to your neighbour, and should expose all your sin
to the world? Or how should you like it if some other man
would make known all your malice? You would doubtless
want every man to be silent, to excuse you and cover up your
evil and pray for you. But now you act contrary to nature
and its law, which says, 'Whatsoever ye would that men
should do to you, do ye even so to them' (Matthew vii. 12).

And do not think that the sins of a slanderer and a back-
biter, and wicked judge will be forgiven; no, neither the
smallest nor the greatest.

And if ever you wish to do something about the sin of
your neighbour, keep the precious noble golden rule of Christ,
which says (Matthew xviii. 15), 'If thy brother shall trespass
against thee, go and tell him his fault between him and thee
alone'. And notice: do not speak to others about it, but keep
it between yourself and him alone.

He who strives to do this noble work; how easily he could
expiate his sin even if he did not do much else. For if he
should fall into sin again, God will say, 'Yes, this man
covered the guilt of his neighbour and forgave him. Draw
nigh, all creation, and cover him, and his sin shall be forgiven
and shall not be remembered for ever'.

*Exposition of the Lord's Prayer for
   simple lay-folk.*   W.A. 2. 120.

> *Then came Peter to him, and said, Lord, how oft shall*
> *my brother sin against me, and I forgive him ? till*
> *seven times ?*   MATTHEW xviii. 21.

God's kingdom or the forgiveness of sins has no limit,
as the text of the Gospel so beautifully shows when Peter
asked the Lord. Jesus answered with the parable in which He
earnestly exhorts us, in fear of the loss of God's grace, to
forgive our neighbour his trespasses, without any reluctance,
because God forgives us such endless sin and guilt. Our debt
which we owe to God is ten thousand pounds, which means
that it is infinite. It is so great we could not pay it, with all our
possessions and with all our powers, for we cannot blot out
even the smallest sin. And since God in His kingdom forgives
us so much out of sheer grace, we ought also to forgive our
neighbour a little.

Christ speaks as follows: 'In My heavenly kingdom, where
there really is nothing but forgiveness of sins, that is, the
Christian Church, I will so do to him who pardons another
man's sin.' And again: 'To him who will not show mercy to
his neighbour will I also show no mercy. I am like a lord and
king with regard to you all, but you are like fellow-servants
among one another'.

Sermons from the year 1524.   W.A. 15. 730 f.

*For if ye love them which love you, what reward have
ye ? do not even the publicans the same ?*
                                   MATTHEW v. 46.

A Christian should have a good and helpful heart and
prove his goodness even to an evildoer. To be helpful to the
good and to thy friends is easy, for even murderers can
render service to their friends, and the heathen can be good,
kind, and helpful so long as they feel sure that the help will
be returned. But when they receive no help in return their
goodness and charity dries up. And then it is openly seen
that there is no well nor living fountain of love, but only
water poured into the sand, which is a pagan kind of helpful-
ness. But if I do a good deed to a man and he repays me with
evil and I say: 'Go on, my heart will not grow weary of
doing good. I will not wish you evil or encourage you to do
evil. I shall rebuke you, but if you do not heed, go on. If the
mayor and judge do not punish you, you will find One in
heaven who will punish you. He has still so many devils, so
many rogues on earth, so much water, fire, logs, stones,
plagues, and pestilence, that He can fully punish you. And
since I know that your sin will not remain unpunished, I will
keep a sweet and charitable heart, which is ready at all times
to give counsel'. And that is called a Christian heart and
Christian love, which the pagans do not have.

A Christian should have a well which cannot be dried up
or exhausted, even if his charity is poured out like water into
sand.

Sermon on the fourth Sunday after   W.A. 37. 101.
    Trinity, 1533.

Put on therefore, as the elect of God, holy and beloved, bowels of mercies, kindness, humbleness of mind, meekness, longsuffering.   COLOSSIANS iii. 12.

It is not enough to be charitable and forgiving towards your neighbour, with countenance, gestures, mouth, or tongue. It must be from the heart, or God will not forgive you, and you will be cast out of His Kingdom of grace. And again, if we feel God's mercy towards us, we should gladly forgive our brethren who have offended us. Our merciful Father forgives us our sin in order that we also should forgive our brethren and show mercy unto them, as He is merciful unto us, and forgives sin, death, guilt, and pain. If we do thus, we are in the Kingdom of God. For the goodness of God lives in our hearts, making us loving and good. Christ is seated at the right hand of the Father and rules nonetheless in the hearts and consciences of all the faithful, so that they both love Him and fear Him, live in awe of Him and obediently follow Him as an obedient people follows its king; and in all their character and conduct they become like Him, as He says: 'Be ye perfect, even as your Father which is in heaven is perfect'. And God is perfect in that He suffers our evil, wretchedness, sin, and imperfection, and forgives us, so that we should likewise forgive our brethren.

Sermons from the year 1524.   W.A. 15. 733.

Fifth Week after Trinity

SANCTIFICATION IS THE WORK OF GOD

Sunday: 1 Peter iii. 8–15

But as he which hath called you is holy, so be ye holy in all manner of conversation; because it is written, Be ye holy; for I am holy. 1 Peter i. 15–16.

Because I am your Lord and God and you are My people, you shall be like Me. For a proper lord causes his people to become like himself, and to be obedient and to follow the will of their lord. And as God our Lord is holy, so is His people holy; therefore we are all holy when we walk in faith. The Scriptures do not speak much about the saints who have died but about those who live here on earth. Thus the Prophet David describes himself in the Psalm vi. 2: 'Preserve my soul, for I am holy'.

For whoever is a Christian is made one with the Lord in all that He possesses; and as Christ is holy, he must be holy, or else he must deny that Christ is holy. If you have been baptised, you have put on the holy garment which is Christ, as St. Paul says. The little word 'holy' means that you are God's own, and that you belong to Him, which means you are 'consecrated'. Thus St. Peter says: 'Ye have consecrated yourselves to God, therefore take heed that ye are not once more led astray into worldly lusts, but let God alone rule, and work, and live within you, so are ye holy as He is holy'.

Exposition of 1 Peter, 1523.　　　　　　　　　W.A. 12. 287.

> *. . . but ye are washed, but ye are sanctified, but ye are*
> *justified in the name of the Lord Jesus, and the Spirit*
> *of our God.*   1 Corinthians vi. 11.

We honour Christ and not ourselves when we praise this
sanctity, which we receive because we enter into His suffering
and sanctity.

That I recognise myself as a sinner is right, as regards my
own person, but since through faith in Christ I am no longer
a child of Adam but a child of God, I am truly holy. There
is a fine distinction: inasmuch as I am man and a child of
Adam, I belong to hell. If I had on my side all manner of
self-appointed piety, austerity, fervent devotion, and good
works, and wished to rely on them, I should be damned and
lost.

But if you believe that through Christ, who died for your
sin and is risen for your salvation, you have become a brother
of Christ and a child of God, and have been baptised in that
faith, you can say: Now I am no longer Adam's child, no
longer a sinner, so long as I belong to this brotherhood. And
if you can be bold and audacious about it, do so. I am still
studying the matter, for it is no easy thing that a sinner should
say: I have a chair in heaven next to St. Peter. And yet we
must praise this sanctity and glory in it. Thus alone is the
golden brotherhood.

Sermons from the year 1530.   w.a. 32. 92 f.

*We are bound to give thanks alway to God for you,
brethren beloved of the Lord, because God hath from
the beginning chosen you to salvation through sanctification of the Spirit and belief of the truth.*

2 THESSALONIANS ii. 13.

Therefore, we ought to regard as holy, and mention together with Christ, those who keep His Word, and earnestly
witness to it, especially when they are suffering persecution
or temptation, even if they are poor and feeble men, having
no appearance of special sanctity. For we can never perceive
it written on a man's forehead whether or not he is holy and
just. But this we can see: where the Word brings forth fruit,
so that men have to suffer for it, etc., these, we know, these
must be living saints.

Then the false humility of our hypocrites speaks: God forbid that any man should be so presumptuous as to allow himself to be called a saint! Are we not all sinners? Answer: All
such thoughts spring from the old illusion that when sanctity
is mentioned, people think of mighty deeds, and look to the
saints in heaven, as if they themselves had won and merited
their position. But we say that the true saints of Christ must
be good strong sinners and remain such saints as are not
ashamed to pray the Lord's Prayer: 'Hallowed be Thy Name,
Thy Kingdom come, forgive us our debts,' etc., for we confess that the name of God is not sanctified in us as it should
be, nor has His Kingdom come, nor is His Will being done.
They are called holy, not because they are without sin, or
sanctified through works. On the contrary, they are sinners
in themselves and are condemned with all their works, but
are made saints with a sanctity which is not their own, but
Christ the Lord's, which is given to them through faith and
becomes their own.

Exposition of John xvi–xx.   w.a. 28. 175 ff.

*. . . that they may receive forgiveness of sins, and
inheritance amongst them which are sanctified by
faith that is in me.*   ACTS xxvi. 18.

God has made provision that we should become holy in
a spiritual way. It is a spiritual word, that in our innermost
spirit we are made holy before God. And He spoke this word
in order to make manifest that there is no holiness save that
which God works in us.

Hence the Gospel calls us holy even while we are still here
on earth, if we have faith.

You must be holy, and yet you must not bear yourself as
though you thought you were holy of yourself or by your
own merit, but because you have God's word that heaven
is yours, that you are devout, and that through Christ you
have become holy. This you must confess if you wish to be
a Christian. For we could show no greater disdain and blasphemy towards the Name of Christ than by denying His
blood the honour that it washes us clean of sin and makes us
holy. Therefore you must believe and confess that you are
holy through this blood and not through your own devotion.
Thus you leave your life and possessions above with Christ
and await and accept whatever may happen to you.

Exposition of 1 Peter, 1523.   W.A. 12. 262 f.

*Not as though I had already attained, either were
already perfect: but I follow after, if that I may
apprehend that for which also I am apprehended of
Christ Jesus.* PHILIPPIANS iii. 12.

Therefore none of the saints regards or confesses himself
to be just, but they always pray to be made just and wait for
those who confess that they are sinners and abhor their sins
to be justified.

Hence the whole life of the new and faithful and spiritual
people consists in the fact that with the inward groaning of
their hearts, with the cry of their works, with the toil of
their bodies they desire and implore for this one gift: that
they may be justified until death; that they may never stand
still, never think themselves to have already attained, never
regard any work as the goal of a justification actually already
attained, but await it as though it were beyond their reach
so long as they still commit sins.

Commentary on Romans. 146, 153 f.

. . . every branch that beareth fruit, he purgeth it.
                                        JOHN XV. 2.

We always understand our own work before it is done,
but we do not understand the work of God until after it is
done. Jeremiah xxiii. 20: 'In the latter days ye shall understand it perfectly'. That is to say, in the beginning, or at first,
we understand only our own plan, but in the end we understand the plan of God. John xiv. 29: 'That when it is come to
pass ye may believe'. As I have said, it is as when an artist
comes across some material which is apt and fitting for the
purpose of his art, which aptness is, as it were, an unexpressed
prayer to be fashioned. The artist understands this and
answers when he prepares to give it form according to its
aptness. Likewise God comes to our thinking and desiring
and sees our silent request and our aptitude. Then He begins
to fashion the form which His art and plan have prepared.
The form and pattern of our thinking must inevitably perish
in the process.

Commentary on Romans.   309.

*The Spirit itself beareth witness with our spirit, that
we are the children of God.* ROMANS viii. 16.

He who with firm faith and hope is confident that he is a
child of God, is a child of God, for no man can have such a
confidence except through the Holy Ghost.

If you believe that your sin can only be cancelled by God,
that is good. But now believe this as well (not that you could
unless the Holy Ghost gave you the power), that through
Christ your sins have really been forgiven. That is the witness which the Holy Ghost gives to your heart; your sins are
forgiven. Thus a man is justified through faith. That is the
Apostle's meaning (you must firmly believe with regard to
yourself, and not only with regard to the elect, that Christ
died for your sins also and has atoned for them).

And the same is true concerning merits. If you believe that
you cannot attain to such merits apart from Him, that is not
yet enough, until the Spirit of Truth testifies to you that you
really have such merits through Him. And this comes to pass
if you firmly trust that the works you are doing are acceptable
and well-pleasing to God, whatever kind of works they may
be. And this is a certain sign of such trust, if you perceive
that, in spite of your works, you are nothing before God,
although they are good and are done for obedience' sake;
for you no longer do evil works. And this very humility and
unrest of conscience with regard to good works makes them
well-pleasing to God.

And the same is true as regards eternal life. It is not enough
to believe that He will give you this life out of sheer grace.
No, you must have the witness of the Spirit that you really
will attain to it through the help of God.

Commentary on Romans.

298 f.

THE MEANING OF BAPTISM

Sunday: ROMANS vi. 3–11

For if we have been planted together in the likeness of his death, we shall be also in the likeness of his resurrection: knowing this, that our old man is crucified with him, that the body of sin might be destroyed, that henceforth we should not serve sin. ROMANS vi. 5-6.

This is a true apostolic saying. What he elsewhere referred to as: 'baptised into Christ's death and buried with Him in baptism', he here describes as 'planted together into the likeness of His death'. Thus he binds and knits together Christ's death and resurrection and our baptism, in order that baptism should not be thought of as a mere sign, but that the power of both Christ's death and resurrection are contained in it. And this is so in order that there should also follow in us both death and resurrection. For our sin is slain through His death, that is, taken away, in order that it may no longer live in us but die and be dead for ever.

Thus, that in baptism we are sunk under the water indicates that we too die in Christ, but that we emerge again means and imparts to us new life in Him, just as He did not remain in death but rose again. But such a life should not and cannot be a life in sin because sin has already been slain in us and we have died unto sin; but it must be a new life of righteousness and holiness. Thus we are now called 'planted into Christ' and 'made one with Him', and, as it were, baked into one loaf, and we receive into ourselves both the power of His death and of His resurrection, and also the fruit or consequence of it is found in us, since we have been baptised in Him.

Sermon on the sixth Sunday after　　　　W.A. 22. 96 f.
Trinity, 1535.

*Know ye not, that so many of us as were baptised
into Jesus Christ were baptised into his death?*

ROMANS vi. 3.

The meaning of this word is a blessed dying unto sin and
a rising in the grace of God, so that the old man conceived
and born in sin is drowned, and a new man emerges or rises,
born of grace. Thus sin is drowned in baptism and justification emerges.

And the meaning of such dying and drowning of sin is not
perfected in this life, not until the body dies and crumbles to
death. The sacrament or sign of baptism is soon performed,
as we see. But the meaning of it, the spiritual baptism and
drowning of sin is continued all through our earthly life and
cannot be fully achieved while we are alive on earth. Only
at the hour of our death is it completed. Then the person is
truly sunk into baptism, and the meaning of it is fulfilled.
Therefore this whole life is nothing but an unceasing baptism
unto death. And whoever is baptised is condemned to death.

Therefore the life of a Christian, from baptism unto the
grave, is nothing but the commencement of a blessed dying,
for at the Last Day God will make him a new and different
man.

Sermon on the holy and venerable   W.A. 2. 727 f.
Sacrament of Baptism, 1519.

*. . . baptising them in the name of the Father, and of
the Son, and of the Holy Ghost.* MATTHEW xxviii. 19.

A child that is born of devout parents and follows them
in every way and is like them is called a devout child. This
child by right possesses and inherits all that his parents have,
their name and their possessions. Thus we Christians are reborn in baptism, and are made God's children, and if we
follow our Father and His ways, His Name and all that He
has is made our eternal inheritance. And our Father's nature
is goodness and mercy, as Christ says: 'Be ye therefore merciful as your Father also is merciful'. Again: 'Learn of me, for
I am meek and lowly of heart'. Thus God is also just, pure,
true, strong, simple, wise, etc., and all these different names
of God are included in the one little word: 'Thy Name'.
For the names of all the virtues are names of God. And as
we are baptised in these names and sanctified and dedicated,
so that they have become our names, it follows that we are
called God's children and must be merciful, good, chaste,
just, true, simple, kind, peaceful, and of a sweet disposition
towards every man, even towards our enemies. For the Name
of God in which people are baptised works all this in them.

Exposition of the Lord's Prayer for　　　W.A. 2. 87 f.
simple lay-folk, 1519.

Likewise reckon ye also yourselves to be dead indeed unto sin, but alive unto God through Jesus Christ our Lord. ROMANS vi. 11.

Thus the person is made quite clean and innocent, sacramentally, which means that he has received the sign of God, namely baptism. This indicates that all his sins are dead, and that he will die in grace and rise again on the Last Day, pure and free from sin, to live eternally. Thus it is true that, because of the sacrament, he is pure and free from sin, but as this is not yet perfected and he is still living in sinful flesh, he is not yet free from sin or pure from all things, but has begun to be made pure and innocent.

But you may say: but what help is baptism to me if it does not completely slay my sin and wash me clean? Here follows the right to understanding and knowledge of the sacrament of baptism.

First, that you submit to the sacrament and its meaning shows that you desire to die to sin and be made new on the Last Day in accordance with the meaning of the sacrament. God accepts this and permits you to be baptised, and from that hour He begins to make you new. He pours into you His grace and the Holy Spirit, who begins to kill your sinful nature and to prepare you to die and rise again on the Last Day.

Further, if you promise to remain thus, and more and more to overcome sin, so long as you live, even until death, God accepts that and prepares you through all your earthly life with many good works and with much suffering. Thus He does what you desired in baptism, and your desire was to be redeemed from sin, and to die and rise on the Last Day in newness of life, and thus to complete the meaning of your baptism.

Sermon on the holy and venerable   W.A. 2. 730.
Sacrament of Holy Baptism, 1519.

He that believeth, and is baptised, shall be saved.
MARK xvi. 16.

If a man has fallen into sin, he should think most intensely of his baptism, of how God there promised to forgive all his sin, if he would fight against it until death. When this truth and promise are joyfully remembered, baptism renews its work and power and the heart is once more joyful and content; but not because of the person's own work or oblation, but because of the mercy of God, who in baptism promised to keep him for ever. And to this faith he must firmly cleave, even if all creatures and all sin fall upon him he must still cling to it, for whoever allows himself to be robbed of this faith makes God a liar, in respect of the promise which He gave in the sacrament of baptism.

Sermon on the holy and venerable   W.A. 2. 733.
Sacrament of Holy Baptism, 1519.

This is he that came by water and blood, even Jesus
Christ; not by water only, but by water and blood.
                                    I JOHN v. 6.

Thus he always mingles blood with baptism in order that
the red and innocent blood of Christ may be seen in it. To
human eyes there appears to be nothing but pure colourless
water. That is true, but St. John wishes to open for us the
inward and spiritual eyes of faith, that we may perceive not
water only but also the blood of our Lord Jesus Christ.

And why? Because holy baptism was won for us through
that blood which He shed for us when He paid for our sin.
This blood and the merit and power of it He has attached to
baptism, that we should thus receive it. For if a man receives
baptism in faith, that is like being openly washed with the
blood of Christ and being made clean from sin. For we do
not attain to forgiveness of sin through our own works, but
through the dying of the Son of God and through the
shedding of His blood. Such forgiveness is contained in the
holy sacrament of baptism.

Sermons from the year 1540.   W.A. 49. 131.

> *But as he which hath called you is holy, so be ye*
> *holy in all manner of conversation.* 1 PETER i. 15.

I will not call myself holy for what I have done nor be called holy by anyone else or praised for my sanctity. I am holy because I can say with firm faith and a pure conscience: Although I am a poor sinner, yet Christ is holy in His Baptism, Word, Sacrament, and the Holy Ghost. That is the one true holiness given unto us by God.

But (you say) how do I attain to it? Or what have I to do with the Holy Ghost? Answer: He has baptised me and preached the Gospel of Christ to me and quickened my heart to believe. Baptism did not spring from me, nor did faith and the Gospel, but He gave them to me. For the fingers which baptised me were not the fingers of man but of the Holy Ghost. And the preacher's mouth and words which I heard were not the preacher's own, but the words and preaching of the Holy Ghost, who gives inward faith, through such outward means, unto sanctification.

Therefore, we should as little deny or doubt that we are holy as that we are baptised and are Christians.

Exposition of John xiv and xv.   W.A. 45. 616 f.

Seventh Week after Trinity

SANCTIFICATION
(as the response of the justified sinner)

Sunday: ROMANS vi. 19–23

*Now being made free from sin, and become servants
to God, ye have your fruit unto holiness, and the end
everlasting life.* ROMANS vi. 22.

Thus St. Paul says: 'Know ye not, that to whom ye yield
yourselves servants to obey, his servants ye are to whom ye
obey: whether of sin unto death, or of obedience unto
righteousness?' and this means, as you now through grace
have received the forgiveness of sins, and are now just, you
are bound to obey God and live according to His Will. For
you must be in the service of one master, either of sin which
brings you into death and the wrath of God, if you remain
in it, or of God in grace, to serve Him in newness of life.
Therefore you must no longer be obedient to sin, for you are
now released from its power and dominion.

Sin will not be able to rule over you, for you are no longer
under the Law but under grace. That is, you can now resist
sin because ye are now in Christ and have received the power
of His resurrection.

Sermon on the seventh Sunday after   W.A. 22. 106 f.
*   Trinity, 1534.*

Sanctify the Lord God in your hearts.   1 PETER iii. 15.

How does St. Peter mean that we should sanctify God?
How can we sanctify Him? Must not He sanctify us? Answer:
We pray likewise in the Lord's Prayer, 'Hallowed be Thy
Name', that we may sanctify His Name, although He sanctifies it Himself. Therefore it comes to pass as follows: you
should sanctify Him in your hearts, which means that, whatsoever our Lord God may send us, be it good or evil, be it
pleasant or unpleasant, shame or honour, good fortune or
bad fortune, I should not only regard it as good, but also
holy, and say, This is a precious, holy thing, and I am not
worthy that it should touch me. If in such things I give praise
to God regarding such works as good, holy, and precious, I
sanctify the Lord in my heart.

Exposition of 1 Peter, 1523.   W.A. 12. 358.

*All things have I seen in the days of my vanity: there
is a just man that perisheth in his righteousness.*
ECCLESIASTES vii. 15.

It is not enough to confess with the mouth that you are a
sinner, for what is easier, especially if your conscience is
quiet and you suffer no temptation? No, if you have confessed
with the mouth that you are a sinner, you must really think
so in your heart and in all your actions and doings bear yourself accordingly. Hence there are few who acknowledge and
believe that they are sinners. For how can a man confess
that he is a sinner if he cannot bear a word directed against
his actions and plans, but immediately flies into a temper and
swears that he is sincere and is doing good, and that it is wrong
to oppose him and perverse to reject him? But immediately
he has to suffer some small affliction he is beside himself and
annoys everyone with his complaints that he alone suffers
unjustly. See, then, the hypocrite, who has confessed that
he is a sinner, and yet is quite unwilling to do and suffer what
is right for a sinner, but desires only what is right for a just
and saintly man.

In which way must a man become a sinner in the spiritual
sense? It is not possible in a natural way, for in that way he
cannot become a sinner because he is one already. Rather the
changes must be wrought in the hidden depths of our innermost heart, that is, in our opinion and estimation of ourselves.
Holy Scripture and all the works of God aim at nothing else
than to change this self-esteem.

Commentary on Romans.   105 ff.

We are his workmanship, created in Christ Jesus unto good works, which God hath before ordained that we should walk in them. EPHESIANS ii. 10.

We must receive before we can give out. Before we can do works of mercy we must first receive mercy from God. We do not lay the first stone, nor does the sheep seek the shepherd, but the shepherd the sheep. Therefore with regard to works, remember that they merit nothing before God, but without merit, we receive everything that we have from God.

After that, we may regard works as a sure sign, like a seal on a letter, assuring me that my faith is right. The reason is that if I feel in my heart that the work flows from love, I am sure that my faith is right. And if I forgive my brother, such forgiving makes me certain that my faith is right and confirms me, and gives me proof of my belief that God has forgiven me and continues to forgive me day after day; but if I do not forgive I must certainly conclude that I lack faith.

Sermon on the fourth Sunday after   W.A. 10. I (ii). 317 f.
Trinity, 1526.

*Make not provision for the flesh, to fulfil the lusts
thereof.* ROMANS xiii. 14. Luther's translation:
*Make provision for the flesh, yet so as not to fulfil the
lusts thereof.*

There is nothing in us more dangerous than our reason
and will. And this is the first and highest work of God in us
and the best discipline—to lay aside our works and to let
go our reason and will, committing ourselves to God in all
things, especially when they are running spiritually and
smoothly.

The discipline of the flesh follows, to mortify its coarse
and evil lust and win peace and rest. Such lusts we must overcome with fasting and watching and work. Thus we learn
why and how much we should fast, watch, and work. There
are unfortunately many blind people who esteem their
discipline, such as fasting, watching, or working, in themselves
good works, and practise them in order to win great merit.
Such fasting is not fasting at all, but a mockery of fasting
and of God.

Therefore I leave it to every man to choose for himself the
days, the food, and the amount of his fasting, but he must not
leave it at that, but keep watch over his flesh; inasmuch as
he finds it lascivious and wanton, he should discipline it with
fasting, watching, working, but no more.

Sermon on good works, 1520.   W.A. 9. 270 f.

The joy of the Lord is your strength.
NEHEMIAH viii. 10.

Behold, how daring and bold the Prophet is! Who gave him such a stout and defiant courage? Or whence did he receive it? From the Saviour alone. The more people would drive us away from Him, the firmer we cling to Him. The more sorrow, misery, and harm people do us, the more we rejoice, for our joy is eternal. And the more people want to drag us away from it, the greater it becomes.

But someone may say: can ever a soul lose such joy? Yes, and as soon as we lose it we are surrounded by everlasting pain, from which, though it is in itself eternal, God saves His people. Hence the joy also is eternal, though we may lose it while we are here on earth. And this should be understood as follows: Christ is my Saviour; if I know and believe it, it is an eternal joy to me, so long as I build upon it. When, however, the heart and conscience are devoid of Christ, the joy has ceased. Grace continues, but the conscience can stumble and fall. And this I say that you may not be offended if many of your number fall away from the Gospel and deny Christ. For where Christ is with His comfort and joy, the cross and persecution are not far away.

But I fear that we have neither the cross nor the joy because we receive so little of the Gospel. We remain for ever in our old nature and despise the dear and precious treasure of the Gospel.

Sermon on the first Sunday in Advent,   E.A. 17. 113
1524, on the greatest blasphemy of the
Papists.

*If ye through the Spirit do mortify the deeds of the
body, ye shall live.*   ROMANS viii. 13.

The mortification of sin through the Spirit comes to pass
when a person who recognises his weakness and sin, feels that
sinful lusts are stirring in him, takes himself in hand, and
remembering the Word of God, and the forgiveness of sins
through faith, strengthens himself and resists his lusts and
does not submit to them, so that they cannot proceed to action.

For this makes the difference between those who are
Christians and are holy, and the others who are without faith
and the Spirit, or have ceased to care and lost them. For,
though the faithful still suffer from sinful lusts of the flesh
as the others do, yet they continue in repentance and in the
fear of God and keep their faith, so that their sins are forgiven
for Christ's sake, because they resist and do not give way to
sin. Therefore they continue in forgiveness, and their weakness is not unto death and condemnation as with the others,
who without repentance and faith go wilfully on in their
lusts, contrary to their conscience, and thus thrust away both
faith and the Holy Ghost.

Sermon on the eighth Sunday after   W.A. 22. 134 f.
   Trinity, 1535.

Eighth Week after Trinity

Sunday: ROMANS viii. 12–17.

Looking for that blessed hope, and the glorious appearing of the great God and our Saviour Jesus Christ.
TITUS ii. 13.

Through the Gospel we have been given a treasure which is not goods and gold, power and honour, joy and happiness of this world, and not even life on this earth, but hope, even a living and blessed hope, which will quicken us into life and blessedness in body and soul, perfectly and eternally. To this treasure the Gospel calls us, and in this treasure we are baptised. Therefore let us live this earthly life bearing in mind that we shall leave it behind, and let us stretch out after that blessed hope as 'toward the mark of the prize of the high calling of God in Jesus Christ' and seek after it and await it at all times.

But how long shall we wait for that blessed hope? Will it remain but a hope for ever, and will it never be fulfilled? No, he says, our blessed hope will not always remain a hope, but it will eventually be made manifest, so that we shall no longer only hope and wait for it, but what we now believe and hope for will then be made manifest in us and we shall possess with full certainty what we now await. But meanwhile we must wait for that blessed hope until it be revealed.

Sermons from the year 1531.　　　　　　　　W.A. 34. II. 117.

He hath begotten us again . . . to an inheritance in-corruptible, and undefiled, and that fadeth not away, reserved in heaven for you. 1 Peter i. 3, 4.

While we live on earth we must live in hope. For although we know that through faith we possess all the riches of God (for faith certainly brings with it the new birth, sonship, and inheritance), we do not yet see it. Therefore it still stands in hope, and is laid aside a little while, so that we cannot see it with our eyes. This he calls the hope of life.

In hope, he says, we await the precious inheritance to which we have attained through faith. For this is the order: out of the Word comes faith, out of faith the new birth, and out of the new birth we enter into hope, so that we are sure of the heavenly good and await it with certainty.

If you are a Christian waiting for your inheritance or salvation, you must keep to this alone and must despise everything that is on earth and must confess that all earthly reason, wisdom, and holiness are nothing. The world will not be able to bear this. Therefore you must consider that you will be condemned and persecuted. And therefore St. Peter gathers faith, hope, and the holy cross into one unity; for the one follows from the other.

Exposition of 1 Peter, 1523. w.a. 12. 267 ff.

We are saved by hope; but hope that is seen is not hope; for what a man seeth, why doth he yet hope for ?
　　　　　　　　　　　　　　　ROMANS viii. 24.

This word is to be understood in its proper sense as expressing a most ardent intent. For hope, which proceeds from a longing for the beloved object, ever increases the fervour of love through the delay. Whence it comes that the beloved object and the love which desire it, are made, as it were, one thing by the ardent intent of hope. Thus love transforms the lover into the thing beloved and hope transforms the person hoping into the thing hoped for, but the thing hoped for is not seen. Thus hope plunges a man into what is unknown and hidden, into inner darkness, so that he does not know what he hopes for, but yet knows what he does not hope for. Thus the soul becomes at the same time hope and the thing hoped for, because it dwells in what it does not see, that is, in hope. If the hope were seen—that is to say, if the person hoping and the thing hoped for should know each other— then the person hoping would not be transformed into the thing hoped for—that is to say, into hope and that which is unknown—but would be powerfully drawn to the things which are seen, and would enjoy the fruits of what he knows.

Commentary on Romans.　　　　　　　　　　　305 ff.

Who forgiveth all thine iniquities; who healeth all thy diseases. PSALM ciii. 3.

Understand it in this way, that Christians are divided into two parts—the inner being, which is faith, and the outer, which is the flesh. If you look on a Christian according to his faith, he is completely pure, for there is no impurity in the Word of God, and where it enters into a heart which clings to it, the Word inevitably makes the heart completely pure. All things are therefore perfect, in faith, and that is why we are kings and priests and the people of God. But as our faith is in the flesh and we are still living on earth, we feel at times evil tendencies, such as impatience and fear of death, etc. Those are all still weaknesses of the old man, for faith has not yet completely penetrated and has not yet complete dominion over the flesh.

This you can see from the parable in the Gospel of St. Luke, chapter x, which tells of the man who went from Jerusalem down towards Jericho and fell among robbers, who wounded him and left him half dead. Afterwards a Samaritan had compassion on him and bound up his wounds and looked after him, and paid the host of the inn to nurse him. There you may see that this man is no longer sick unto death, because his neighbour took care of him; rather, he is certain that he will live. And yet there is still something lacking, for he is not yet completely well. His life is saved, but his health is not yet perfect. He is still under the doctor, and needing attention.

In the same way, we have the Lord Christ and are sure of eternal life, but there is still something of the old Adam in our flesh.

Exposition of 1 Peter, 1523.   w.a. 12. 322 f.

*Increasing in the knowledge of God; strengthened
with all might, according to his glorious power.*

COLOSSIANS i. 10, 11.

We must earnestly and diligently study the Word of God
and pray not simply that we may learn to know the Will of
God, but that we may be filled with it and always walk in
His way and continue in it, and so seek strength and comfort.

For it is the nature of the riches of this knowledge that
whoever has it has never enough and never tires of it, rather,
the more and the longer he drinks of it, the more is his heart
filled with joy and the more he thirsts for it, as the Scriptures
say, 'whosoever drinketh of me will thirst after me all the
more' (Ecclesiasticus xxiv. 21).

For, as St. Peter says, the dear angels in heaven also never
tire of it but have everlasting joy in it and desire to look into
what is revealed and preached to us (1 Peter i. 12).

Therefore, unless we too hunger and thirst (as we ought
much more than the angels) to know and to understand God's
Will more perfectly until we also attain to an everlasting
vision in the life hereafter, there is nothing more of it in us
than a mere froth which can neither quench our thirst nor
satisfy us and can neither comfort us nor make us better.

Sermon on the twenty-fourth Sunday   W.A. 22. 378 f.
after Trinity, 1536.

*We, according to his promise, look for new heavens
and a new earth.*   2 PETER iii. 13.

Because we are to be new men God wills that we shall have
new and different thoughts, minds, and understanding, not
judging things as they appear, to reason and to the world,
but as they are before His eyes, and that we should rule ourselves according to the invisible and new nature that is to
be, for which we hope and which is to follow these earthly
sufferings and this wretched nature. Therefore we should
not covet this life and mourn and lament that we must leave
it, nor that this whole world and all that there is in it and so
many great and famous people must perish. Rather we should
have mercy on the poor dear Christians, both the living who
now suffer oppression, and the dead who are lying in their
graves longing to rise and be transformed, like the grain
which is turned in the ground in the winter, or the sap in
the trees which cannot rise because of the cold and waits for
the summer to come, that they may come forth and produce
green leaves and blossoms.

Sermons from the year 1531.   W.A. 34. II. 481.

> *Father, I will that they also, whom thou hast given*
> *me, be with me where I am; that they may behold my*
> *glory, which thou hast given me.*   JOHN xvii. 24.

My dear Christians should not only be with Me, but should receive a bright and clear view of My glory, as He has said shortly before in other words: 'The glory which thou gavest me I have given them'. For now, on earth, we know and hold it in faith, but we do not see it except through a mirror and in a veiled Word, namely, that we hear the preaching and understand it with our hearts, that Christ is risen from the dead and ascended into heaven where He is seated in the glory and Majesty of the Father as the only mighty Lord over all creation. But it is still a veiled knowledge, like a thick cloud over the bright sun. For no man's heart can hold it and no man's understanding can comprehend that the glory is so great, especially as Christ now, in His Christians, appears so different. But there, in the world to come, another light will shine, so that we shall no longer hold it only in faith and in the preaching and teaching of the Word, but we shall see it all radiant before our eyes and shall look upon it with unspeakable and eternal joy.

Exposition of John xvi–xx, 1528.   W.A. 28. 194 f.

Trinity II : St. Lawrence

THE CHURCH OF LOVE

Ninth Week after Trinity

THE CHRISTIAN IN HIS SECULAR ESTATE

Sunday: LUKE xvi. 1–12

The lord commended the unjust steward, because he had done wisely; for the children of this world are in their generation wiser than the children of light.

LUKE xvi. 8.

It says here, the Lord commended the unjust steward. This must not be taken to mean that it pleases Him if we are unjust towards others; He praises only the swiftness and prudence, and desires that we should be as earnest and diligent in a good cause as this steward was in a bad cause, for his own benefit and for his master's harm.

On the contrary, we see how the children of light, that is, the true Christians, are lazy, weary, careless, and slow with regard to the things of God. Therefore Christ judges right when He says that the children of the world are more diligent and wise than His children, for it is found that the devil has a hundred servants at work where Christ has hardly one. What shall we do about it? We cannot alter it, for the world will not hearken to our words. We must preach and continue to rebuke, threaten, and admonish people, the lazy, weary Christians as well, and we must all remind ourselves to take as an example the industry with which the world serves the devil, so that we should exercise ourselves in good works as the children of Adam do in evil works. We might attain a little of their industry, especially as we are children of light.

Sermon on the ninth Sunday after Trinity, 1544.　　　　　　　　W.A. 52. 430 ff.

*With good will doing service, as to the Lord, and not
to men.* EPHESIANS vi. 7.

God needs many and various ministries and states. Therefore He gives many and various gifts and ordains that we
need one another. What were princes, noblemen, rulers, if
there were not at the same time pastors, preachers, teachers,
and others who till the soil, and craftsmen, and the like?

Therefore, although a man's state may be lower than your
own, you must not forget that it is likewise created and
ordained by God. And again you must know, that you have
been given your state that you may humble yourself and serve
others, as a nobleman serves his prince at court or at war, or
a manservant or maidservant their masters and mistresses.
All this you must do because it is God's Will.

God does not ask whether you are a lord or a servant,
husband or wife: do remain in the state to which you have
been called, and learn to serve God in it by serving your
neighbour.

Sermons from the year 1544.   W.A. 49. 611 f.

*Except the Lord build the house, they labour in vain
that build it.*   PSALM cxxvii. 1.

Let the Lord build your house and look after it. Do not
interfere with His work. It falls to Him, not you, to look after
it. Leave Him, who is Master of the house and runs it, to look
after it. If much is needed in a house, do not worry, God is
greater than a house. He who fills heaven and earth will
surely be able to fill a house, all the more so because He has
undertaken to do so and allows the Psalmist to praise Him
for it.

But this does not mean that He forbids you to work. Work
you should and must, but do not ascribe the fact that you
have food to eat and that your house is furnished to your
work, but to God's grace and blessing alone. For where it is
ascribed to a man's own work, covetousness and worry immediately raise their heads and the thought that much work
will mean many possessions. Hence the strange contradiction
occurs that some, who work extremely hard, have scarcely
enough to eat, while others who work leisurely are blessed
with all good things. This means that God will have the
honour, for He alone makes things grow. For even if you
were to till the earth for a hundred years, and do all the work
in the world, you could not make it bring forth one blade
of grass; but while you are asleep, and without your work,
God will bring the blade out of the little grain, and He adds
many grains according to His will.

Exposition of Psalm cxxvii.   W.A. 15. 365 f.

Thou also hast wrought all our works in us.
ISAIAH xxvi. 12.

What is our work in field and garden, in town and house, in battling and in ruling, to God, but the work of children, through which He bestows His gifts on the land, in the house, and everywhere? Our works are God's masks, behind which He remains hidden, although He does all things. If Gideon had not obeyed and gone to battle with Midian, the Midianites would never have been conquered, although God could, of course, have conquered them without Gideon. He could also give you corn and fruit without your ploughing and planting, but that is not His will; neither is it His will that your ploughing and planting should produce corn and fruit; but you must plough and plant and say a blessing on your work and pray: Now help, O God; give us now corn and fruit, dear Lord; for our ploughing and planting will not yield us anything. It is Thy gift.

God is the giver of all good gifts; but you must fall to, and take the bull by the horns, which means you must work to give God an occasion and a mask.

Exposition of Psalm cxlvii.   W.A. 31. I. 435 f.

Having ministry, let us wait on our ministering.
                                            ROMANS xii. 7.

There must be difference of ministries and states, for there is not *one* state but many. But the many varied states can be gathered up in one unity of the Spirit. So the body has many members: not all can be eyes, but the eyes are eyes, and each member is itself and has its own office, and yet there is but *one* life, and drink, and food, to sustain all the members and the one body, although there are many various members. See, then, how in like manner, under the great diversity of the various states and persons called for in this life and ordained by Him, God has created one being and one unity with this intent, that each one in fulfilling his ministry shall do the work allotted to him as his state demands, performing it with that humility which regards all states and persons as equal before God, as being all created equal and having the one as much favour with Him as the other, so that no one may pride himself before God and his neighbour, thinking highly of himself because his state is high, but may perceive that unless he preserves, in his higher state, the spirit of true humility, he sins much more shamefully, and will be condemned much more severely than any man of lower degree.

Therefore let every man fight the good fight in his own calling. If you are a man or woman and say to yourself: I will fulfil my ministry; I will not run away into a monastery but will do the work which God has given me and seek no other, you are fighting the right battle. . . . If you are a husband or wife, you have your calling from God, and so have the servant, the maid, and the mayor.

It is probable that servants will continue to murmur against their masters. Would that such would say to them-selves—I have not sinned against my master, but against God. For if this knowledge were to remain in us, that our work does not concern a man, but God, it would help us.

Sermons from the year 1531.   W.A. 34. I. 578.

*In the sweat of thy face shalt thou eat bread, till thou
return unto the ground; for out of it wast thou taken.*
GENESIS iii. 19.

The man is not burdened with child-bearing; that is the woman's affliction. He has a different calling, namely, that he should look after his wife and child and keep them. This demands so much care and labour that every man shuns it, and none is willing to bear the burden, and yet it must be borne. For if you do not take a wife and do not eat your bread in the sweat of your brow, God takes the punishment which He has laid on your body and lays it upon your soul. That is a poor exchange. He desires to be gracious and helpful to your soul; but He chastens your body.

If man and woman are truly joined in wedlock, they do not have an easy time, for married life means labour and sorrow, or else it is not right before God. Wherefore, if in your married life you have to endure much sorrow and labour, be of good cheer and remember that it is so ordained that it is God's holy will that people should marry. Therefore in the name of God, I burden myself with trouble and give myself to marriage, willingly and cheerfully. If you refuse to do this, and wish to do better, your soul will be lost, however well it may go with your body.

Therefore God curses the soil, that of all that it bears not half should be corn, but most should be thorns and thistles, which otherwise would not grow. Because He wills that man should labour, He ordains that far the greater part shall be thorns and thistles. Therefore the sum and substance is that He in this way wills to keep us in check.

Exposition of Genesis, 1527.   W.A. 24. 103 f.

Marriage is honourable in all.   HEBREWS xiii. 4.

Touching marriage, as touching any other estate which God has called into being, the cardinal point is that each man should know of a certainty that matrimony is ordained and appointed by God. Almost the chief thing to know in married life is that we should learn to look on marriage in the light of its highest honour, which is that it is ordained by God and is supported by God's Word.

If we consider it in godly and in Christian wise, the greatest thing is, that on wife and on husband the Word of God is written. If you can look upon your wife as though she were the only woman in the world and there were none besides; if you can look upon your husband as though he was the only man in the world and there were none besides, then no king, and not even the sun, will shine brighter and clearer in your eyes than your wife and your husband. For here you have the Word of God which gives you your husband and your wife and says: The man shall be yours; the woman shall be yours. That pleases Me well. All angels and all creatures find pleasure and rejoice therein. For no adornment is above the Word of God, through which you look upon your wife as a gift from God.

Would to God that every man might go through life with such a mind, that he could say from the bottom of his heart: I am certain and I doubt it not, that God is well pleased that I remain here and live with this woman to whom I am joined in holy matrimony, for He Himself has ordained it thus and His word tells me so. This Word comforts those who are joined together in married life and gives them a good conscience.

A marriage sermon on Hebrews   W.A. 34. I. 50 ff.
  xiii. 4, 1531.

PEOPLE AND STATE

Sunday: LUKE xix. 41–48

*If thou hadst known, even thou, at least in this thy
day, the things which belong unto thy peace! but now
they are hid from thine eyes.* LUKE xix. 42.

Thus it shall fare with all who have no fear of God and
look more to their own selves than to Him. In this manner
God avenged the death of all His holy Prophets. I am distressed at heart for Germany. For now she has the day of
her gracious and merciful visitation. If she makes light of it
and does not receive it, but scoffs and sneers at it, then Germany will lose the splendour of this glorious day, and God
have mercy on her, she is ruined. The wind blows ill; for
even now, at the time of the grace of her Lord, she remains
unmindful of the eternal good. As the Lord says: If you
comprehended it, you would weep, and you would receive
forgiveness of your iniquities. And again, Now I have not
come as a hangman, judge, and persecutor, to destroy you;
I have come as a Father, preacher, and Saviour, to give you
counsel and to help you. But if you let the sun go down,
you will be lost.

The Lord spent three days preaching in the Temple,
because He had never before been so deeply moved, for He
sensed the peril of the hour pressing upon Him. The dear
Lord Jesus would gladly have seen a different response.

Sermons from the year 1531.   W.A. 34. II. 84 ff.

THE RULING POWERS ARE ORDAINED OF GOD, AND SUSTAINED
BY THE PRAYERS OF THE CHRISTIANS

Be of good courage, and let us play the men for our people, and for the cities of our God: and the Lord do that which seemeth him good. 2 SAMUEL X. 12.

We Christians must understand that all worldly rule and power, until its time is run, is grounded in an ordinance or commandment of God and in the prayer of Christians. Those are the two pillars which carry the whole world. If they give way, all must tumble to the ground, as will be seen on Judgement Day. And even now, in our time, it is apparent that all kingdoms and powers are enfeebled and beginning to crumble, because those two pillars are wellnigh sinking and breaking. The world does not want it otherwise, for it will not receive the Word of God (although the Word honours and sustains it), but persecutes and kills innocent Christian folk and does not cease to rage against the pillars which support it; like an insane husband tearing his own house to pieces. We shall withstand and breast the tide as long as we can hold out, though we shall gain no thanks for it. But if her fall and destruction come to pass, and the Word of God and Christian prayer cease, then may the devil, the world's god, have mercy on her.

Exposition of John xiv and xv.   W.A. 45. 535.

Seek the peace of the city.   JEREMIAH xxix. 7.

Hence it is the duty of the Council and the Magistrates to devote great care and attention to the young. All the town's goods, honour, life, and limbs are entrusted to their faithful hands, and they would not act honestly before God and man if they failed to seek the town's well-being and improvement day and night. But the well-being of a town does not consist only in gathering treasures, building firm walls and fine houses, and making many firearms and armour; rather, where there is much of that and fools get it into their hands the town will be the worse for it. But this is the town's greatest and highest good, that it has many fine, scholarly, dignified, sensible, and honourable citizens, for they would be able to gather and treasure goods and keep them and use them aright.

Hence, since a town must have such people, and since there are complaints on every hand because of the lack of them, we must not wait until they grow of themselves. We cannot build them of stones, or carve them from wood, and God will not perform a miracle as long as we are able to meet the need by means which are in our hands already. Therefore we must undertake the work, whatever the cost and labour involved, and train them ourselves. For who is to blame, that capable people are now so few in every town, except the Councils and Magistrates, who have left the young folk to grow like trees in the forest and have not seen to it that they are trained and trimmed? Now the tree has grown so irregular that it is of no use for building, but is crooked lumber which will only do for firewood.

And now it has become a dire necessity, not only for the sake of the young, but for the maintaining of both spiritual and secular estates, that we devote ourselves seriously and earnestly to this matter while there is still time.

To the Mayors and Councillors of all German   W.A. 15. 34 f.
  cities that they should establish and maintain
  Christian schools.

He is the minister of God to thee for good.
ROMANS xiii. 4.

Secular authority is an image, symbol, and likeness of the authority of Christ; for the ministry of the Word brings eternal justification, eternal peace, and eternal life, and the secular authority maintains temporal peace, justice, and life, yet it is a glorious divine ordinance and a wonderful gift of God, who has instituted and appointed it, and wills that it shall remain as a necessity for all time, for if it were lacking no man could save himself from his neighbour, but they would all devour each other like unreasoning beasts. Secular authority protects your body that no one may kill you; your wife that no one may take her and abuse her; your children, daughter and son, that no one may abduct them and take possession of them. It protects your house and home, that no one may break into it and plunder it, and your fields, cattle, and all your possessions, that no one may seize and steal and run away with them, or damage them.

Do you not think that if the birds and animals could speak, when they see worldly government among men, they would say: 'O great and noble men, compared with us you are not human beings but gods. You enjoy secure possession of life and land, while we are not safe from each other in respect of life or home or food, not even for an hour. Woe to your ingratitude, that you do not see what glorious life our God has given you compared with us beasts'.

A sermon on keeping children at school.   w.a. 32. ii. 554 f.

*Wherefore ye must needs be subject, not only for
wrath, but also for conscience sake.*   ROMANS xiii. 5.

Holy Scripture has fine, clear eyes, and looks in the right
way upon the worldly sword as that which must be merciless
for mercy's sake and exercise severity out of sheer goodness.
Paul and Peter say it is the minister of God for wrath,
revenge, and punishment of the evil and for the defence,
praise, and honour of the good. It looks upon the saintly and
has mercy on them, and to prevent them suffering it fights,
bites, cuts, strikes, and murders, as God has commanded and
knows that it is His servant in doing this!

But that rogues and rascals are thus punished without
mercy is not only done in order that the wicked may be
punished and the desire for their blood satisfied, but that the
good may be defended, and peace and security maintained,
and these are without doubt Christian works of great mercy,
love, and goodness.

Worldly authority is not ordained in order that the rulers
may exploit and abuse their subjects, but that they get the
best and greatest profit for them. The Romans used to call
their princes Patres Patriae. We should blush that we never
call or regard our princes as fathers of the land. Our prince
is our father, and so is our mayor, for through him, as through
a father, God gives us food and protects our home. Therefore
we must honour, obey, and love them, so that a subject should
regard his prince as the greatest treasure and should beware
of rebellion.

On the fifth Commandment, 1528.   W.A. 30. I. 70.

Behold the works of the Lord, what desolations he
hath made in the earth. He maketh wars to cease unto
the end of the earth; he breaketh the bow, and cutteth
the spear in sunder; he burneth the chariot in the fire.

PSALM xlvi. 8–9.

When I look at war, how it punishes the wicked, slays
wrongdoers and makes such desolation in the earth, it appears
to be a very unchristian thing and altogether contrary to
Christian love. But when I consider how it defends the godly
and protects wife and child, house and home, earthly possessions and honour and keeps them in peace, it is seen to
be a good and godly thing. For if the sword did not defend
and maintain peace, everything in the world would go to
rack and ruin. Therefore such a war is nothing but a short
absence of peace to prevent everlasting and unbounded
strife; a small misery preventing a great misery.

What is said and written about war as a terrible plague is
all true, but it should be remembered at the same time how
much greater is the plague which war prevents. If people
were saintly and willing to keep peace, then war would be
the greatest plague on earth. But do you not see that the
world is evil, that people do not desire to live in peace but
want to rob and steal, and kill and abuse your wife and child,
and take away your honour and possessions? All over the
world man fights man. No single person could save himself
from this unending strife unless the little strife which is called
war should check it. Therefore God has honoured the sword
so highly that He calls it His own ordinance, and does not
will that we should say or think that man has invented it and
ordained it. For the hand which holds this sword and kills
with it is no longer a human hand, but the hand of God, so
that it is not man but God that hangs, breaks human limbs
on the wheel, hacks off heads, slays, and makes war. It is all
His work and judgement.

On whether soldiers can be saved, 1526.   W.A. 19. 626.

*He said unto them, Render therefore unto Cæsar the
things which be Cæsar's, and unto God the things
which be God's.* LUKE xx. 25.

The Scriptures say the Holy Ghost, not the world, prince,
or emperor, shall be judge, through the Word of God, and
the world shall be judged and punished and shall submit to
such judgement. But where it resists and makes itself judge,
and superior to the Word of God, in the matter of condemning or ruling us, we must know that such a judgement stands
condemned, and is of the devil, and we must resist and say:
'O my prince, emperor, and world, I am in your power as
regards life and possessions in matters that touch your rule,
and in respect of life and possessions I should and shall be
obedient to you; but if you try to reach further into the
things which are God's, where you should not and cannot
be judge, but must, like me and all creatures, be judged
through His Word, then I must not and will not follow you,
but will do the opposite, so that I may obey Him and continue in His Word.'

Beloved, we are not baptised in the name of kings, princes,
and the multitude, but in the name of Christ and God Himself; neither are we called kings or princes or the multitude;
but we are called Christians. No one must attempt to guide
souls unless he knows how to show them the way to heaven.
But no man can do that, but God alone. Therefore, in those
things which concern the soul's salvation, nothing must be
taught and received but the Word of God alone.

Exposition of John xvi.   W.A. 46. 48.

Eleventh Week after Trinity

OUR NEIGHBOURS

Sunday: LUKE xviii. 9–14

Two men went up into the temple to pray; the one a Pharisee, and the other a publican. LUKE xviii. 10.

Let us consider this fool, the Pharisee. He does the most glorious works! First, he thanks God. He fasts twice a week for the glory of God. He gives a tenth of all his worldly goods. He has not committed adultery, has never done violence to any man or stolen any man's goods. He has led such a saintly life. Would you not call that a wonderfully honourable life? According to the judgement of the world no man could scold him. Indeed, the world would have to praise him, and in fact, he praises himself. But there, at that moment, God's judgement falls upon him saying that all his works are blasphemy. Lord God, have mercy! How terrible is this judgement! We are shocked to the limit, for not one of us is half as saintly as the Pharisee!

Mark, then, how deeply the sword of God cuts and how it pierces to the innermost soul! Here everything must be laid in ruins or smitten to the ground and humbled, or the soul cannot exist before God. Thus, touching this matter, a godly woman must fall down and kiss the feet of the worst harlot, yea, even her footsteps.

The publican stands there and humbles himself. He makes no mention of fasts or works or anything. And yet the Lord says that his sin is not so great as that of the hypocrite. Let us take care that no one exalt himself above the most insignificant sinner. If I lift myself up above my brother, even by the breadth of a finger, yes, above the worst sinner, I shall be thrown down.

Sermons from the year 1522. W.A. 10. III. 300 f.

The Pharisee stood and prayed thus with himself,
God, I thank thee, that I am not as other men are,
extortioners, unjust, adulterers, or even as this
publican.   LUKE xviii. 11.

Behold how he also tramples on the other table of the Law,
and rages against his fellow-men. There is no Christian love
in him at all, nothing to show any love and concern about
his neighbour's honour and salvation. He treats him in a
scandalous way and tramples him under his feet and does
not regard him as worth treating as a human being. Where
he ought to save him and help him that he should suffer no
evil or injustice, he himself inflicts on him the greatest wrong.
For where he knows and perceives his brother sinning against
God, he does not consider for a moment how to convert him
or save him from the wrath of God and from condemnation,
so that he may alter himself. There is in his heart no mercy
or compassion for a poor sinner's misery and distress. To
his mind it is but fit and proper that the publican should be
left in his misery and condemnation. He withholds from him
all the proper ministry of love and service.

What service can such a man render to the Kingdom of
God, one who can rejoice and find great pleasure in the sin
and disobedience of all the world towards God and who
would be grieved if anyone's heart were inclined towards
God, intending to keep his commands, one who would be
loath to help him in the slightest way, even where he might,
and unwilling to ward off from his brother evil and destruction? What could one hope for, or look for, in a man whose
heart is so bad that he cannot desire his neighbour's salvation?

Sermon on the eleventh Sunday after   W.A. 22. 200 f.
   Trinity, 1544.

Look not every man on his own things, but every man also on the things of others. PHILIPPIANS ii. 4.

Mark here how St. Paul sets before us a clear picture of a Christian life. He shows that all our work should be directed towards the good of our neighbour, because for each of us our faith suffices and all our works and all our life are left to him to use in a free service of love to our neighbour.

Well, then, my God has given to me an unworthy and condemned man, without any merit on my part, freely and out of pure mercy, through and in Christ, the unsearchable riches of salvation and piety, so that henceforth I need nothing more than to believe that this is true. Yet shall I not in return gladly and freely serve such a Father, who has thus poured His superabundant blessings upon me, and do whatever pleases Him, and also become a Christian to my neighbour, as Christ has become to me, and do for him everything that is helpful towards his salvation: because through my faith all my wants are satisfied in Christ?

Behold, thus springs forth from faith, love, and desire for God, and out of love a free, willing, and cheerful life spent in free service to our neighbour.

On the freedom of a Christian. W.A. 7. 35 f.

THE CHRISTIAN AS REGARDS HIS FAITH AND VOCATION

If ministry is given to us, let us wait on our ministering.   ROMANS xii. 7.

I have stated that Christians living with each other, and within their own flock, require for themselves neither magistrates nor sword; they have neither need nor use for them. But since a true Christian on this earth lives not unto himself but unto his neighbour, and serves him, he does, because of his spiritual nature, do what he himself does not, if it is helpful and needful to his neighbour. Therefore, as all the world needs the sword that peace may be kept, sin punished, and evil warded off, he submits most willingly to the rule of the sword, pays taxes, respects the magistrates, serves as a soldier, and is helpful and does everything he can to strengthen the worldly authority that it may be maintained in fear and honour.

Thus the two go well together, that at the same time you do justice to the kingdom of God and to the kingdom of this world, both outwardly and inwardly, at the same time suffer evil and injustice and yet punish evil and injustice, at the same time do not resist evil and yet do resist it. For in doing the one you look upon yourself and your own interests, and in doing the other you look upon your neighbour and his interests. In what concerns yourself and your own interests you hold to the Gospel and as a true Christian suffer injustice for yourself; in what concerns your neighbour and his interests you hold to love and do not tolerate any injustice for your neighbour. This the Gospel does not forbid. Rather it commands it in another place. This is the way in which all the saints have used the sword from the beginning of the world.

On civil Government.   W.A. 11. 253 f.

*The servant of the Lord must not strive; but be
gentle unto all men, apt to teach, patient, in meekness
instructing those that oppose themselves.*

2 TIMOTHY ii. 24–25.

If you are truly meek, your heart grieves over any evil that
befalls your enemy. Those who do that are the true children
and heirs of God and brothers of Christ, who did the same
for us all on the holy cross. Thus we see that a godly judge
is pained when he has to pronounce judgement on the evildoer, and that he grieves over the death which the Law inflicts upon such an one. But the deed is not what it seems;
for it appears to be full of wrath and severity. But so funda-
mentally good is meekness that it remains even under such
angry deeds, and the heart suffers most grief when duty calls
to anger and severity.

Yet we must take heed that our meekness does not run
counter to the honour and the command of God. Thus it is
not right that the magistrates should look on, leaving sin to
rule, and that we should remain silent about it. Our possessions, and honour, and loss we should not regard, and should
not be angry because of anything that may happen to them,
but God's honour and command we must defend, and the
loss and injustice which our neighbour suffers we must re-
dress, the magistrates with the sword, other people with
words and penalties, yet always grieving over those who have
deserved such punishments.

Sermon on good works, 1520.   w.a. 9. 292 f.

Rule thou in the midst of thine enemies.   PSALM CX. 2.

That is not among your friends, not in the midst of roses and lilies, but in the midst of thorns and foes I have appointed your rod. And thence it follows that all who want to serve God and follow Christ must suffer much disappointment and pricking, as Christ Himself says, 'In the world ye shall have tribulations, but in me alone is peace'. Thus it is ordained by God and will not be otherwise; Thy reign shall be in the midst of thine enemies. And whoever will not suffer thus will not be found in the kingdom of Christ. He wants to be in the midst of friends, to sit among lilies and roses and not live with wicked people but with saints.

O, you blasphemers and betrayers of Christ! If Christ had done as you are doing, who would ever have been saved? He emptied Himself of His Godhead, His piety, and His wisdom, and He desired to be with sinners, that He might make them full; yea, and He took them to Himself, and did not wish to have to do with the spiritually minded, the pious, and the just. And what are you doing? The very opposite. You are unwilling to bear your brother's sin, and load yourselves with your own justification and wisdom, but Christ emptied Himself of His own justice and wisdom and burdened Himself with the sin and iniquities of others. Behold, how faithfully you follow Christ!

The children of God do not flee the company of evil men, rather do they seek it that they may help them. They do not want to go to heaven alone, they want to bring with them the greatest sinner, if they can.

Exposition of Psalm cx, 1518.   W.A. I. 696.

Him that is weak in the faith receive ye, but not to doubtful disputations.   ROMANS xiv. 1.

The Apostle desires, first and foremost, that those who are of little faith should be supported and built up by those who are stronger; then, that the weaker should not rashly pronounce judgement upon the others. Thus He admonishes them to preserve peace and unity. Again, since the faith of the weak may not carry them into blessedness, we must look after them, that they may grow strong. We must not leave them to themselves in their weakness, like those who turn away from them in disgust and only think of their own salvation.

And what God does not forbid but leaves free, that must remain free to everyone; and no one is to be obeyed who forbids what God has left free. Rather it is the duty of everyone to fight against such prohibitions with words and deeds, and to do the thing in a spirit of defiance.

Commentary on Romans.   473.

Twelfth Week after Trinity

SICKNESS

Sunday: MARK vii. 31–37

There is no riches above a sound body.
ECCLESIASTICUS XXX. 16.

O, dear Lord God, what a precious thing is a healthy body! How little do we give Him thanks for it! God has burdened our poor flesh with many kinds of sickness and disease, and still we fail to understand. We ought every day to perceive how sinful we are by nature. O, blindness upon blindness!

When our heart is grieved and sad, the weakness of the body follows. Sickness of the heart is true sickness, such as sadness, temptation, and the like. I am a true Lazarus, and well tried in sickness.

It is true that our sufferings are great, but what are they compared with the sufferings of Christ, the Son of God, the Crucified? There we may well be put to silence.

Table-Talk.   w.a. Tischreden. 4. 202.

For whom the Lord loveth he chasteneth, and
scourgeth every son whom he receiveth.

HEBREWS xii. 6.

Therefore, it is with us as with a good child that loves his
father with all his heart and is obedient to him and knows that
the father returns his love, for though he is flogged by his
father, he will yet kiss the rod and say: 'Beloved rod, you do
me much good; how well you have flogged me'; and he suffers
the punishment willingly, bearing still deeper love to his
father, for the child's love and confidence in his father makes
all punishment sweet. Similarly with us: when we perceive
the good deeds of Christ our hearts rejoice within us and when
He sends us misfortune, grief, and peril, we beg to thank Him
and say: to God be praise for evermore because He chastens
me thus. Formerly I should have thought that God had forsaken me, but now my sickness is as dear to me as health, and
a tower and a prison is like a royal palace to me. God is my
gracious Father and therefore all this suffering is lovely and
very precious unto me.

Exposition of John i, 1537.   W.A. 46. 662.

> *My heart is sore pained within me; and the terrors*
> *of death are fallen upon me.*   PSALM lv. 4.

All suffering laid upon the flesh can be endured. The heart
can even despise all physical suffering and rejoice in it, but
when the heart is tormented and broken, that is the greatest
anguish and suffering of all. In bodily afflictions you suffer
but half, for joy and happiness may still fill the soul and heart,
but when the heart alone must bear the burden, it takes great
and lofty spirits, and special grace and strength to endure it.

Why, then, does God let such suffering and affliction befall
those whom He loves most?

First, because He wants to save His people from pride, so
that the great saints who have received such special grace
from Him should not venture to put their trust in themselves.
Therefore it must be thus mingled and salted for them that
they do not always possess the power of the Spirit, but that,
at times, their faith grows restless and their hearts faint, so
that they perceive what they are and confess that they can
achieve nothing unless the pure grace of God sustains them.

Again, God lets such affliction befall them as an example to
others, to shake the self-confident souls, and to comfort those
who are afraid.

In the third place comes the right and true cause why God
acts thus, namely, in order to teach His saints where they
should seek true comfort, and be content to find Christ and
to abide with Him.

Sermon on the first Sunday after   W.A. 17. II. 22 f.
Epiphany, 1525.

I am not alone, because the Father is with me.

JOHN xvi. 32.

Whoever wants to be a true Christian should seek such help and strength as to be so disposed and equipped that he needs no other man, but is strong in himself, so that, if he falls on evil he does not need to stare about seeking help from other people. Christ must be our example, that we may learn and know that our strength comes alone through His grace. David had experienced this; therefore he says in Psalm cxlii: 'I looked on my right hand, and beheld, but there was no man that would know me; refuge failed me; no man cared for my soul'.

Such is the lot of Christians at all times. They are forsaken and left to themselves. Those who would like to stand by them and help them have little faith and therefore cannot help; and those who could and should help turn away and become their worst enemies. Therefore we must have our strength in ourselves, and not in other men.

This example of our Lord Christ we must learn and mark well because the suffering of a Christian begins in loneliness, for the time is sure to come when you are left alone, and if it does not occur in this life it occurs at the hour of death. Therefore every Christian should arm himself with the strength which is Christ and be united to Him who is our only help and comfort, according to His promise.

Exposition of John xvi–xx, 1528.   W.A. 28. 214 f.

I wait for the Lord.   PSALM CXXX. 5.

There are some people who want to show God the goal and to determine the time and the manner and at the same time suggest how they wish to be helped; and if things do not turn out as they wish, they become faint-hearted, or, if they can, they seek help elsewhere. They do not wait upon God, rather God should wait for them and be ready at once to help them in the way they have planned. But those who truly wait upon God ask for grace, and they leave it free to God's good pleasure how, where, and by what means He shall help them. They do not despair of help, yet they do not give it a name. They rather leave it to God to baptise and name it, however long it may be delayed. But whoever names the help does not receive it, for he does not await and suffer the counsel, will, and tarrying of God.

Exposition of four comforting   E.A. 37. 423 f.
  Psalms, 1526.

*Forsake me not, O Lord: O my God, be not far from
me.* PSALM xxxviii. 21.

I am alone, forsaken and despised by all, therefore do Thou
receive me and do not forsake me. It is the nature of God that
He creates out of nothing; therefore, God cannot make anything out of him who has not yet become nothing. Men, on
the other hand, change one thing into another, which is a
futile occupation.

Therefore God receives none but those who are forsaken,
restores health to none but those who are sick, gives sight to
none but the blind, and life to none but the dead. He does not
give saintliness to any but sinners, nor wisdom to any but
fools. In short: He has mercy on none but the wretched and
gives grace to none but those who are in disgrace. Therefore
no arrogant saint, or just or wise man can be material for God,
neither can he do the work of God, but he remains confined
within his own work and makes of himself a fictitious, osten-
sible, false, and deceitful saint, that is, a hypocrite.

The seven penitential Psalms, 1517.   W.A. 1. 183 f.

*But know that the Lord hath set apart him that is
godly for himself.*   PSALM iv. 3.

God works wonders in His saints and leads them wonderfully, against all human reason and wisdom, so that those who fear God and are Christians learn to cling to things invisible and are brought back to life through being given over unto death. For the Word of God is a light that shines in a dark place, as every example of faith shows.

God deals with His saints and Christians as with the godless and the enemies of Christ; at times, even worse. He treats them as the master of the house treats his son and servants. His son he strikes and flogs more often than the servants, and yet for him he saves a treasure for an inheritance. Otherwise I should be at a loss to say why God allows His dear children to have such hard times in this world.

Table-Talk.   w.a. Tischreden I. 519 f.

Thirteenth Week after Trinity

GOOD WORKS

Sunday: Luke x. 25–37

*Thou shalt love the Lord thy God with all thy heart
. . . and thy neighbour as thyself.* Luke x. 27.

There you have the good works described all together.
These we should practise towards one another as our heavenly
Father has done towards us and is still doing unceasingly.
You have often heard that we need no works to please God,
but we need them for our neighbour. We cannot make God
any more powerful or richer through our works, but we can
make our neighbour stronger and richer by them. He needs
them and they should be directed towards him and not to
God. You have often heard this, and it is still ringing in your
ears; would to God that it would go into your hands and be
expressed in works!

Faith is due to God alone; faith receives divine works
which God alone can do, and these works of God we can
receive alone through faith. Then we should be busy for our
neighbour's sake and direct our works towards him, that
they may serve him.

My faith I must bring inwardly and upwards to God, but
my works I must do outwardly and downwards to my
neighbour.

Sermon on the fourth Sunday after   w.a. 10. i (ii). 314 f.
Trinity, 1526.

> *By the deeds of the law there shall no flesh be justified*
> *in his sight.* ROMANS iii. 20.

I have often warned you that you should keep works and
faith separate, for although this has been so often said and
preached to you that you know it well, yet, whenever it comes
to the point, that you should judge according to it and do
right, everybody does wrong. Faith, I say, you must have
towards God in your conscience and no law must strike
against it, be it the law of man or the Law of God. Therefore,
if you hear someone saying, 'You must do this', wanting to
force such work or deed upon your conscience and setting it
in opposition to God, remember that that is surely the devil's
teaching. And you should keep the two as far apart as heaven
and earth, or day and night, so that your faith remains within
your heart and conscience alone, but your works are drawn
away from the conscience to the body. Faith belongs to
heaven above; works must be related to earth. Faith is
directed to God, works to the neighbour. Faith is above the
Law and is without the Law. Works are placed under the
Law and are the bond-servants of the Law.

Sermons from the year 1525.   W.A. 17. I. 105 f.

*Inasmuch as ye have done it unto one of the least of
these my brethren, ye have done it unto me.*

MATTHEW XXV. 40.

Dear Lord God, we are so blind that we do not take such
love to heart. Who could ever have discerned that God lets
Himself so low, that He receives all these works which we do
to the poor and needy as if they had been done to Him? Thus
the world is full of God. In every yard, in every lane you may
find Christ. Do not gaze up into the sky and say: If I could
but once see our Lord God, how readily I should render Him
any service in my power! You are a liar, says St. John. Listen,
thou wretched man, do you wish to serve God? You have
Him in your home, with your servants and children; teach
them to fear God and put their trust in Him alone, and love
Him; go and comfort your sad and sick neighbours, help
them with all your possessions, wisdom, and skill. Bring up
your children that they may know Me, give them a good and
saintly schoolmaster; spare no cost with them; I shall reward
you richly.

See that you do not fail to see Me. I shall be close to you
in every poor and wretched man, who is in need of your help
and teaching; I am there, right in the midst. Whether you do
little for him or much, you do it unto Me. You will not give
the cup of cold water in vain. You will receive fruit a thousandfold, not because of your work, but because of My promise.

Sermons from the year 1526. W.A. 20. 514 f.

> *But when thou doest alms, let not thy left hand*
> *know what thy right hand doeth; that thine alms may*
> *be in secret.*   MATTHEW vi. 3-4.

St. Paul speaks in the same way in Romans xii. and elsewhere: 'he that giveth, let him do it with simplicity'. Giving
with simplicity means not seeking honour, favour, gratitude, or
reward, and not regarding persons, whether they are ungrateful or not, but freely giving what you intended, just as God
daily gives and lets His sun shine, regardless of man's gratitude or ingratitude. That is a simple heart and mind which
seeks no reward and wants no reward, but only considers
God's Will and honour.

Therefore the world is in a shameful state. Whether it is
devout or evil, it is never right. For either it wants to be a
public devil doing evil works, or it wants to be God Himself
doing good works. And neither can be endured. Therefore,
no man can do a good work unless he is a Christian, for if he
does it as man, he does it not for the honour of God but for
his own honour and pleasure; or if he pretends to do it for the
honour of God, it is an evil-smelling lie.

But this is giving alms secretly: when the heart does not
reveal itself, wanting neither honour nor name, but gives the
gift freely, regardless of whether it is seen and praised by men.
Your gift shall be concealed under that simplicity of heart
which never asks or considers whether it will earn gratitude or
ingratitude, good or evil, but leave that to God.

Sermons on Matthew v–vii, 1532.   W.A. 32. 410 f.

Freely ye have received, freely give.
MATTHEW x. 8.

For, if the saints did their good works in order to win the kingdom of Heaven, they would never win it. Rather they would be counted among the wicked, for they would be considering with evil eyes their own good, and that in the highest spiritual things, and even in regard to God.

For the saintly children of God do their good deeds out of sheer good will, seeking no reward but alone God's honour and Will, and are ready and eager to do good, and would be even if there were neither heaven nor hell. And this is proved fully by the words of Christ, when He says: 'Come ye blessed of my Father, inherit the kingdom prepared for you from the foundation of the world'. Now, could they merit, as a reward of their deeds, that Kingdom, which is prepared for them before they are created? The Kingdom is not being prepared, for it is prepared already, but the children are being prepared for the Kingdom, and they do not prepare the Kingdom, that is to say: the Kingdom wins the children and not the children the Kingdom.

On the enslaved will.   163 f.

Love your enemies. MATTHEW v. 44.

What sort of a good deed is it if we are kind only towards our friends? Does not even a wicked man so behave towards his friend? Even dumb beasts are good and gentle towards their kind. Therefore a Christian must seek for something higher and serve with meekness even undeserving and ungrateful people, and wicked men and enemies, so our heavenly Father makes His sun to rise on the evil and on the good and sends rain on the ungrateful as on the grateful.

Yet here we shall find how hard it is to do good works according to the will of God, how our nature writhes and winces at it, although we are quite ready and willing to do the good works of our own choice. So, turn to your enemies, to the ungrateful, and do them good, and you will find out how near you are to this commandment or how far you are away from it, and how all through life you will be occupied in practising this work. For, if your enemy is in need of you and you do not help him if you can, it is like stealing what belongs to him, for it was your duty to help him.

Sermon on good works, 1520.   W.A. 9. 297 f.

> *Let every one of us please his neighbour for his good*
> *to edification.*   ROMANS xv. 2.

A Christian lives for one purpose only, namely, to do good to others, and not to destroy men but their vices, and this he cannot do unless he is willing to have to do with the weak. It would be a foolish work of charity if you feed the hungry, give drink to the thirsty, clothe the naked, visit the sick, but would not suffer the hungry, naked, sick, and thirsty to visit you and be in your company. And if thou would not suffer the wicked and the frail to be with you, that would be the same as saying that you did not wish to help one soul to sanctity.

Therefore let us learn from this Epistle that the Christian way of living does not consist in *finding* saintly, righteous, and holy people, but in *making* them. And let this be the Christian's work and practice on earth, to make such people, whether by punishment, or prayer, or by suffering for them, or in what ever way they can. Likewise, a Christian lives not to find rich, strong, and healthy people, but to make the poor, the weak, and sick, rich, strong, and healthy.

Sermon on the second Sunday in   W.A. 10. I (ii). 69.
Advent, 1522.

FRUIT

Sunday: GALATIANS v. 16-24

*Abide in me, and I in you. As the branch cannot bear
fruit of itself, except it abide in the vine; no more can
ye, except ye abide in me.* JOHN xv. 4.

Whoever wants to be a Christian must be born, and grow
out of the vine which is Christ.

When I am baptised or converted through the Gospel, the
Holy Ghost is present and takes me like a piece of clay, and
makes me into a new creature, who now receives a new mind,
heart, and thoughts, namely, a right knowledge of God and a
heartfelt trust in His grace. In short, the innermost being of
my heart is made new and changed, that I become a new
branch planted into the vine which is Christ and growing out
of Him. For my holiness, righteousness, and purity do not
grow from myself, nor do they rest upon myself, but are in
Christ alone and come from Him, into whom I am rooted
through faith, as the sap passes into the grapes, and I have
been made like Him, that He and I are now of one nature and
substance, and through Him I bear fruit, which is not mine
but the vine's. Thus Christ and Christian become one loaf
and one body, and Christians bear the proper fruit, not
Adam's, and not their own, but Christ's.

Exposition of John xiv and xv.   w.a. 45. 667.

*Ye have not chosen me, but I have chosen you, and
ordained you, that ye should go and bring forth
fruit, and that your fruit should remain.*

JOHN xv. 16.

Thereunto have I chosen you and have given unto you all
these things, that you should bear much fruit and live in such
a manner that men may see that you are truly my disciples.
It is not given to you to destroy sin; that is for you too lofty
a thing, and it belongs to My calling alone: but you should
bear fruit, first, that God be thereby honoured and praised,
and that you may show your obedience; thereafter to the good
and betterment of your neighbour, so that it can be seen that
you truly believe in Christ and belong to Him. This happens
when the fruits appear, so that men see that you are kind and
generous and patient, and that you cause no grief or harm to
others.

Exposition of John xiv and xv.   W.A. 45. 700 f.

Without me ye can do nothing.   JOHN XV. 5.

It is a tremendous comfort and inspiration when a man knows that he does not live and work to no purpose but that his works are well-pleasing to God and are called true fruit, and when he can say from the bottom of his heart: I am baptised into Christ; this is not my own idea nor is it an invention of men, but my Lord Christ Himself has done it; of that I am certain. Secondly, I know and I witness to it before all the world, that through the grace of God I am able to believe in this Man, and mean to stay with Him, and to yield up both life and blood and everything, before I would betray Him; such is the faith in which I stand and live. After that I go out, eat and drink, sleep and wake, rule and serve, and work and act and suffer, and all in the faith in Him into whom I am baptised, and I know that in this manner I bear fruit which is good and well-pleasing to God.

For such a man, wherever he lives, whatever he does, be it great or small, and whatever it be called, he is always bearing fruit, and he cannot help bearing fruit. And whatever he does he does easily and without unpleasantness and strain and boredom. Nothing is too heavy or too big for him, that he could not suffer and bear it.

Exposition of John xiv and xv.   W.A. 45. 671.

*Even so every good tree bringeth forth good fruit; but
a corrupt tree bringeth forth evil fruit.*

MATTHEW vii. 17.

No good work helps a man who has no faith towards
saintliness or salvation. The opposite is also true. No evil
work can make him evil and condemned, but only unbelief,
which makes both the person and the tree evil, and then he
does the evil works. Therefore, if we grow saintly or wicked,
it does not begin with works but with faith, as the wise man
says (Ecclesiasticus x. 12): 'The beginning of all sin is the turning away from God and not trusting in Him'. So also Christ
teaches that we must not begin with works, and says: 'Either
make the tree good and its fruit good, or make the tree corrupt and its fruit corrupt', as though He would say: Whosoever would have good fruit must begin with the tree and make
it good. Therefore, whoever would do good works must
begin not with the works, but with the *person* who is to do
the works. But the person cannot be made good except
through faith, neither can he be made evil except through unbelief. It is true that works make a person saintly or evil
before man, that is to say, they indicate outwardly who is
saintly and who is wicked, as Christ says (Matthew vii. 20),
'By their fruits shall ye know them'. But all this is in outward
appearance only.

On the freedom of a Christian, 1520.   W.A. 7. 32 f.

Seest thou how faith wrought with his works, and by works was faith made perfect?   JAMES ii. 22.
Love is the fulfilling of the law.   ROMANS xiii. 10.

Faith and love should be thus distinguished, that faith is concerned with the person and love with the works.

This is said in order that the nature and meaning of faith, love, and the law may be rightly perceived, and that to each is ascribed what properly belongs to it, namely, that faith justifies but it does not fulfil the law; that love does not justify but it fulfils the law; the law demands love and works, but does not mention the person; the person feels the law, but love does not feel it at all.

Faith, then, although it cannot fulfil the law, yet possesses that with which the law can be fulfilled, for it gains the Spirit and the love with which it can be fulfilled. And again, though love does not justify, yet it gives proof of what makes a person just, namely, faith. To sum up, as St. Paul himself here says: 'love is the fulfilling of the law'; as if he said: It is one thing to fulfil the law, and another to make possible the fulfilling of the law. Love fulfils the law in the sense that it is itself the fulfilling of the law, but faith fulfils it in the sense that it provides the doer and love remains the deed.

Sermon on the fourth Sunday after   W.A. 17. II. 97 f.
    Epiphany, 1525.

> *Be ye therefore perfect, even as your Father which is*
> *in heaven is perfect.*   MATTHEW V. 48.

We can never be perfect or attain to perfection in the sense
of being completely free from sin, as some dream of perfection. But this is the meaning of perfection here and everywhere in Holy Scripture, that, in the first instance, the teaching is right and perfect, and then that our life is ruled by it and
lived in accordance with it.

But the teaching and the life of the Jews is both imperfect
and wrong because they teach love only towards their friends,
and they live accordingly. That is a broken and partial love,
but God desires a whole, round and complete love, so that we
love our enemy and do him good, as much as our friend.
Thus I am called a truly perfect man, who keeps the teaching
whole and complete.

But if life does not run so smoothly and perfectly, and it
cannot because flesh and blood hinder it unceasingly, that
does not destroy perfection, if only we strive after it and
continue to walk in it daily, so that the spirit is master of the
flesh and bridles it, and constrains it and holds it back, and
keeps it from making headway to act against this teaching.
Thus I am called to keep my love on the middle path, the
same towards all, and omitting no one. In this way I shall
possess the true Christian perfection which does not consist in
special offices or states, but is common to all Christians, and
should be.

Exposition of Matthew v–vii, 1532.   W.A. 32. 406.

> *He that is mighty hath done to me great things; and*
> *holy is his name.* LUKE i. 49.

It may be that someone will be frightened by such great deeds of God, unless he not only believes that God has the power and the knowledge to do such great deeds, but also that He has the will and the love to act thus, and then he will be comforted. Yet it is not enough to believe that He wills to do great deeds with others, but not with you, thus excluding yourself from such divine action, as those do who do not fear God in the height of their power, but give in faint-heartedly when they are in trouble. For such a faith is futile and dead, like a delusion taken into the mind from a fairy-tale. But without any hesitation or doubt you must picture His Will for you and firmly believe that He wills to do great things for you and that He will do them. Such a faith lives and works. It penetrates and changes the whole man. It constrains you to live in fear if you are prosperous, and to be comforted if you are in need, and the more prosperous you are the more you should live in fear, and the deeper you are cast down the more you should be comforted. Such a faith can do all things; as Christ says, it stands firm by itself. It comes also to experience the divine working, and thus the divine love, and thence it is moved to hymn God's praise, so that the believer thinks highly of God and regards Him as very great.

The Magnificat, translated into German,   W.A. 7. 553 f.
 and expounded, 1521.

Fifteenth Week after Trinity

ON ANXIETY AND TRUST IN GOD

Sunday: MATTHEW vi. 24-34

Behold the fowls of the air, for they sow not, neither do they reap, nor gather into barns; yet your heavenly Father feedeth them. Are ye not much better than they?
MATTHEW vi. 26.

Thus God sets before us the example of the creatures, that we may learn from them to trust in God and not to be anxious. For the little birds fly before our eyes, to shame us, and we should take off our hats to them and say: 'My dear Doctor, I must confess, I cannot do what you do. You sleep the whole night through in your little nest without any anxiety. At dawn you rise and are happy and gay. You perch on a little flower and sing your praise and thanks to God. Then you seek your food and find it. Shame on me! What a fool I am, that I fail to do the same, although I have so much reason to do it!'

If the little bird can live without anxiety and bear itself in that respect like a living saint, though it has neither field nor barn, neither chest nor cellar, and sings and praises God and is happy and gay because it knows that there is One who cares for it, whose name is 'Our Father in heaven', why do we not do the same, we, who have the advantage that we can work, till the soil, gather the fruit, and store it and lay it up till we need it? And yet we cannot leave off living in such shameful anxiety.

Sermon on the fifteenth Sunday after Trinity, 1544.   W.A. 52. 473 f.

I would have you without carefulness.

1 CORINTHIANS vii. 32.

Despairing unbelief is still so deep in us, that we always live in anxiety about food and drink. The reason is that we want to know how God will sustain us. We want to have our barn well full of corn, and our chest full of gold, and to bind God to our barn and chest, but His Will is to be free and Master over all, over time and place and person and everything. Leave it to Him, to determine how He will feed us, He will give corn and gold as and when we need them, but our course is to say : I will do my work today and I shall see whence He will give me food, and the same again tomorrow, and thus we should understand that He will feed us and we shall have no need to be anxious.

Therefore we should leave all care to Him. The work we do and the pains we take are not contrary to faith, but are useful for the training of the flesh ; but anxiety is contrary to God. The woman should mind the children, run the house, and wait for God to show what is His Will for her. Similarly, the man should work and commit himself to God. God will not desert him. He has promised that very clearly. All that we achieve with our anxiety is that we stand in God's way and hinder His work in us.

Sermons on Genesis, 1527.   W.A. 24. 115 f.

*The eyes of all wait upon thee; and thou givest them
their meat in due season.*   PSALM cxlv. 15.

Mark now, that no animal works for its food, but each hath
its peculiar task, and thereafter it seeks and finds its meal.
The bird sings and flies, builds it nest and rears its young
ones; that is its work, but its work does not feed it. Oxen
plough, horses carry loads and go to battle, sheep produce
wool; that is their work, but they do not live by it; but the
earth brings forth grass and feeds them through the blessing
of God.

In the same way man must work, but yet he must know
that it is Another who feeds him, and not his work. It is the
blessing of God, although his work appears to feed him,
because God gives him nothing without his work: like the
bird which neither sows nor reaps, and yet would die of
hunger if it did not look for food. But that it finds food is not
due to its own work but to the goodness of God. For who has
provided the food that the bird may find it? For, where God
does not provide no one can find, even though all the world
should search and work themselves to death. This we can see
with our eyes and grasp with our hands; and yet we do not
believe. And again, where He is not the counsellor and pre-
server nothing is secure; though it may be fastened with a
hundred thousand locks. It will be scattered to the winds,
that no man will know where it has gone.

Exposition of Psalm cxxvii, 1524.   W.A. 15. 367 f.

*Cast thy burden upon the Lord, and he shall sustain
thee: he shall never suffer the righteous to be moved.*

PSALM lv. 22.

Whoever desires to be a Christian must learn to believe
this, and to exercise this faith in all his affairs, in physical
and in spiritual things, in doing and in suffering, in living and
dying, and to cast aside all anxious thoughts and cares and
throw them cheerfully off. Yet he must not throw them into
a corner, as some have vainly tried to do, for they will not
let themselves be stripped of their power so long as they are
allowed to dwell in the heart, but you must cast both your
heart and your care upon God's back, for He has a strong
neck and shoulders, and can well carry them. And, moreover,
He bids us cast them upon Him, and the more we cast on
Him, the more He is pleased, for He promises that He will bear
your burden for you, and everything that concerns you.

'Cast ye all your care upon him; for he careth for you.'

O, if a man could learn this casting off of his care, he would
know by experience that it is true. But he who does not learn
such casting off of his care, must remain a downcast, dejected,
defeated, rejected, and hopelessly confused man.

Sermon on the third Sunday after   W.A. 22. 34 f.
Trinity, 1544.

*Why standest thou afar off, O Lord? Why hidest
thou thyself in times of trouble?*   Psalm x. 1.

When we suffer in respect of our body, or possessions, or
honour, or friends, or whatever we have, let us ask if we believe that we are not well-pleasing unto God, and if, whether
our sufferings and afflictions are small or great, God has
graciously ordained them for us.

Faith sees through what to our feelings and understanding
is the expression of His anger and holds a sure confidence in
His good purpose. God is hidden here, as the bride sings in
the Songs of Songs; behold, He standeth behind our wall, He
looketh forth at the window showing Himself through the
lattice, which means that He is hidden beneath the sufferings
which seek to separate us from Him, like a wall, and He sees
us and does not leave us. For there He stands ever ready with
His gracious help, and is seen through the windows of a
struggling faith.

Sermon on good works, 1520.   W.A. 9. 233.

*I will instruct thee and teach thee in the way which
thou shalt go: I will guide thee with mine eye.*

PSALM xxxii. 8.

You ask that I should redeem you. Do not grow weary.
Do not teach Me, and do not teach yourself. Leave yourself
to Me. I will be your Master; I will lead you in the way in
which I desire that you should walk. You think that all is lost
when it does not work out as you desire. Your thinking is
harmful to you, and it hinders Me. It must not work out
according to your understanding but must be superior to
your understanding; sink yourself into not-knowing and I
will give you My knowledge. Not-knowing is true knowledge;
not knowing where you are going is truly knowing where
you are going. To know Me makes you simple. Thus Abraham
went out from his fatherland and he knew not whither he
went. He committed himself to My knowing and cast aside
his own knowing, and went the true way and reached the
right end.

Behold, this is the way of the cross, which you cannot find,
but I must lead you, like a blind man. Therefore, not yourself, not a man, not a creature, but I will teach you, through
My Word and Spirit, the way wherein you are to walk. You
should follow the work which you choose and not the suffering which you devise, but that which comes to you against
your choosing, thinking, and devising. It is there that I call
you. There you should be a pupil. There is the time. There
your Master has come to you.

The seven penitential Psalms, 1517.   W.A. I. 171 f.

We know that tribulation worketh patience, and patience, experience, and experience, hope.

ROMANS V. 3-4.

When God wants to strengthen a man's faith He first weakens it by feigning to break faith with him. He thrusts him into many tribulations and makes him so weary that he is driven to despair, and yet He gives him strength to be still and persevere. Such quietness is patience and patience produces experience, so that when God returns to him and lets His sun rise and shine again, and when the storm is over he opens his eyes in amazement and says: 'The Lord shall be praised, that I have been delivered from evil. God dwells here. I did not think that all would end so well'.

Within a day or two, within a week or a year, or even within the next hour, sin brings another cross to us: the loss of honour or possessions, bodily injury or some mishap which brings such trouble. Then it all begins again and the storm breaks out once more. But now we glory in our afflictions because we remember that on the former occasion God was gracious to us, and we know that it is His good will to chastise us, that we may have reason to run to Him and to cry, 'He who has helped me so often will help me now'. And that self-same longing in your heart (which makes you cry, Oh that I were free! Oh that God would come! Oh that I might receive help!) is hope, which putteth not to shame, for God must help such a person.

In this way God hides life under death, heaven under hell, wisdom under folly, and grace under sin.

Sermons from the year 1527.   W.A. 17. II. 274 f.

TO BECOME STRENGTHENED IN THE INNER MAN

Sunday: EPHESIANS iii. 13-21

... that he would grant you, according to the riches of his glory, to be strengthened with might by his Spirit in the inner man. EPHESIANS iii. 16.

Worldly people are full of courage and of high spirits, and so are Christians. Christians are much stronger through the Holy Spirit, for they fear neither the world nor the devil, neither death nor misfortune. This is called spiritual strength. For the little word 'spirit' rightly means courage, which is bold and daring. For spiritual strength is not the flesh and bones, but the heart and courage itself, and again weakness, on the other hand, means timidity and cowardice and lack of courage.

Therefore St. Paul says: 'This is what I desire and pray for you from God, that He may give you such a strong and daring mind, such a powerful and joyful spirit, as fears no shame, poverty, sin, devil, and death, that you will be certain that nothing can harm you and that you will not want'. Worldly courage endures no longer than there is some earthly good on which to rely; but the true courage trusts in God alone and has no other good or gold than God alone; in Him it withstands all evil and wins an altogether different heart and courage from that of the world.

Sermons from the year 1525.   W.A. 17. I. 435.

For our gospel came not unto you in word only, but also in power, and in the Holy Ghost, and in much assurance.   1 THESSALONIANS i. 5.

We Christians must be sure of our Gospel and must be able firmly and without any wavering to say YES or NO and stand by it. How often the Apostle uses the Greek word 'plerophoria', which means such a certainty and fullness of faith that our hearts never waver but are full of certainty at all times. As I have said before, Christians must know for certain what they believe, and must witness to their belief. Therefore, if you take away that certain affirmation so that Christians are no longer sure of what they believe, they have ceased to be Christians, and you have taken away their faith. For the Holy Spirit is given to them from heaven in order that He may sanctify the hearts of the faithful and make them firm and sure in their witness to Christ, so that they will live and die for it. And is not this the greatest certainty if I stand so firmly by my YES that I am ready to die for it? Yes, it is.

The Holy Spirit is no sceptic. He has not written an uncertain delusion in our hearts, but a strong, great certainty, which does not let us waver, and (may it please God) will not let us waver: but (praise be to God) makes us as sure as we are that we are now alive, and that two and three make five.

On the enslaved will.   8 ff.

The Lord shall be thy confidence.   PROVERBS iii. 26.

Christ who is your righteousness is greater than your sin and all the world's sin. His life and comfort are stronger and mightier than your death and hell.

Hence a heart that is so strengthened and unafraid can despise the devil and all his terrors and plagues and can stand up against all his power, saying: 'Sin, if you would condemn me you must first condemn Christ, my dear Saviour, Priest, and Advocate with the Father. Death, if you would devour me, begin on high with Christ, my Head. Devil and world, if you would plague and frighten me, first drag Him down from His seat'. In short: I must not and will not be afraid of anything, even if the lightning should strike down at this instant and throw everything into confusion. For Christ is mine in His suffering, His death, and His life, the Holy Spirit with His comfort, and the Father Himself with all His grace in which He sends the Holy Spirit that He may preach Christ to my heart and fill it with His comfort.

Exposition of John xiv and xv.   W.A. 45. 727.

*Being confident of this very thing, that he which hath
begun a good work in you will perform it until the day
of Jesus Christ.*   PHILIPPIANS i. 6.

Only keep a firm hold on Me. Through My Word I have
made a beginning with you and brought you to Myself. But
if you wish to give proof that you are abiding in Me, you will
have a hard struggle at first and will think that you are alone,
and that I have forsaken you and left you in the grip of fear
and misery. But only keep a firm hold and I will give you
proof that I love you, and you will feel in your heart how
well-pleased God is with your faith, your suffering, and your
witness. From such experiences you will increasingly understand who I am, what I can do, and what My plan is for you,
and I will reveal Myself to you from day to day until you are
so strengthened through temptations that in the name of
Heaven you can defy the devil and beat him off.

This power to defy the devil comes from experiencing in
times of temptation the doctrine which we already believe.
Thus we perceive that we are in Christ and Christ is in us.
And where there was previously wrath and anger there is
nothing of that kind now, for Christ is our dear bishop and
Mediator with God and He alone is our Master and Lord, and
no one shall accuse or frighten us, or teach or rule us.

Exposition of John xiv and xv.   W.A. 45. 600 f.

*Give attendance to reading, to exhortation, to doc-
trine.* 1 TIMOTHY iv. 13.

I am often aware of temptation, and even to this day can
scarcely guard myself sufficiently against it. This I confess
openly as an example to any who are interested, although I
am an old doctor and preacher and am so much more versed
in the Scriptures, or at least ought to be, than all those wise
ones who attack me; I must still grow daily, like a child, saying aloud early every morning the Lord's Prayer, the Ten
Commandments, the Creed, and such precious psalms and
sayings as I choose, just as the children are now being
taught to do, although I have daily to study the Scriptures
and to fight the devil. I may not say in my heart: You know
the Lord's Prayer, you know the Ten Commandments, you
know the Creed by heart, etc. No, I must go on learning every
day and remain a pupil of the Catechism. I feel how notice-
ably it helps me, and I find by experience that the Word of
God can never be exhausted, but that it is really true as
Psalm cxlvii. says: 'His understanding is infinite'.

Exposition of Psalm cxvii.   W.A. 31. I. 227.

I give thanks unto thee for thou hast chastened me sore,
and art become my salvation. PSALM cxviii. 21.

This is a joyful verse. It sings and dances along in sheer delight. Art Thou not a wonderful and precious God, who dost rule over us so wonderfully and so graciously? Thou exaltest us when Thou humblest us. Thou justifiest us when Thou showest us to be sinners. Thou leadest us into heaven when Thou cast us into hell. Thou givest us victory when thou allowest us to be defeated. Thou bestowest life upon us when Thou givest us over to death. Thou comfortest us when thou allowest us to grieve. Thou makest us joyful when Thou allowest us to weep and lament. Thou makest us sing when Thou allowest us to weep. Thou makest us strong when we suffer. Thou makest us wise when Thou makest us fools. Thou makest us rich when Thou makest us poor. Thou makest us masters when Thou allowest us to serve— and innumerable similar wonders which are all contained in this one verse and for all of which Christians give thanks in these few words: 'I give thanks to Thee, for Thou hast chastened me sore and art become my salvation'.

Sermons from the year 1532.   W.A. 36. 171.

The Spirit also helpeth our infirmities.

ROMANS viii. 26.

Let no man think that he will be freed from all sin, lust, and evil thoughts, yet each must continue to yearn for such freedom and cry to God: 'Ah, if only I could be set free from sin'. The voice of the Holy Spirit will thus cry in us till the Last Day. Therefore sin always abides in us poor Christians. We fall into sin, but not wilfully or out of wickedness, but from weakness, which God can well forgive. Therefore it is the best comfort that we have within us the testimony of the Holy Spirit, which means that when we are in need and cry to God He will be gracious to us and will help us. For our position is now so different from what it was before when we were in need. Now we can trust in God and know that He will not forsake us, and thus we show that we are truly Christians.

On many important matters, 1537.   W.A. 45. 405.

Trinity III: St. Michael

THE CHURCH MILITANT

ONE HOLY CATHOLIC CHURCH

Sunday: EPHESIANS iv. 1–6

That they all may be one. JOHN xvii. 21.

For to everyone who believes through the word of the Apostles, the promise is given for Christ's sake and by the power of this prayer, that he shall be one body and one loaf with all Christians; that what happens to him as a member for good or ill, shall happen to the whole body for good or ill, and not only one or two saints, but all the prophets, martyrs, apostles, all Christians, both on earth and with God in Heaven, shall suffer and conquer with him, shall fight for him, help, protect, and save him, and shall undertake for him such a gracious exchange that they will all bear his sufferings, want, and afflictions and he partake of all their blessings, comfort, and joy.

How could a man wish for anything more blessed than to come into this fellowship or brotherhood and be made a member of this body, which is called Christendom? For who can harm or injure a man who has this confidence, who knows that heaven and earth, and all the angels and the saints will cry to God when the smallest suffering befalls him? If a sin attacks him to frighten, bite, and oppress his conscience, threatening him with the devil, death, and hell, God speaks with the great company of heaven: 'Sin, leave him to Me unmolested! Hell, leave him undevoured; Death, leave him unslain.' But this cannot be done without faith, because to the eyes of the world and of reason the opposite appears to happen.

Sermons on John xvi–xx, 1528.   W.A. 28. 182.

Your life is hid with Christ in God.
COLOSSIANS iii. 3

The Church is ruled by the Holy Spirit, and the saints are likewise ruled and quickened by Him (Romans viii.), and Christ is with His Church until the end of the world.

Yet we must ask whether it is certain that those who are called the Church are really the Church, or whether they have been astray all through their lifetime, and have at last come back to the right way. For mark that at the time of the Prophet Elijah all of the people of Israel who were in high places, those exercising authority with regard to ruling, teaching, and other offices, had fallen away into idolatry, so that Elijah thought that he alone had remained faithful. Yet the Lord had saved seven thousand! But who could see them and who knew that they were the people of God?

And what happened in the time of the Lord Christ Himself, when all the Apostles were offended and fled, when the whole great and glorious people were united in betraying, rejecting, condemning, and crucifying Christ, and only one or two, such as Nicodemus, Joseph, Mary, and the thief on the cross were saved? But were not the many also called the people of God? Or was there no true people of God left? O yes, there was, but it had neither the name nor the honour.

And has it not been so from the beginning with the Church and the children of God (for the work of God is altogether different from the work and reason of man) that many have been called saints and the people of God, and they were not, while some, a little despised company, were not given the name but were the faithful?

On the enslaved will.   78 f.

*I have given unto them the words which thou gavest
me.*   JOHN xvii. 8.

This convinces and assures us that a devout Christian
knows that the Church does not appoint or ordain anything
outside the Word of God. And if there is a Church which
does that, it is only a Church by name, as Christ says. The
Word is not the Word of God because the Church says it,
but the fact that the Word of God is preached constitutes the
Church. The Word is not created by the Church, but the
Church is created by the Word. And a certain sign by which
we may know where the Church be, is the Word of God.

How can we know where the Church is, if we do not hear
her preaching and the testimony of the Spirit?

On the misuse of the Mass, 1521.   W.A. 8. 491 f.

The people that dwell therein shall be forgiven their iniquity.   ISAIAH xxxiii. 24.

The Kingdom of Christ does not consist in condemnation. 'I have not come to condemn but to forgive sins. For no one can enter My Kingdom unless his sins are forgiven. My Kingdom is not barren. All who are called and have entered it are sinners. And as they are sinners they cannot live without forgiveness of their sins.'

Thus, none but sinners can enter the Kingdom. Such is the Kingdom of Christ. He admits no saint, He sweeps them all out. And if anyone wants to be a saint, He thrusts him out of His Church. But if sinners enter His Kingdom they do not remain sinners. He spreads His cloak over them, saying: 'If you have fallen into sin, I forgive you and cover your sin'. It is true that sin is present, but the Lord of this Kingdom will not look upon it. He rather covers it over, forgives it and does not count it against you. Thus you are made a living saint and a true member of Christ.

Sermons on John vi–viii.   W.A. 33. 509.

TO THE CHURCH ARE GIVEN THE KEYS OF HEAVEN AND OF HELL

Verily I say unto you, Whatsoever ye shall bind on earth shall be bound in heaven; and whatsoever ye shall loose on earth shall be loosed in heaven.

MATTHEW xviii. 18.

Whatsoever is bound on earth is bound in heaven. God here binds Himself to the judgement of the Holy Christian Church on earth, when she uses her judgement aright, so that the judgement of the Church becomes God's judgement. Holy Scripture teaches here that the Lord Christ has ordained in the Church a great spiritual order, that He and she shall have power with regard to public sins and vices to bind and banish those responsible through the Word. He does not say that He reserves some power to Himself, but what the Church binds shall be bound in His sight—that, and nothing else.

Therefore, wherever you see that sin is punished or forgiven, publicly or otherwise, you may know that the people of God is there. Where there is not the people of God, there are not the keys either. For Christ has left them behind so that there shall be a public symbol and sanctuary where the Holy Spirit can sanctify sinners and where Christians can bear witness that they are one holy people under Christ in this world. And those who will not turn away from their sins and be sanctified must be expelled from this holy people—that is, bound and locked out by the keys.

On the Councils and Churches, 1539.　　　W.A. 50. 632.

Blessed are ye, when men shall revile you; and
persecute you; and shall say all manner of evil
against you falsely.   MATTHEW V. II.

Outwardly the holy Christian people can be recognised by
the sacred sign of the Holy Cross, for they must suffer misfortune and persecution, all kinds of affliction and temptation
from the devil, the world, and the flesh (as the Lord's Prayer
says), must sorrow in spirit, be meek, alarmed, outwardly
poor, despised, ill, and weak that they may be made like Christ
their Head. And all this suffering must be brought upon them
for no other reason than that they are holding firmly to Christ
and to the Word of God, and are thus suffering for Christ
alone. They must be devout, quiet, and obedient, ready to serve
their country and everyone with their body and their goods,
and do no harm to anyone. But no people on earth will suffer
so much bitter hatred. Their life will be harder than that of
Jews, Heathen, or Turks: in short, they will be called heretics,
villains, devils. They will be cursed and called the most in-
famous people on earth, so that those by whom they are
pursued, hanged, drowned, murdered, and tortured (and no
one has pity on them, and when they thirst they are given only
myrrh and gall to drink) may render God a service, and all
this not because they are adulterers, murderers, thieves, and
villains, but because they confess Christ alone, and no other,
as their God. And wherever you see and hear such things,
you may know that there is the holy Christian Church, as He
says: 'Rejoice ye in that day and leap for joy, for behold, your
reward is great in heaven'. For by this sacred sign the Holy
Spirit not only sanctifies His people but also makes them
blessed.

On the Councils and Churches, 1539.   W.A. 50. 641.

THE UNITY OF THE SPIRIT THROUGH THE LORD'S SUPPER

The cup of blessing which we bless, is it not the communion of the blood of Christ? The bread which we break, is it not the communion of the body of Christ?
1 CORINTHIANS X. 16.

And where you see this Sacrament being duly administered you may be certain that God's people is present. For as was said afore concerning the Word, that where the Word of God is, there is the Church, so also where Baptism and this Sacrament are, there is God's people. For no one possesses or uses or observes these sacred things but the people of God, although there are some false and faithless Christians secretly among them, but they do not profane the people of God.

See that you exercise and confirm your faith, so that when you are troubled or when sin is besetting you, you go to the Sacrament and heartily desire it, and what it signifies, and do not doubt that it will be done unto you as the Sacrament declares, that Christ and all His saints will draw near to you with all their virtues, sufferings, and graces, to live, work, rest, suffer, and die with you, and be so fully yours that they have all things common with you. If you are willing to practise this belief and confirm it, you will experience what a rich and joyful wedding-meal your God has prepared for you on the altar.

On the Councils and Churches, 1539.   W.A. 50. 631.

Eighteenth Week after Trinity

TEACHING AND UNDERSTANDING

Sunday: 1 CORINTHIANS i. 4–9

And if Christ be not raised, your faith is vain; ye are yet in your sins. 1 CORINTHIANS xv. 17.

If a man desires to preach the Gospel, he must above all else preach that Christ is risen. Whoever does not preach this is no apostle, for it is the main article of our belief, and those are the purest and noblest books which teach most about this. The greatest power lies in this article of our belief, for if there were no Resurrection we should have no comfort or hope, and everything else that Christ has done and suffered would be in vain. Therefore we must teach this: Behold, Christ died for you: He took upon Himself your sin, death, and hell, and bore the burden of it all. But nothing could hold Him down. He was too strong. He rose from beneath it all and overcame it and subjected it to Himself, and He did this only that you should be freed from it and made lord over it. If you believe it, it is yours. O, how well we Christians should know this; how clear and distinct should this Epistle be to us!

Exposition of 1 Peter, 1523.   W.A. 12. 268 f.

*God hath chosen the foolish things of the world to con-
found the wise.*   I CORINTHIANS i. 27.

Unless we are weak Christ cannot exercise His strength on
us. If it were our strength and power with which we resist our
enemies, we should have the glory and not Christ. But experience teaches us that we are not such as can help themselves,
but God must do it. Thus God is glorified in our infirmity.

The Lord Christ comforts us in that we know for certain
that at times we shall be weak whilst our enemies are strong
and boastful, but Christ wins the victory in the end.

Thus God deals with us when we ourselves and all that we
stand for are yielding and going to pieces before the world,
when we are outwardly weak in the eyes of the world, or
when each single Christian is hard-pressed, so that we are not
afraid or dispirited. Here we learn that our Lord God does not
jest when He feigns to be weak, but is in earnest, for He will
cast down the mighty through the weak and will exalt the
weak. But we must not look upon these things with the eyes
of worldly reason, as is generally done, or we shall be lost.
We must know that it is God's Will to overcome the mighty
through the weak. We must believe this and straightway
shut our eyes.

Sermons on John vi–viii.   W.A. 33. 339 ff.

THE WORD SHOWS WHETHER THE CHURCH IS PRESENT

Thine they were, and thou gavest them me; and they have kept thy word. JOHN xvii. 6.

There is no argument about whether there is on earth a Church which man should obey. The battle begins when men must decide which is the true Church. As long as we judge according to human words and understanding we cannot settle this quarrel, nor can we find the true Church, but we can reach certainty in the matter if we hear how Christ our Lord Himself describes and portrays the Church. Here He christens and depicts her as the little company which loves Christ and keeps His Word (for thus is such love known and felt). 'My Word', He says, 'must remain and be kept, or there can be no Church'. The Word of Christ is here the rule and test whereby one can find and know the true Church, and by which she must set her course, for there must be a rule and order according to which the Church shall preach and act. It is not right that any man speak and act as he likes, and claim that the Church has spoken, and acted, by the Holy Spirit.

And that is why Christ binds His Church to His Word and gives it to her as a sign whereby men may enquire and test whether she possesses the Word, and teaches and preaches in accordance with it and does everything for the love of Christ.

Sermon on Whitsunday, 1544.   W.A. 21. 461.

He that heareth you heareth me.   LUKE X. 16.

God speaks through the holy Prophets and men of God, as St. Peter says in his Epistle: 'Holy men of God spake as they were moved by the Holy Ghost'. God and man must not be separated and severed from each other according to the understanding and judgement of human reason; but we must immediately say: 'Whatever this man, Prophet, Apostle, or sound preacher and teacher says and does by the command and Word of God, God Himself says and does, for he is God's mouthpiece and instrument'. Those who hear him should say with conviction: 'At this instant I am not listening to Paul, Peter, or any man, but I am listening to God Himself speaking, baptising, pronouncing absolution, punishing, excommunicating, or administering the Sacrament'.

O my Lord God, what a great comfort a poor, contrite, and broken conscience may receive from such a preacher, when it believes that such words and comfort really are God's Word and comfort, and that God means it so. Therefore we most certainly believe that God works through His Word, which is like an instrument through which the heart may truly learn to know Him.

Table-Talk.   W.A. Tischreden 3. 673 f.

> *Beloved, believe not every spirit, but try the spirits*
> *whether they are of God; because many false prophets*
> *are gone out into the world.* 1 JOHN iv. 1.

He is called the Spirit of truth because He is opposed to all
lies and false spirits, for the world is full of spirits, as the
proverb says: where God builds a church the devil builds a
chapel beside it—that is, where the pure Word of God is
preached, the devil introduces sects and mobs and many false
spirits, which take to themselves the glory and the name of
Christ and His Church. But at bottom it is all false and there
is no truth nor certainty in it. 'But I will give unto you the
Spirit', says Christ, 'who will make you sure and certain of
the truth, so that you will no longer doubt any article concerning your eternal blessedness, but will be sure of the
matter and will be able to be judges and judge all other teaching'. Thus He will make you not only soldiers and victors,
but He will give you a scarlet robe and make you doctors and
masters who can discern with certainty which teaching is true
or which false in the Church. The devil will not be sufficiently
clever and no traitor sufficiently nimble to make your teaching false or lead you astray.

And thus the Christian Church has held her own from the
beginning until now among innumerable false spirits which
have been from the beginning and may still come. And yet
she goes on standing firmly by her Baptism, Lord's Supper,
Gospel, Christ, the Ten Commandments, and true and pure
prayer, and thus she judges and separates from herself all
false teaching which is opposed to her—yes, even though the
devil should become an angel of light and as a beautiful and
radiant figure should present himself as God.

Exposition of John xiv. and xv.   w.a. 45. 727 ff.

LET US HOLD FAST THE PROFESSION OF OUR FAITH

*Let us hold fast the profession of our hope without
wavering; for he is faithful who hath promised it.*
Luther's translation of HEBREWS x. 23.

Therefore take heed and let nothing on earth, however
great, nor even angels from heaven, drive you against your
conscience away from that teaching which you know and
esteem to be of God. St. Paul says (Galatians i. 8): 'But though
an angel from heaven preach any other Gospel unto you than
that ye have received, let him be accursed'. You are not the
first, nor the only one, nor will you be the last to be persecuted for the Word of God. Christ says (Matthew v. 10):
'Blessed are they which are persecuted for righteousness' sake';
again (Matthew xxiv. 9): 'Ye shall be hated by all men for my
name's sake'; again (John xvi. 2): 'The time cometh that whosoever killeth you will think that he doeth God service'. We
must remember such sayings and fortify ourselves with them,
yes, we must give praise and thanks to God and beseech Him
that we may be made worthy to suffer for His Word. Remember that it has been revealed that at the time of the antichrist
no man will be free to preach, and all who teach and hear the
Word of God will be deemed accursed. Thus it is now and
thus it has been for more than a hundred years.

Instruction to those making confession—   W.A. 7. 295 f.
on forbidden books, 1521.

*Verily, verily, I say unto you, He that believeth on me,
the works that I do shall he do also; and greater works
than these shall he do; because I go to my Father.*
JOHN xiv. 12.

Because we have such a treasure we have all things and
are lords above all lords. We are beggars on earth as Christ
was Himself, but before God we are laden with an abundance
of riches, so that the world is poor and wretched compared
with us and cannot even keep her own possessions without
us. And what is the reason that Christians shall do such great
and even greater works than He Himself? No other, He says,
than this: 'because I go to my Father'.

This is what Christ means by going to the Father, that He
shall be made Lord and seated on the throne at the right hand
of the Father and be given all authority in heaven and on
earth. And this is why you will have power to do such works,
because you are of Me and believe in Me, and you shall be in
Me and I shall be in you. For through the power which I
shall have at the right hand of the Father, being of the same
divine Majesty and openly transfigured and shown forth as
very God and Lord over all creatures, I shall work in you who
believe in Me and who, having received My Word, Baptism,
and Sacrament, steadfastly abide in them. And as I am Lord
over sin, death, the world, the devil, and everything, so shall
you be also, so that you will be able to glory in the selfsame
power, not that you will have it of your own worthiness or
strength, but solely because I go to the Father. Through the
Word and through prayer My Word will work mightily in
you.

Exposition of John xiv. and xv. W.A. 45. 537 ff.

Nineteenth Week after Trinity

THE SANCTIFYING POWER OF THE CHURCH

Sunday: EPHESIANS iv. 22–32

Give no offence in any thing, that the ministry be not blamed. 2 CORINTHIANS vi. 3.

A Christian should be careful to give no offence to any man so that the Name of God shall not be blasphemed. It is a great thing to be a Christian—that is, a new man created after God, and a true image of God in whom God Himself is clearly seen. Therefore, whatever a Christian does, be it good or evil (under the name of a Christian), will be counted to the honour or dishonour of the Name of God. Therefore, if you follow your lusts and obey the old Adam within you, you do nothing but give occasion to the blasphemer and cause the Name of God to be blasphemed because of you.

In this respect a Christian should take the greatest care, even if he cares for nothing else, to protect and honour the Name of his dear God and Saviour Jesus Christ.

Sermon on the nineteenth Sunday after Trinity, 1544.　　　W.A. 22. 321.

Let no man so account of us, as of the ministers of Christ, and stewards of the mysteries of God.

1 CORINTHIANS iv. i.

St. Paul might well have said here: We are stewards of the wisdom of God, or the righteousness of God, or the like. But that would be speaking fragmentarily. Therefore to comprise everything that is offered in Christ he uses the one word 'mysteries'. As if he wished to say: we are spiritual stewards and we distribute the grace of God, the truth of God, and who could count all His innumerable virtues? I will include them all in one word and say, they are the mysteries of God; and I call them mysteries and hidden things because they can be obtained by faith alone.

The mysteries of God are those hidden things which God gives and which dwell in God. The devil also has his mysteries, as is said in the Book of Revelation xvii. 5. 'And upon her forehead was a name written, MYSTERY, BABYLON THE GREAT, MOTHER OF HARLOTS AND ABOMINATIONS OF THE EARTH'. They pretend that their teaching and work leads to heaven, but there is nothing in it but death and hell for all who believe in it. But the mysteries of God contain life and blessedness.

Thus we learn from these words that the Apostle regards the servant of Christ as a steward of the mysteries of God; that is, he shall regard himself and be regarded by others as a man who preaches and gives to the people of God nothing but Christ and what belongs to Christ; that is, he shall preach the pure Gospel and the pure faith, that Christ alone is our life, way, wisdom, power, prize, and blessedness, and that without Him we have nothing but death, error, folly, helplessness, shame, and damnation. And whoever preaches anything else shall not be deemed a servant of Christ or a steward of the mysteries of God.

Sermon on the third Sunday in Advent,   W.A. 10. I (ii). 128 f. *1522.*

... as poor, yet making many rich; as having nothing,
and yet possessing all things.   2 CORINTHIANS vi. 10.

Every single Christian is a man such as the Lord Christ
Himself was when He was on earth, and performs such great
deeds, that in things divine he can rule the whole world, and
help and serve everyone and do the greatest works which can
be done on earth. For in the sight of God he is esteemed
higher than the whole world, so that for his sake God sustains the world and gives it all it has. Hence if there were no
Christians on earth, no town or land would have peace, yes,
in one single day the devil would ruin everything there is on
earth. The fact that there is still corn growing in the fields,
that men recover from their illnesses, that they have food,
peace and security, all this they owe to the Christians.

Indeed we are poor beggars, and yet we make many rich.
In very truth we possess nothing, and yet we have all things;
and whatever kings, princes, citizens, and peasants have in
this world, they have it, not because of their fair hair, but
because of Christ and His Christians.

To them is given the Gospel, Baptism, and the Sacrament
to convert the people, to win souls from the devil, to snatch
them out of hell and death, and take them up to heaven; and
again to strengthen, comfort and uphold the poor and instruct
and advise the afflicted consciences in their sore temptation;
and again to teach all people in all occupations how to do
their work as good Christians.

This sort of work kings and emperors, the mighty and the
rich, the learned and the wise cannot perform, nor could they
pay for it with all their possessions. For there is not one
amongst them who could comfort and cheer a single soul,
when it is burdened and weighed down by sin.

Exposition of John xiv and xv.   W.A. 45. 532.

Let all your things be done with charity.

1 CORINTHIANS xvi. 14.

The true brotherhood is divine and heavenly; it is the noblest, surpassing all the others as gold surpasses copper or lead; it is the communion of saints, in which we all are brothers and sisters, so near to one another that greater nearness could never be conceived. For there is *one* baptism, *one* Christ, *one* Sacrament, *one* meal, *one* Gospel, *one* faith, *one* Spirit, *one* spiritual body, and each one is a member of the other; no other brotherhood is so deep and close.

But if you say, 'Unless I get something through the brotherhood, of what use is it?' the answer is: 'You serve the congregation and other people as love does, and you will have your reward without any seeking or desiring it'. But if love's service and reward seem mean to you, that is a sign that your brotherhood is not of the right spirit. Love serves freely and therefore God gives to her freely all His riches. Forasmuch as all things must be done in love, if they are to be well-pleasing unto God, the brotherhood must also be in love. Yet what is done in love can by its nature not seek its own, rather it seeks the benefit of others, and especially the congregation.

The more you find you are being grafted into Christ and His fellowship of saints, the more firmly are you able to stand, that is, as you find your trust in Christ and His dear saints growing in strength, your certainty grows of their love towards you, and of their succour in all the troubles of life and death. And again, if you take to heart the decline of all Christians and of the whole Church, or the fall of any one, Christian, and your love is given to them all, so that you would readily help any man, hate none, sympathise with all, and pray for them, then all is well.

Sermon on the Sacrament of the   W.A. 2. 756 f.
Body of Christ, 1519.

For we being many are one bread, and one body;
for we are all partakers of that one bread.
1 CORINTHIANS X. 17.

To receive this Sacrament in bread and wine is to receive a certain sign of fellowship and incorporation with Christ and all the saints.

Just as bread is made by crushing many grains of corn together and the bodies of many grains of corn become one loaf of bread, in which each grain loses its own body and form and takes on the common body of the loaf, and as the grapes similarly lose their own form and become one form of wine and drink, so must we if we rightly use the Sacrament. Out of love, Christ, with all His saints, takes on our form and fights with us against sin, death, and all evil, so that we, being kindled with love, take His form, trust ourselves to His righteousness, His life and blessedness, and so through the fellowship of the good that belongs to Him and the wretchedness that belongs to us, we become *one* loaf, *one* bread, *one* body, *one* drink, and all is common. Oh! What a great Sacrament this is, that Christ and His Church are *one* flesh and *one* bone. And again, through the selfsame love we should be transformed and should accept the infirmities of all other Christians, and take upon us their form and their afflictions, and give to them whatever we can, that they may enjoy it. This is the right communion and true meaning of the Sacrament.

Sermon on the Sacrament of the   W.A. 2. 743.
   Body of Christ, 1519.

We have also a more sure word of prophecy; whereunto
ye do well that ye take heed.   2 PETER i. 19.

We have the comforting promise in defiance of all opposition that what we (as Christians) speak, and do, and suffer
is true and comes from the Spirit of truth; and again, whatever
is done, said, preached, and undertaken against it must be false
and full of lies before God, however right it may appear, and
whatever claim may be made by it as pure truth, highest holiness, and spirituality, yes, even when the world fights for it
with all its might, to maintain it, and most cruelly slanders us
and storms against us. For our Gospel and deeds are not
founded upon us, neither are they for our sakes, but everything is for the sake of this Lord Christ, from whom we
have all things and for whose sake we preach, and live, and
suffer. Since, then, all things are for His sake, we leave the
caring to Him who says He will bring all these things to fulfilment and give us the spirit and the courage we need; and
what He does through His Christians is pure and certain
truth.

Exposition of John xiv and xv.   w.a. 45. 569 f.

There is no respect of persons with God. ROMANS ii. 11.

Thus all is made even and no man has more than another wherein to glory before God, who will suffer no man to be despised, censured, or cast out. It is said, 'Ye shall preach and proclaim this Gospel to all creatures'. In this respect the greatest, wisest, holiest, noblest man is no better than the meanest, simplest, and most despised on earth. They are all lumped together, and no one is singled out or separated, for sorrow, or for love, or for praise and privilege. It is written plainly and without exception—those who believe, whoever they are, and no matter to what people, nation, or class they belong, and however unequal they may be in the eyes of the world. But in the life of the world there must be inequality and variety, as there is among the creatures, where each is of its own kind and differs from the others.

Yet though all this works in perfect order, no one can say: whoever does this or that will be saved. Therefore in this Kingdom of Christ all is heaped together, and comprised in one word in one sentence: not this man or that man doing this or that, but, 'he that believeth shall be saved'. There you have it all in one, whether you be Jew or Gentile, master or servant, virgin or husband. 'If you believe', says Christ, 'you are in My Kingdom, a saved man, redeemed from sin and death.'

Sermon on the Ascension of Christ, 1544.   W.A. 21. 393 f.

Twentieth Week after Trinity

THE CHURCH'S WORSHIP

Sunday: EPHESIANS V. 15–21

. . . that ye may with one mind and one mouth glorify God, even the Father of our Lord Jesus Christ.
ROMANS XV. 6.

All that we can give to God is praise and thanksgiving. This is the only true service, as He Himself says.

But how could we give God praise and adoration, the only true service, if we did not love Him and accept His gifts? But how can we love Him unless we know Him and His gifts? But how can we know Him and His gifts if no man preaches about them and the Gospel is left lying under the bushel? For where there is no Gospel God cannot be known; hence there can be no praise or love of God. Thus there can be no worship.

St. Paul admonishes us that we shall with *one* mind and *one* mouth glorify God. That happens when we are of *one* mind and know that we are all equal, having received the same gifts in Christ, so that no man exalts himself above another, and none claims any special gift.

Sermon on the second Sunday in   W.A. 10. I (ii). 80 f.
Advent, 1522.

*... for I had gone with the multitude ... to the house of
God, with the voice of joy and praise, with the multitude
that kept holyday.* PSALM xlii. 4.

The multitude needs a certain place and certain days and
hours suitable for listening to the Word of God; and therefore God has ordained and instituted the Holy Sacraments to
be administered to the congregation at a place where all
gather together for prayer and thanksgiving.

The advantage of this is that when Christians gather
together, prayer is more powerful than at other times. We can
and should most certainly pray at all places and hours, but
prayer is nowhere so strong and powerful as when, in unity of
Spirit, the whole congregation is gathered together to pray.

And this is said that we Christians might know in what way,
to what end, and to what degree we should use it, which means
that we should gather at a certain place and time to study and
hear the Word of God and to bring before Him our own and
other general and particular needs, and thus send up to
heaven a strong and powerful prayer, as well as to join in
praising and glorifying God for all His benefits. And this we
know is the true service, which is well-pleasing to Him and
which He honours with His Presence.

And whatsoever is done at such a gathering of the congregation or Church is pure and holy and divine—a holy Sabbath
whereby God is worshipped in holiness and men are suc-
coured.

Sermons from the year 1544.   W.A. 49. 593 f.

I exhort therefore, that, first of all, supplications,
prayers, intercessions, and giving of thanks, be made
for all men.　I TIMOTHY ii. 1.

Common prayer is a precious and most powerful thing. That is why we gather together to pray. The Church is called a house of prayer that we may gather together there in unity of spirit and bethink ourselves of the needs and sorrows of all men and carry them up in prayer before the throne of God and invoke His grace. And this must be done earnestly and with genuine affection because we feel all men's need and therefore pray to God with real sympathy for them, in sure trust and confidence.

Would to God that some multitude might so pray that one common and genuine heart-cry of the whole people should soar up to God! What immeasurable help and virtue would follow such a prayer! What greater calamity could befall all evil spirits? What greater thing could be wrought on earth, whereby so many sinners would be won, so many saints upheld!

And, indeed, it is not that places and buildings are lacking where we can gather together, lofty, great, and glorious Churches, spires or bells, but only this unconquerable prayer, that we should unite and offer it to God.

Sermon on good works, 1520.　　　　　W.A. 9. 263 f.

Close to "enuff prayers".

Till I come, give attendance to reading, to exhortation,
to doctrine.   1 TIMOTHY iv. 13.

My advice is that people should not dispute about secret
and hidden things, but that they should stay simply by the
Word of God and especially the Catechism, for therein is
contained a good and true summary of the whole Christian
religion and the most important articles put together in brief.
For God Himself gave the Ten Commandments, Christ composed and taught the Lord's Prayer, and the Holy Spirit set
down the articles of the Creed in the shortest and most appro-
priate words. But it is despised as a bad, unworthy thing,
because the children have to say it off by heart every day.

The Catechism is the true lay-bible containing the whole
Christian teaching as each Christian must know it for his
eternal blessedness.

The Catechism contains the best and most perfect Christian
teaching. Therefore it should be preached again and again
without ceasing, and all the common preaching should be
founded on it and related to it. I wish men would preach it
every day and simply read it from the book.

Table-Talk.   W.A. Tischreden 2. 523.

He sent his servant at supper time to say to them that
were bidden, Come; for all things are now ready.
LUKE xiv. 17.

Friend, if you had no occasion or need to go to the Sacrament, would it not be a serious and wicked thing to feel cold and disinclined towards it? What else could that mean than that you were disinclined to believe, to thank and to remember your dear Saviour and all the goodness which He has shown towards you through His bitter suffering, endured that He might redeem you from sin, death, and the devil, and justify and quicken and save you. But wherewith shall you warm yourself against such coldness and disinclination? Wherewith shall you awaken your faith? Wherewith shall you stir yourself to give thanks? Will you wait until prayer breaks in upon you or till the devil makes a place for it? That will never happen. You must stir yourself by this Sacrament and hold fast to it. Here is the fire that can kindle the heart. You must remember your need and thirst, and hear and believe the good that your Saviour wrought for you! and your heart will be renewed and your thoughts be changed.

Exhortation to the Sacrament of the Body   E.A. 23. 196.
and Blood of our Lord, 1530.

The sacrifices of God are a broken spirit. PSALM li. 17.

It is a very precious promise, if only we could believe it, that our afflictions are to God the most pleasing sacrifices. The Lord God delights in our preaching, suffering, and sadness; they are the highest sacrifice. But He is not speaking here of the sacrifice of praise and thanksgiving, but teaches that sorrow and contrition are the greatest sacrifices, for they stay the old man. If I preach, I do it in praise of our Lord God, so that I offer the morning and the evening sacrifice, for He is well pleased when His Word is preached, and preaching is the loftiest sacrifice a man can give. If a man preaches in the right manner, he gives praise to our Lord God. If he is thrown into prison for it, he willingly offers the further sacrifice; and such affliction and suffering is well pleasing to God and is to Him like a thousand sacrifices. The broken and contrite heart is to God a greater sacrifice than the whole Levitical Sacrifice. Would that we could believe it!

Short writings on the Psalms,   W.A. 31. I. 542.
  1530–1532.

> *Distributing to the necessity of <u>saints;</u> given to hospitality.* ROMANS xii. 13.

How strange! Every day we ask and desire the saints to care for our necessities, and St. Paul teaches us to distribute to theirs.

St. Paul mentions the necessities of the saints in order to stimulate and inflame us all the more to do good to Christians. He points out to us the true saints, namely, those who are in dire need; that is, they don't look like saints at all, rather do they look like poor, forlorn, hungry, naked, imprisoned, killed people who are in need of everybody's help and cannot help themselves. The world regards them as wretched evil-doers who deserve to suffer all kinds of misery. Christ will bring forward such saints on the Day of Judgement, saying: 'What ye have done unto the least of these My brethren ye have done it unto Me'. And then the great saint-worshippers will stand in shame and fear before these saints, whom they would not look upon on earth because of their disgrace.

Be given to hospitality! Here he begins to enumerate some of the necessities of the saints and to teach how we should care for them, namely, this cannot be done by words alone but by deeds, such as to give them hospitality when they need it. It also includes all other bodily needs such as feeding the hungry, giving drink to the thirsty, and clothing the naked.

Sermon on the second Sunday after   W.A. 17. II. 49 f.
  Epiphany, 1525.

Twenty-first Week after Trinity

THE CHURCH MILITANT

Sunday: Ephesians vi. 10–17

Finally, my brethren, be strong in the Lord, and in the power of his might. Ephesians vi. 10.

He acts like a proper god-fearing general who preaches a sermon to his men drawn up in battle array, admonishing them to stand firm and fight boldly and confidently, so that it might well be called a battle-sermon for Christians. For he shows here that those who are baptised into Christ and would hold fast to Him must be warriors, always equipped with their armour and weapons, and that the lot of a Christian is no leisurely existence, nor one of peace and security; rather he is always on campaign, attacking and defending his position.

Therefore he here warns and musters his soldiers, saying, 'You are in my army and under my flag; see to it that you are on the look-out for the enemy, ready to defend yourselves against his angels, for he is never far away from you'. As long as you do that, you need have no fear. For we belong to a Lord who has angels Himself and power enough, and is called the Lord of hosts and the true victor over the dragon, and He stands by us, even fights for us, so that the devil and all his angels will fall down and be cast out. For the Word of the Lord abides for ever. It may suffer temptation and the Church may have no peace from the enemy, and some who let the Word be taken out of their heart may fall; yet the Word must abide for ever.

Sermons from the year 1544.　　　　　　　w.a. 49. 583 f.

> *There was war in heaven; Michael and his angels*
> *fought against the dragon; and the dragon fought and*
> *his angels.*   REVELATION xii. 7.

What is said here about the fight in heaven must also come to pass here on earth within the visible Churches, and the fight must not be understood in reference to the spirits in heaven but to all Christians who belong through faith to the Kingdom of Christ.

They fight against the devil who leads the world astray, and there is here on earth no other war than the fight against this seduction. And that is why this war is not waged with armour, sword, pike, or musket, or with bodily or human power, but with the Word alone, as it is written, 'they overcame him by the word of their testimony' (Revelation xii. 11). With this testimony (that is, by preaching the Word and witnessing to it) they drive the devil out of heaven when he tries to go in and out among them to rob them of their salvation which hereafter will be seen and now is believed.

Sermons from the year 1544.   W.A. 49. 575 f.

*Then answered the Jews and said unto him, Say
we not well that thou art a Samaritan, and hast a
devil? Jesus answered, I have not a devil; but I honour
my Father, and ye do dishonour me.* JOHN viii. 48–49.

What does Christ do here? He suffers His life to be
covered with shame and He endures it in silence; but He
defends the teaching, for the teaching is not ours but God's,
and God must not suffer. There patience ceases and I must
venture for it all that I have and suffer all that they inflict
upon me, in order that the honour of God and His Word
shall not suffer. For that I perish, matters little, but if I let
God's Word perish and remain silent, I do harm to God and
all the world.

Thus, then, must we act. When they threaten our life we
must suffer it and give love for hate and good for evil.

But when they attack the Gospel they attack God's honour,
Then love and patience must end and we must not remain
silent, but we also must speak out and say: I honour my
Father, therefore ye dishonour me, but I do not ask about
you dishonouring me because I also do not seek my own
honour. But take heed, there is One who seeks my honour,
and He will pronounce judgement, that is the Father Himself,
and He will demand it of you, and judge you, and He will not
let you go unpunished. He does not seek His honour only,
but also mine, because I seek His honour, as He says 'those
who honour Me will I honour'. And that is our comfort, that
we can be cheerful if all the world heaps upon us shame and
disgrace, for we know that God will demand our honour, and
for the sake of it He will execute judgement, punishment, and
vengeance. Would that we should believe it and wait for it,
for He shall surely come!

Sermons from the year 1525.   W.A. 17. II. 233.

For we can do nothing against the truth, but for the truth. 2 CORINTHIANS xiii. 8.

This is so great a good that no human heart can grasp it (therefore it necessitates such a great and hard fight). It must not be treated lightly, as the world maintains and many people who do not understand, saying we should not fight so hard about an article and thus trample on Christian love; rather, although we err on one small point, if we agree on everything else, we should give in and overlook the difference in order to preserve brotherly and Christian unity and fellowship.

No, my dear man, do not recommend to me peace and unity when thereby God's Word is lost, for then eternal life and everything else would be lost. In this matter there can be no yielding nor giving way, no, not for love of you or any other person, but everything must yield to the Word, whether it be friend or foe. The Word was given unto us for eternal life and not to further outward peace and unity. The Word and doctrine will create Christian unity or fellowship. Where they reign all else will follow. Where they are not no concord will ever abide. Therefore do not talk to me about love and friendship, if that means breaking with the Word, or the faith, for the Gospel does not say love brings eternal life, God's grace, and all heavenly treasures, but the Word.

Sermons from the year 1531.   W.A. 34. II. 387.

*Take . . . the sword of the Spirit, which is the word of
God.* EPHESIANS vi. 17.

Christendom must also have people who can beat down
their adversaries and opponents and tear off the devil's equip-
ment and armour, that he may be brought into disgrace. But
for this work powerful warriors are needed, who are thoroughly familiar with the Scriptures and can contradict all false
interpretations and take the sword from false teachers—that is,
those very verses which the false teachers use and turn them
round upon them so that they fall back, defeated. But as not
all Christians can be so capable in defending the Word and
articles of their Creed, they must have teachers and preachers
who study the Scripture and have daily fellowship with it, so
that they can fight for all the others. Yet each Christian should
be so armed that he himself is sure of his belief and of the
doctrine and is so equipped with sayings from the Word
of God that he can stand up against the devil and defend himself, when men seek to lead him astray, and so can help to
fight the battle for the maintaining of true doctrine.

Sermons from the year 1531.   W.A. 34. II. 378 f.

> *Resist, stedfast in the faith, knowing that the same*
> *afflictions are accomplished in your brethren that are in*
> *the world.*   1 PETER v. 9.

In such temptations St. Peter comforts the suffering Christians by telling them that they are not the only nor the first souls to be so tempted, as though they had to bear a peculiar, rare, and unheard-of cross and suffering and should think and feel that they alone had to bear it; rather they should know that all their brethren in Christ scattered everywhere have at all times had to suffer thus from the devil and his on-slaughts because they were in the world. For it is an immense help and comfort when the sufferer knows that he is not alone but is suffering with a great multitude.

Therefore no man should regard his own anguish and distress as so horrible, as if it were new and had never happened to anyone before. It may well be new to you and you may not have experienced it before, but look around you at all the Christians in our beloved Church from the beginning to this hour, planted in the world to run the devil's gauntlet and unceasingly winnowed and fanned like wheat.

For where God through His Word and faith has gathered together a Church, the devil cannot be at peace, and where he cannot achieve her destruction through sectarianism he strikes at her with persecution and violence, so that we must risk our body and life in the fight, and all we have.

Sermon on the third Sunday after   W.A. 22. 47 f.
  Trinity, 1544.

Take the shield of faith . . . and the helmet of salvation,
and the sword of the Spirit. EPHESIANS vi. 16–17.

We must prepare for battle, and what we need most is a good strong shield. Faith is such a shield, as the Apostle indicates, as he takes it and clings to the Word of Christ, and answers the devil: 'Though I am a sinner, though I have not lived as I ought and have done too little, yet there is the Man, holy and pure, who gave Himself for me, and died for me, and was given to me by the Father to be mine, with His holiness and righteousness. You must leave me in peace and unaccused. I hold fast to him. My life and deeds must remain as best they can'.

'And the sword of the spirit, which is the Word of God.'

This is the last, but it is the strongest and the right weapon for smiting the devil and overcoming him. For it is not enough to have defended ourselves against the enemy, and to be able to stand against him when he attacks us, so that we are not defeated; that is called defence. We must also be able to take the offensive—that is, to pursue the enemy, and put him to flight. Similarly, here it is not enough to ward off the devil with faith and hope as our shield and helmet, but we must draw the sword, hit back at him, hunt him down, and make him flee, thus gaining the victory ourselves. And that sword, he says, is the Word of God. For a sword of steel and iron would avail us nothing against the devil; it must be the sword of the Spirit.

Sermons from the year 1531.   W.A. 34. II. 402 ff.

Twenty-second Week after Trinity

THE PERFECTING OF THE CHURCH

Sunday: PHILIPPIANS i. 3–11

I am confident of this very thing, that he which hath begun a good work in you will perform it until the day of Jesus Christ. PHILIPPIANS i. 6.

Such is a Christian heart and such is its appearance and form, as St. Paul says in these words, namely, that from the bottom of his heart he is thrilled and delighted and gives thanks to God that others are coming into the fellowship of the Gospel; and he is full of confidence towards those who have begun to believe and takes their salvation to heart, and rejoices in it as much as in his own salvation and does not know how to thank God enough for it. He asks God unceasingly that he may live to see many come with him into that fellowship, and to be kept in it until the day of the Lord Jesus Christ, who will perfect all things and make whole what is deficient here, and that they may remain unobjectionable in such faith and hope until they reach that selfsame joyful day.

Thus speaks the holy Apostle as he pours out the bottom of his heart, filled with the rich and wondrous fruit of his spirit and faith, which is all on fire with joy and happiness when he sees that the Gospel is understood, accepted, and honoured, and so filled with love for the Church that he knows of nothing higher to wish her and to ask of God than that she may increase and abide in the Gospel. He regards it as so great and precious a treasure when men can hear the Word of God and keep it.

Sermon on the third Sunday after   W.A. 22. 35 f.
Trinity, 1544.

388

> *. . . until ye be endued with power from on high.*
> LUKE xxiv. 49.

We, who preach the Gospel and witness to it and are persecuted by the world for it, know that we may place our comfort in Christ, the faithful counsellor, and rely on His power. Because we do that we see and experience that He is the true Victor, who without striking a blow preserves so many souls from the devil's kingdom simply by the breath of His mouth. Further, He not only shows His fighting power to His enemies but also to us every day, in that He, or we through Him, strikes the devil dead—that is, sin and death in our own hearts.

This is the manner in which this hero fights: wherever the Gospel gets a hold it does not stop striking and attacking the world so that many souls are won and the Kingdom of Christ extends. This is a blessed fight and a blessed war, for by it men are delivered from the devil and brought into the Kingdom of Christ. What a hero and giant Christ is: thus it is written in Psalm cxlix: 'Let the saints hold a two-edged sword in their hands'. Those are not the material swords of this world, but spiritual swords of the mouth of Christ. With these swords and with their wisdom Christians must rush into battle and smite down the heathen nations and kings, with all their visions of holiness, and take them prisoner and subject them to Christ. Such is the honour of God's warriors and saints.

(Context cannot be found; given as E.A. 6. 298 f.*)*

Verily thou art a God that hidest thyself, O God of Israel, the Saviour.   ISAIAH xlv. 15.

The Prophet Isaiah speaks the truth about Him, for He hides His omnipotence, His wisdom, power, and strength and makes it appear as though He could do nothing, knew nothing, understood nothing, or does not wish to do. Now He lets our enemies do as they like with His Word, Sacraments, and Christians; He lets us call and cry, and keeps silence, as though He were writing a poem, or were occupied with something else, or were out in the fields, or were asleep and could not hear us. But that day will come when He will manifest His greatness and His power and His omnipotence.

Meanwhile Christians who are baptised in His name must keep still and must put up with being trampled upon, and must be patient. For in the life of believing it is His will to appear small; but in the life of seeing He will not be small but very great. Then He will show that He saw the suffering of His people and heard their cries and that His will was inclined towards them to help them, and that He had the power to help them. Now He hides His good will, His power and strength; but when He appears He will reveal His will and power and strength. He could help and save now. He has the power to do so, nor does He lack the will, but all this is concealed in the Word so that we cannot see it but must take hold of it by faith. But on the day of His Advent He will take away the veil and He will appear as a great God and will do justice to His Name, so that people will say: 'Behold, He is the Lord and Saviour'.

Sermons from the year 1531.   W.A. 34. II. 128.

*The Lord said unto my Lord, Sit thou at my right
hand, until I make thine enemies thy footstool.*
PSALM CX. I.

The Prophet here depicts the Kingdom of Christ as an
eternal kingdom which is always engaged in battle. For it is
written, 'until I make thine enemies thy footstool'. And yet
that does not seem right to us. Such a king ought not to have
many enemies, and He should drive them out swiftly with one
stroke of His sword. Yes, and He will do so when the time is
come, but while we are here on earth the warfare goes on.
Sectaries, human wit and reason, our own flesh, conscience,
death, and the devil, press in upon us to produce anxiety and
fear. Therefore, whoever wants to be a Christian should consider this, and learn to know the nature of the Kingdom.

There will be discord, it cannot be otherwise. Therefore
when men thus rage and rave, I say: 'It must be so. Do you
not know who Christ is, namely, a Man whom the world, the
devil, sin, and death and everything resists?' For He must
have enemies, and here on earth His Kingdom knows no
settled peace. In the hereafter, in the life to come, there will be
peace; but the Kingdom on this earth shall not know peace.

Sermons from the year 1531.   W.A. 34. II. 68 f.

His name shall be called Wonderful.   ISAIAH ix. 6.

Christ is called 'Wonderful' because it is wonderful and strange that He withholds from our eyes, reason, and senses all that He does for His Christian Churches, and hides it away in His Word. Justification, holiness, wisdom, strength, life, salvation, and everything which the Church has in Christ is incomprehensible to reason and hidden from the world. If you judge the Church according to reason and outward appearance you are wrong, for you see men who are sinful, weak, afraid, sad, wretched, persecuted, and hunted out of house and home. But when you see that they are baptised, believe in Christ, give evidence of their faith by bearing good fruits, take up their cross with patience and hope, you have seen the truth. That is the true colour by which men may know the Christian Church.

The Christian Church is holy and righteous, yet she does not appear holy and righteous. Men see nothing but sin and death, and hear nothing but the slandering of the devil and the world. And the reason is that Christian righteousness has its basis outside of us and is found in Christ and through faith in Him. Hence the whole Christian Church and each single Christian confesses: 'I know that I am sinful and impure, lying in prison, danger, death, shame, and disgrace, and I feel in myself nothing but sin; and yet I am just and holy, not of myself, but through Jesus Christ whom God has made my wisdom, justification, sanctification, and salvation'.

Sermon on the Feast of the beheading   E.A. 6. 281 ff.
   of John the Baptist.

The Lord is the strength of my life; of whom shall I be afraid?   PSALM xxvii. 1.

Yes, He gives peace even in the midst of temptation, yet He does it in such a way that all the time you are going uphill and downhill and uphill again. One moment it is night, the next day, and then it is soon night again. It is not always night and not always day, it changes from one to the other, so that at one time it is night, at another day, and soon it is night again. That is how He rules His Christian Church, as we can see from all the stories of the Old and the New Testaments.

And this is called the power of the Lord, that He is not a counsellor and comforter who, when He has given us His Word turns away from us and does nothing more for us, but He helps in order to bring our sufferings to an end. If we are led into temptation, He gives us His faithful counsel, and fortifies us with His Word, so that we do not sink to the ground from weakness, but are able to remain on our feet. But when the hour is come and we have suffered enough, He comes with His power and we win through and gain the victory. We need both counsel, to comfort and uphold us in our sufferings, and power to win through to the end. All the Psalms give Christians strength in suffering—that is, they comfort us in our afflictions, so that our backs do not break, but we continue in hope and patience. Thus He leads all Christians. That is His way. Anyone who does not know that does not know what sort of a king Christ is.

Sermon on St. Peter and St. Paul's Day.   E.A. 6. 294 f.

He sent redemption unto his people.   PSALM cxi. 9.

Those who have believed in Me, suffered for My sake, and died in faith in Me need have no fear. Those may be afraid who have not believed, but do not you fear, for it must come to pass so. If the world is to crash in ruins, there must first be some cracking and bursting, otherwise such a great structure cannot collapse. Everything must shake and sway, like a sick man, who when death strikes him, twists and writhes and rolls his eyes and twists his mouth. His face turns pale and his appearance changes. So it will be with the world.

Therefore I say unto you, Fear not, but lift up your heads, like people who rejoice to see it, for, behold, your redemption is near.

So the Lord speaks to His saints, for they too will be afraid when the sun and moon so affect their eyes and the sky is filled with fire. For the saints are not so strong; even St. Peter and St. Paul would be afraid, if they were alive. But our Lord says, Be of good cheer; it will indeed be a terrible sight, but it is not against you but against the devil and unbelievers. To you salvation is come and the joy of redemption, for which you have so long been sighing and praying, that My Kingdom might come to you, cleansing you from all your sins and redeeming you from all evil. And what you have so long been praying for with all your heart shall then be given to you.

Sermon on the second Sunday in Advent,   W.A. 52. 19.
1544.

Trinity IV: The End of the Church Year

THE CHURCH OF THE CONSUMMATION

Twenty-third Week after Trinity

OUR CONVERSATION IS IN HEAVEN

Sunday: PHILIPPIANS iii. 17–21

*Our conversation is in heaven, from whence also we
look for our Saviour, the Lord Jesus Christ.*
PHILIPPIANS iii. 20.

We who are baptised into Christ and believe in Him, he
says, have not based our existence and comfort on the
righteousness of this temporal and worldly life on earth. We
have a righteousness which cleaves, through faith, to Christ
in heaven, and stands and abides in Him alone (for otherwise
it would be nothing before God), and only aims to be eternally in Him, that He through His Coming may make an end
of this earthly life, and of this earthly body, and give us
another life, which shall be new, pure, and holy, and like the
life and body of Christ.

Therefore we are no longer called citizens on earth, but
whoever is a baptised Christian is, through Baptism, a proper citizen of heaven. Therefore we should walk and bear
ourselves as those who belong there and have their home
there, and we should comfort ourselves in the knowledge
that God has accepted us and will bring us to heaven. In the
meantime we wait for the Saviour who will bring down to us
from heaven eternal righteousness, life, honour, and glory.

Sermon on the twenty-third Sunday   W.A. 22. 371.
  after Trinity, 1544.

If any man be in Christ, he is a new creature.
2 CORINTHIANS V. 17.

For a Christian is a new creature, or newly-created work of God, and he speaks, thinks, and judges all things in a different way from the world's speaking and judging. Because he is a new man, all things do become new to him, here in this life through faith, and afterwards in the life to come, through openly revealing their nature. Now the world cannot help judging death according to its old nature and ways, that it is the most terrifying and frightening thing on earth, and the end of life and of all joy.

But a Christian, on the other hand, as a new man, is equipped with very different and even contrary thoughts, so that he can be courageous and happy, even when he is passing through hard times; and in his heart he remembers that he possesses a great treasure even though he is poor; he is a powerful prince and lord when he is in prison; and surpassing strong when he is weak and ill, and in highest honour when he is disdained and reviled. Similarly, he will be quickened into newness of life, if he now has to die. In short: he wins a new heart and courage through which he makes all things new here on earth, and thus has a foretaste here of the future life, where everything will become new before his eyes and in the full light of day made new, as he now thinks and envisages it through faith, according to his new nature.

Sermon preached at the Castle at   W.A. 36. 255.
Wittenberg, 1532.

*If we hope for that we see not, then do we with patience
wait for it.* ROMANS viii. 25.

Such is rightly taught, but not soon learned: rightly
preached, but not soon believed; it is well advised, but not
easily followed; well said, but hard to do. For there are very
few people on earth waiting for the blessed hope and the
coming eternal Kingdom and inheritance, and waiting with
such conviction as they might, being only lightly attached to
this present life. There are few who only look at this temporal
life through a coloured glass, as it were blindly, but look at
that eternal life with clear and open eyes. Alas, the blessed
hope and the heavenly inheritance are all too often forgotten,
but the temporal life and the transitory realm on earth are all
too much remembered. This transitory life we have unceasingly before our eyes, we think about it and care for it and are
happy in it, but we turn our back towards the everlasting life.
Day and night we pursue this earthly life, but the eternal life
we throw to the winds.

But this should certainly not be so with Christians; rather
the opposite should obtain. A Christian should look at this
temporal life with closed or blinking eyes, but he should look
at the future eternal life with his eyes wide open and in clear
bright light, and he should have only his left hand in this life
here on earth; but with his right hand, with his soul, and with
his whole heart he should be in the other life, in heaven, and
should wait for it always with certain hope and a joyful mind.

Sermons from the year 1531. W.A. 34. II. 110 f.

WE ARE STRANGERS AND PILGRIMS ON THE EARTH

*. . . and confessed that they were strangers and pilgrims
on the earth.* HEBREWS xi. 13.

The Apostle here desires to show that we should look upon
this life as a stranger and pilgrim looks upon a land in which
he is a stranger or a guest. A stranger cannot say, Here is my
fatherland, for he is not at home there. A pilgrim does not
think of remaining in the land to which he makes his pilgrimage, or in the inn where he stays the night, but his heart and
thoughts are directed elsewhere. He feeds in the inn and rests,
and then he continues his journey to the place where his home
is.

Therefore conduct yourselves as guests and strangers in
this strange land and strange inn, and take nothing from it
but food and drink, clothing and shoes, and what you need
for your night's rest, and keep your thoughts on your
fatherland where you are citizens.

We must note this carefully. We must not seek to build
for ourselves eternal life here in this world and pursue it and
cleave to it as if it were our greatest treasure and heavenly
kingdom, and as if we wished to exploit the Lord Christ and
the Gospel and achieve wealth and power through Him. No,
but because we have to live on earth, and so long as it is God's
will, we should eat, drink, woo, plant, build, and have house
and home and what God grants, and use them as guests and
strangers in a strange land, who know they must leave all
such things behind and take our staff out of this strange land
and evil, unsafe inn, homeward bound for our true fatherland
where there is nothing but security, peace, rest, and joy for
evermore.

Sermons from the year 1531.　　　　　W.A. 34. II. 113 f.

The hope of the righteous shall be gladness.

PROVERBS x. 28.

Although the world may impose on us all manner of plagues and sorrows, and pain our hearts and give us a bitter, sour drink, to say nothing of other daily troubles, such as accidents, or illness, disease, hard times, and war, which hurt the body or the outward man, we must endure it as though biting a sour apple and tasting a bitter draught, that the sweetness that follows may taste the better, and we be driven by this experience to yearn for that day with greater longing. Otherwise we should continue our way so cold and numb that in the end we should no longer feel our misery, like the confident and unrepentant world, till at last we should no longer take notice of the Word of God and should perish with the godless. But now, God in His grace maketh us weary and tired of this life and gives us the comfort of a better—that is, that He will soon appear in the clouds with great power and glory, and lift us up out of all misery to everlasting joy, so that as far as we are concerned nothing better or more to be desired could happen to us. But for the godless there will then be no such joyful sight.

Sermons from the year 1531. W.A. 34. II. 472 f.

I die daily.   I CORINTHIANS XV. 31.

How strange this saying sounds, 'I die daily'. Did I ever (says the world) see you being carried to the grave? I see you walking and standing still, eating and drinking, going about and preaching and following your trade. Is that called dying or being dead? But not every man knows and understands what he means, or what this dying is, or how it comes to pass, that he always carries death upon his neck and is unceasingly tormented by it so that he feels more of death than life. And yet at the same time he says he has the honour or glory of eternal life, although he has only a dim feeling of it, and often none at all. Thus there is a constant struggling and striving between life and death, sin and sanctity, a good and an evil conscience, joy and sorrow, hope and fear, faith and doubt; in short God and the devil and heaven and hell.

It is of this struggle that he speaks here, which he alone could fully understand because he was a great Apostle, ceaselessly engaged in the battle and therefore well practised in it. Therefore he protests that we should believe him to be speaking the truth, although others do not feel it or understand it so.

Sermons from the year 1532.   W.A. 36. 610 f.

*Verily, verily, I say unto you, If a man keep my say-
ing, he shall never see death.* JOHN viii. 51.

Here we must note that Christ makes a distinction between
death and seeing or tasting death. We must all die. But a
Christian does not taste or see death, that is, he does not feel
it or fear it, but passes quietly and gently into death, as though
he were falling asleep and not dying. But a godless man feels
it and dreads it eternally. So that to taste death may well refer
to the power and might or bitterness of death.

It is the Word that makes this difference. A Christian has
the Word and holds firmly on to it in death. Therefore he does
not see death, but in the Word he sees life and therefore he
does not feel death. But the godless man has not the Word;
therefore he sees no life but only death, and therefore he feels
it, for it is a bitter and eternal death.

And this is why Christ promises that whoever cleaves to
His Word shall not see or feel death, not even in the hour of
death.

Thus we see what a great thing it means to a Christian,
that he is already eternally redeemed from death and can
never die. For though the death and dying of a Christian
appears outwardly like the dying of a godless man, they
differ inwardly as much as heaven differs from earth. For
a Christian falls asleep as he dies and he passes through
death into life; but the godless man passes out of life and feels
death eternally.

Sermons from the year 1525.   W.A. 17. II. 234 f.

Twenty-fourth Week after Trinity

THE INHERITANCE OF THE SAINTS

Sunday: COLOSSIANS i. 9–14

He hath begotten us again . . . to an inheritance incorruptible, and undefiled, and that fadeth not away, reserved in heaven for you. 1 PETER i. 3, 4.

This means that our hope is not set on possessions or an inheritance present here on earth, but we live in the hope of an inheritance which is at hand and which is incorruptible, and which is also undefiled, and that does not fade away. We possess this good eternally, only we cannot see it yet. These are mighty and precious words, and whoever can grasp their meaning will not be very concerned (I hold) about temporal goods and pleasures. How could a man still cleave to temporal goods and pleasures if he really believed this? For if you compare earthly things with these you perceive that they last but a short time and then all perish. But these things remain for ever and do not perish. Further, earthly things are all impure and they contaminate us, for there is none so pure and holy that earthly things do not defile him, but this inheritance is altogether pure and the man who possesses it is eternally undefiled. It will not rot or fade or wither. All things that are on earth, even though they be as hard as iron and stone, are perishable and cannot last. Man, as he grows old, grows ugly; but the eternal good does not change, but remains fresh and green for ever. On earth there is no pleasure so great that it does not pall in time. We see that men grow tired of everything, but this good is of a different nature. And this is all ours through the mercy of God in Christ, if we believe it, and it is all given to us freely.

Exposition of 1 Peter, 1523.   W.A. 12. 269.

Wherein ye greatly rejoice, though now for a season, if need be, ye are in heaviness through manifold temptations. 1 PETER i. 6.

Here the Apostle indicates how Christians fare in the world. Before God on high they are dearly beloved children, certain of the heavenly inheritance and of blessedness, but here on earth they are not only sad and sorrowful, and forsaken, but they must suffer also many temptations from the devil and from the wicked world. And what is their offence? Their greatest sin is that they believe in Christ and praise and glorify the unspeakable grace which God has shown in Him to all the world, namely, that He alone can redeem us from sin and death and make us just and blessed, that they believe that human reason cannot of its own free will, its own might and good works prepare itself to receive the grace of God, much less can it merit eternal life, but with all its thoughts and deeds, however glorious and beautiful, it cannot reconcile God, but makes Him the more angry because it undertakes all things without, and even against His Word and command, despising the promise and choosing for itself some special work of its own devising. Then the fire is kindled, for the world will not and cannot allow that its good opinion and piety, its saintliness and all its admirable works shall be punished and condemned as of no worth before God, so they strike and persecute and slay them that preach the Word and testify to it, and think they are rendering God a service. Therefore faith is not a dreamy thought in the heart, but whoever has faith confesses it and speaks of what is in his heart, and for that reason troubles beset him. That is why St. Peter says 'though now for a season ye are in heaviness', thus gathering in one, faith, hope, and the holy cross, for the one follows from the other.

Exposition of 1 Peter.   E.A. 52. 21 f.

Looking for that blessed hope, and the glorious appearing of the great God and our Saviour Jesus Christ.
TITUS ii. 13.

Let us meditate upon these words. He calls it a blessed hope, and sets it against this wretched and unhappy life where there is nothing but misfortune, danger, and sin, which hunt and torture us so that everything which belongs to this life should become tiresome to us and should strengthen such hope in us. This happens with those who honestly try to live a sober, righteous, and godly life. Tribulation we esteem a precious thing and glory in it, for we know that sorrow helps to teach us patience, and patience brings us experience, and experience teaches us to hope, and hope does not put us to shame.

Thus our eyes are kept shut towards the earthly and visible things, and we hope rather for the things eternal and invisible. And all this is wrought by grace through the cross. This establishes the divine life in us, which is intolerable to the world.

Sermon for Christmas Eve, 1522.   W.A. 10. I (i). 43.

I reckon that the sufferings of this present time are not worthy to be compared with the glory which shall be revealed in us.   ROMANS viii. 18.

The sun is now such a clear, bright light that no man, however bright and keen his eyes, can steadily gaze into its brightness. But what will happen hereafter when the radiance of the sun will be seven times as bright as now? What bright, clear eyes will be needed to bear such a sun! If Adam had retained the innocence in which he was created, he would have had clear, bright eyes and would have been able to gaze into the sun like an eagle. But through sin and the fall we humans have become so weakened, poisoned, and corrupted in body, soul, eyes, ears, and everywhere, that our eyes are not the hundredth part as sharp as Adam's were before the fall. Our bodies are unclean, and all creatures have become subject to vanity (Romans viii). The sun, moon, stars, clouds, air, earth, and water are no longer so pure, and beautiful, and lovely as they were. But on that day all things will be made new and will once more be beautiful, as St. Paul says, Romans viii: 'The creature itself also shall be delivered from the bondage of corruption into the glorious liberty of the children of God'.

Sermons from the year 1537.   W.A. 45. 231 f.

Thursday

*I am the way, the truth, and the life: no man cometh
unto the Father, but by me.*   JOHN xiv. 6.

When the hour comes when our life and work must cease,
when we have no longer to stay here, and the question arises,
where do I now find a plank or bridge by which I can pass
with certainty to the other life—when you reach that point,
I say, do not look around for any human way, such as your
own good, and holy life or works, but let all such things be
covered by the Prayer of our Lord and say of them: 'Forgive
us our trespasses' etc., and hold fast to Him who says: 'I am
the Way'. See that in that hour you have this Word firmly
and deeply engraved in your heart, as though you heard
Christ really present and saying to you: 'Why should you
seek another way? Keep your eyes fixed on Me, and do not
trouble with other thoughts about how you may get to
heaven. Thrust all such thoughts entirely away from your
heart and only think of what I say: "I am the Way". Only
see that you come to Me, that is, hold on to Me with firm
faith and the complete confidence of your heart. I will be the
bridge and carry you across, so that in a moment you will
pass out of death and the fear of hell into everlasting life. For
I am the One who Myself built the way or path, and I Myself
have trodden it and passed across, so that I might bring
you and all who cling to Me across. But you must put your
trust in Me, nothing doubting, must venture all on Me, and
with a joyous heart go and die confidently in My Name.'

Exposition of John xiv and xv.   W.A. 45. 498 f.

The righteous hath hope in his death.
PROVERBS xiv. 32.

If there were no death, sin would never die. Through death alone is sin restrained, and there is no other way of getting rid of it. Such gracious and wholesome punishment He gives to us, that sin is slain through death. Therefore we should receive death with joyful heart and bear it as coming from a gracious Father, as the faithful do. For our Father's goodness is so great that even death must serve to slay and to uproot all misfortune.

Therefore death is nothing but sheer grace, yes, even the beginning of life. For since it ministers to the restoration of the soul, our bodily system and all that is associated with it, such as illness, danger, pain, and labour, must also serve for our good, so that we could desire nothing better.

For Adam must die and decay before Christ can completely rise, and that begins with the life of repentance, and is perfected through death. Therefore death is a wholesome thing to all who believe in Christ, for all that is born of Adam death brings to decay and dust, that Christ alone may abide in us.

The seven penitential Psalms, 1517.   W.A. I. 188.

> *. . . increasing in the knowledge of God; strengthened*
> *with all might, according to his glorious power, unto*
> *all patience and longsuffering with joyfulness.*
>   COLOSSIANS i. 10, 11.

With such might and glorious power we too must be strengthened in faith, must strive for it and cleave to it through the Word of God and pray that we may not only make a beginning but press on and win through, and so grow stronger and stronger in the power of the Lord.

But to be so strengthened and to overcome cannot be done without much patience, and not only patience but longsuffering too, which he distinguishes from patience as something greater and stronger. For it is the way of the devil, where he cannot overcome a heart with suffering and sorrow to beset it continuously, and so that it is too much and too long for the patience and it appears as though it would never end, so that at last it makes the person weak and weary and robs him of courage, and the hope of overcoming the enemy.

Against this not only is patience needed but longsuffering too, which holds on firmly and steadfastly and perseveres in suffering, and says: you cannot trouble me too much or too long, even if it should last until the end of the world. This is the true and knightly Christian strength, which can endure all length of time in battle and in suffering. But thereunto we need most of all the power and the might of God through prayer, so that we are not overcome in such hard fighting, but reach the end.

Such patience and longsuffering you should have and practise joyfully.

Sermon on the twenty-fourth Sunday   W.A. 22. 386 f.
   after Trinity, 1544.

Twenty-fifth Week after Trinity

THE RESURRECTION OF THE DEAD

Sunday: 1 THESSALONIANS iv. 13–18

If we believe that Jesus died and rose again, even so them also which sleep in Jesus will God bring with him.
1 THESSALONIANS iv. 14.

He leads us out of death and the grave of sin to resurrection and life, both of the spirit and of the body. But if we die, both spiritually to our sin and bodily to the world and to ourselves, what are we profited? Does a Christian not fare otherwise than that he dies and is buried? Certainly, for we know through faith that we shall also live, as Christ rose from death and the grave and lives, for we have died with Him and with Him are planted in His death. For through His death He slew our sin and death, and therefore we shall be partakers of His resurrection and His life, so that there will be neither sin nor death in our soul and body as there is no death in Him.

This is our comfort against the weakness of the poor and wretched flesh which is horrified at the thought of death. For if you are a Christian you know that your Lord Christ has risen from the dead and cannot die again and death has no power over Him: and that is why it has no power over you.

Sermon on the sixth Sunday after Trinity, 1544.   W.A. 22. 103 f.

> *It is sown a natural body; it is raised a spiritual body.*
> *There is a natural body, and there is a spiritual body.*
> 1 CORINTHIANS XV. 44.

I live in hope that we shall also die in such a manner and pass as wretched sinners into heaven, if we can only keep this ornament, and wrap ourselves in the death of the Son of God, and cloak and cover ourselves with His resurrection. If we stand firmly in Him and do not waver, our righteousness is so great that all our sins, whatever their name and nature may be, are like a little spark, and our righteousness is like an ocean and our death is much less than a sleep and a dream. Further, our shame which we shall bury so ingloriously is covered with a glory which is called 'The Resurrection of Jesus Christ', and with this it is so beautifully adorned that even the sun will blush when it sees it and the dear angels will never be able to turn their eyes away from it. With such great beauty are we arrayed and adorned, that all other filthiness of our poor bodies like death and other things do not count at all in comparison.

Therefore we must look upon the death of a Christian differently and we must not count Christians who have died as dead and buried. To our five senses it does appear so, and as far as they lead us it does hurt. Therefore we must listen diligently to what St. Paul says, namely, that they sleep in Christ and that God will bring them with Christ. Learn to comfort yourselves with such words. God cannot lie. Think only of this, for whoever lacks this comfort finds no other comfort and no joy.

Sermons from the year 1532.   W.A. 36. 249 f.

*And that which thou sowest, thou sowest not that body
that shall be, but bare grain, it may chance of wheat,
or of some other grain; but God giveth it a body as it
hath pleased him, and to every seed his own body.*

1 CORINTHIANS xv. 37–38.

Thus the Apostle relates this article about the resurrection
to the article about the creation, and he proves the one by the
other, as if He would say: Whoever has God's Word that
there is a resurrection of the dead, and who believes and confesses that God who has spoken such a Word is the Father
Almighty, the Maker of heaven and earth, as the children say
in the Creed, and of which the corn in the fields and all creatures are a convincing proof and example, he also believes and
confesses that there is a resurrection of the dead. And whosoever denies and gainsays that there is a resurrection of the
dead, also denies and gainsays at the same time that God is the
Almighty Maker of heaven and earth and that He spoke this
Word about the resurrection of the dead. But whoever confesses this article that God is almighty does not dispute in
subtle fashion whether it is possible or not that the dead shall
rise, for there stands the Word of God which says that it shall
be so.

God who says so is an almighty God, Maker of heaven and
earth and of all creatures; therefore the resurrection must
come to pass and it cannot be otherwise, because God has said
so. Otherwise He would not be an almighty God, and
Creator.

Sermons from the year 1544.   W.A. 49. 399 f.

*He hath raised us up together, and made us sit together
in heavenly places in Christ Jesus.*   EPHESIANS ii. 6.

If we had such faith we should live well and die well, for it should teach us that He did not rise for Himself only. We should cleave together, knowing that it holds for us and that we too are contained in that 'Resurrexit'. Because of it, or by means of it, we too shall rise and live with Him eternally, which means that our resurrection and life in Christ has already begun and is as certain as if it were already perfected; but it is still hidden and not yet made manifest. Henceforth we should fix our eyes steadily on this article that all other sights are nothing in comparison with it, though you could see nothing else in the whole heaven and earth; so that, if you see a Christian die and be buried, and before both your eyes and ears there is nothing but death, you will discern by faith in and beneath it all another picture instead of that picture of death. It will be as if you did not see a grave but unmixed life in a lovely Summer garden, or a green meadow in which there is nothing but new, lively, happy people.

For if it is true that Christ is risen from the dead, we already have the best and noblest part of our resurrection, so that the bodily rising of the flesh out of the grave (which is still in the future) must be counted insignificant in comparison.

Sermons from the year 1533.   W.A. 37. 68.

*For we know that if our earthly house of this taber-
nacle were dissolved, we have a building of God, an
house not made with hands, eternal in the heavens.*
2 CORINTHIANS V. I.

This body is, as St. Paul says, only a tabernacle of the soul,
made of earth or clay, and like an old garment. But because
the soul is already in a new, eternal, and heavenly life through
faith, and can neither die nor be buried, we have nothing more
to wait for than that this poor tabernacle may likewise be
made new and incorruptible, because our better part is above
and cannot leave our flesh behind. And as He who is called
'Resurrexit' is risen from death and grave, so he that says
'Credo' and cleaves to Him must also follow. For He has gone
before us that we should follow, and He has begun the work in
us, that, through His Word and Baptism, we may be daily
raised in Him.

If you receive the Word in faith, you are given other eyes
which can see through death to the resurrection and apprehend the pure thoughts and image of life. If I would judge
according to my reason what I can see and understand, I
should be lost. But I possess an understanding loftier than
what the eyes can see and senses feel, which faith has taught
me. For there stands the text which says 'Resurrexit' 'He is
risen', not for Himself but for our sake, that His resurrection
may be made ours, that we may also rise in Him, and not
remain in death and the grave, but with Him may celebrate
in the body an everlasting Easter.

Sermons from the year 1533.   W.A. 37. 69 f.

*So also is the resurrection of the dead. It is sown in cor-
ruption; it is raised in incorruption.*

1 CORINTHIANS XV. 42.

Behold the farmer who sows seed in the field: he throws
the grain on the ground and it looks as if it were completely
lost. Yet he is not troubled about whether it is in vain. He
even forgets it entirely. He does not ask how it is getting on,
whether the worms are eating it, or it is perishing for some
other reason. On the contrary, he knows that towards Easter
or Whitsun-tide beautiful stalks will appear which will bear
many more ears and grains than he sowed. And if you were
to ask him about it, he would answer: 'My friend, I knew that
I should not throw the seed away in vain, but I do not do it
that the grain may perish in the ground, but rather that through
decaying in the ground it may attain another form and bear
abundant fruit'. That is how any man thinks who does the
same thing or sees it done.

Since in this earthly existence we must do the same, we
should learn from this article (which we cannot grasp and
understand by reason)—because we have the Word of God
and the disciples' experience as well—that Christ rose from
the dead; and we should not judge according to what our
eyes perceive, namely, that our body is buried or burned or
becometh dust in some other way, but we should leave it to
God to care and to fashion what is to be. For if we could see
it before our eyes we should not need faith, and God would
have no means whereby to prove that His wisdom and power
are greater than our wisdom and understanding. Thereforethis
is called the Christian's skill and wisdom that in the midst
of wailing and lamentation he can hold comforting and happy
thoughts, namely, that God suffers us to be buried in the earth
and to decay in the winter, so that we may shoot forth in the
Summer brighter than the sun, as though the grave were not a
grave but a lovely garden in which lovely gentians and roses
are planted which all through the lovely Summer-time will be
green and full of blossom.

Sermons from the year 1533.   W.A. 37. 70.

*Death is swallowed up in victory. O death, where is thy
sting? O grave, where is thy victory?*

1 CORINTHIANS XV. 54, 55.

This song we sing now in reference to the Person of Christ
and of those who are risen with Christ from the dead, for they
have passed through and have won the victory over death.
But when we too shall rise we shall sing the song in reference
to ourselves. Then we too shall laugh at death, and mock him
and say: 'Death, where art thou now? Here is nothing but
life, and I am lord and master over thee. Previously, thou hast
devoured me and hast lorded it over me; but now thou
leavest me undevoured and I am lord over thee. Previously I
was in fear of thee, but now thou canst no longer harm me;
previously thou didst put me into the grave among the worms
and thou madest my appearance horrible to behold; now I
am risen from the dead and I shine brighter than the sun.
How dost thou like me now? Before, thou didst make me
afraid; now I dare thee to touch a hair of my head'.

Sermons from the year 1545.   W.A. 49. 769 f.

Twenty-sixth Week after Trinity

THE END OF TIME

Sunday: 2 THESSALONIANS i. 3–10

So that we ourselves glory in you in the churches of God for your patience and faith in all your persecutions and tribulations that ye endure, . . .

2 THESSALONIANS i. 4–5.

First, St. Paul here praises his Church in Thessalonica. . . . And he provokes them unto further growth that he may present to others an example and image of the fruits which the preaching and understanding of the Gospel should yield. And he shows in what the building and increase of the true Church of Christ consists. He then comforts them (concerning their sufferings and patience) with the glorious advent of the Lord Christ for their redemption, and the requital of their sorrows with rest and joy, and the eternal vengeance upon those who persecuted them.

But it cannot continue thus for ever, nor can it be the will of God that His Christians should so suffer eternally and without ceasing, and then die and remain in death, . . . for He testifies by His Word, that He will be the God of the saints, who fear and trust Him, to whom He has given such great promises. Therefore it follows that His purpose must be to give a different gift, and that this is one of the foremost reasons why He permits Christians to suffer on earth, namely, that His will to give to both their due reward may be thus revealed. Therefore must both Christians' sufferings and the world's wretchedness, tyranny, wrath and persecution of the saints become a certain testimony of another life to come and of the last judgement of God, through which all men, good and evil, shall receive their due reward eternally and without ceasing.

Sermon on the twenty-sixth Sunday after Trinity, 1544.

W.A. 22. 407 f.

*If we are children, then heirs; heirs of God, and joint-
heirs with Christ; if so be that we suffer with him, that
we may be also glorified together.* ROMANS viii. 17.

Because of such suffering with Him St. Paul here says that
we are brothers and joint-heirs with Christ. And now he
begins to comfort Christians in such sufferings, and he speaks
as a man who has been tried and has become quite certain.
And he speaks as though he can see this life only dimly, or as
through coloured glass, while he sees the other life with clear
eyes.

Notice how he turns his back to the world and his eyes
toward the revelation which is to come, as though he could
perceive no sorrow or affliction anywhere on earth, but only
joy. Indeed, he says, when we do have to suffer evil, what is
our suffering in comparison with the unspeakable joy and
glory which shall be made manifest in us? It is not worthy to
be compared with such joy nor even to be called suffering.
The only difficulty is that we cannot see with our eyes and
touch with our hands that great and exquisite glory for which
we must wait, namely, that we shall not die for evermore
neither shall we hunger nor thirst, and over and above shall
be given a body which cannot ever suffer or sicken, etc. Whoever could grasp the meaning of this in his heart, would be
compelled to say: even if I should be burnt or drowned ten
times (if that were possible), that would be nothing in comparison with the glory of the life hereafter. For what is this
temporal life, however long it may last, in comparison with
the life eternal? It is not worthy to be called suffering or
thought of as a merit.

Sermons from the year 1535.   W.A. 41. 302 f.

. . . waiting for the redemption of our body.
ROMANS viii. 23

Thus our daily Lord's Prayer teaches us that with joy we should long for that day and should cry to God, that at length He should avenge His Name, goodness, and blood on the despairing, ungodly world, and that no Christian can or should pray otherwise. And who else should pray thus but a Christian, who is thus tormented and afflicted because of his Baptism and the Gospel, or God's Name and Kingdom, that he has no other help or comfort on earth? And whoever has not yet learned by experience to long for that day has not yet a true understanding of the Lord's Prayer, much less can he pray it from the heart; as I myself used to feel that I was so hostile to the Lord's Prayer that I would much rather have said another prayer. But if you are in great tribulation, the Lord's Prayer will be sweet to you and you will gladly pray it from the bottom of your heart. For who would not wish and pray with all his heart: 'deliver us from evil', that there may be at last an end to our grief and sorrow in this world? For we see that the world wills to stay as it is and will not cast off its old skin, and neither will nor can become better, but rather gets worse every day. Wherefore there is no better thing than to flee away from it, and the sooner the better.

Sermons from the year 1531.   W.A. 34. II. 474 f.

For yourselves know perfectly that the day of the Lord
so cometh as a thief in the night.

1 THESSALONIANS V. 2.

The Last Day will come to all true and faithful Christians
as a day of joy and glory. But it will be a day of dire distress
for all unbelievers, godless men and coveters, usurers, and
false Christians. For thus it will happen: we shall not all receive
the Sacrament in our bed, nor be laid in a coffin and
carried to the grave. For he uses the term 'fallen asleep' of
one who gives up the ghost as he lies in bed; and afterwards
is carried out and buried in the earth. There will be no need
of that (he says) on the Last Day. For then the word will not
be "Come, hear this man's confession, absolve him from his
sins, administer to him the Sacrament, bury him, etc.", but as
you sit at the table at meal-time, or stand before the cash-box
counting your coins, or lie in bed asleep, or sit in the tavern
drinking, or are at a dance, suddenly in the twinkling of an
eye you will be changed, that is, you will be dead and alive.

Whoever will receive advice, let him repent and become a
better man. For the Last Day will come upon us and God's
trumpet will sound before we expect.

Sermons from the year 1545. w.a. 49. 732 ff.

> *Watch therefore: for ye know not what hour your*
> *Lord doth come.*   MATTHEW xxiv. 42.

No man is rightly prepared for the Last Day except he who desires to be free from sin. If that is your desire, why are you afraid? For on this account you are in agreement with it. It comes in order to set free from their sins all who desire it, and you too long to be thus free. Give thanks unto God and continue in that opinion. Christ says that His Advent is your redemption.

But take care that you do not deceive yourself when you say that you would be free from sin and do not fear that Day. Perhaps your heart is false and you do fear it. Perhaps you do not truly desire to be free from sin. Perhaps you are deterred from sinning freely and confidently because of that Day. Take heed that the light that is in you be not darkness. For a heart which truly desires to be free from sin rejoices in the expectation of the day when this desire will be fulfilled. If it does not rejoice in it, then is there no true longing to be set free from sin.

Therefore we must, above all, lay aside hatred and fear of this Advent, and be diligent and earnest in our desire to be free from sin. If we do that, we may not only await that Day with confidence but pray for it with great joy and with ardent hope.

Sermon on the second Sunday in Advent, 1522.

W.A. 10. I (ii). 111.

*Thanks be to God, which giveth us the victory through
our Lord Jesus Christ.*   I CORINTHIANS XV. 57.

St. Paul speaks of two kinds of victory. The first is that of
death which overcomes and lords it over all mankind from
the first man Adam till the end of the world. Of that victory
he speaks in Romans v. 12: 'By *one* man sin entered into the
world and death by sin and so death passed upon all men for
that they all have sinned'. That is death's victory and triumph,
that death rules through sin, and has power and authority
over all men, so that there is no man, whether he be emperor,
king, prince or lord; or however rich, strong, and great he may
be, who must not admit that death will lord it over him.

The other victory is that of life, which rules in and through
Christ, and is victorious over death. Of that victory, too, he
speaks, in Romans v. 17: 'for if by one man's offence death
reigneth by one; much more they which receive abundance
of grace and of the gift of righteousness shall reign in life by
one, Christ Jesus'. That is life's victory and triumph, that in
Christ life reigns and triumphs in opposition to death, and
that death has no power to hold not only Christ but also those
who are baptised in Christ and believe in Him.

It is that that the Apostle speaks of here. He means to say:
death lies on the ground. It has lost its kingdom, might, and
victory. For over against the kingdom and victory of death,
our Lord God, the Lord of Hosts, has brought about another
victory, which is the resurrection of the dead in Christ. Here
is pure life and no death. Death is conquered in Christ and is
dead itself. Life has won the victory and retains it.

Sermons from the year 1545.   W.A. 49. 767 f.

We shall ever be with the Lord.　1 THESSALONIANS iv. 17.

There is for a Christian no more precious thought than that he lives in God while he does his work here on earth. But when the Great Day comes, and it does not matter when, because He is my Lord, then I shall be redeemed. Yet this comfort belongs to none but Christians.

This Judge, who will come with such great power that He will awaken even the devil and all the dead, will be a brother and father and patron of Christians. O! the unspeakable joy when He will call us His friends and brothers and see in us His gift, and the Holy Spirit. And again it will be a joyous thing to the dead. Though nature must be terrified by such divine Majesty, yet the spirit will behold that Majesty with joy. But whoever lacks this comfort will be tormented by the devil. May all bear this in mind and act accordingly. No man will find a hiding-place. All will have to come forth, even though they lie a thousand fathoms down in the sea or under the earth or in the abyss of hell. When Christ is judge all things must come forth into the light.

Sermons from the year 1525.　　　　　W.A. 17. I. 221.

Twenty-seventh Week after Trinity

THE DAY OF THE SON OF MAN

Sunday: MATTHEW xv. 1–13

Then shall they see the Son of man coming in a cloud with power and great glory. LUKE xxi. 27.

Here you may interpret the power with reference to the host of angels, saints, and all the creatures which will come with Christ to the judgement; or as indicating that the Second Coming of Christ will be as impressive in its power as His first coming was insignificant in its weakness and poverty. Further, he not only says; 'He will come', but 'they will see Him come'. For, in His physical birth, He also came, yet none perceived Him. And He still comes every day in a spiritual way, in His Gospel, into the hearts of those who believe; yet no one perceives Him. But this Coming will occur openly, so that no one can help seeing it, as it is said (Revelation i. 7): 'Every eye shall see Him', and they shall perceive that He is none other than the Man Christ Jesus in the flesh as He was born of Mary and walked upon this earth.

Otherwise He might well have said: 'They will see Me', which need not have expressly referred to the physical form. But since He says 'They will see the Son of Man', it is clearly expressed that He means a physical advent, and a physical seeing of a physical form, yet in great power, with the multitudes of angels and all the heavenly glory, and He will be seated on a shining cloud and all His saints will be with Him. Holy Scripture says much about that Day and all things are directed towards it.

Sermons from the year 1522.   W.A. 10. 1 (i). 109.

Then shall he say also unto them on the left hand,
Depart from me, ye cursed, into everlasting fire,
prepared for the devil and his angels.

MATTHEW XXV. 41.

What an awful sight that will be for the godless when they
see not only all the angels and creatures but also the Judge in
His divine Majesty, and hear the judgement of eternal condemnation and of the eternal fire of hell pronounced on them.
That ought to be a strong and earnest warning that we as
Christians should study so to live that we shall be able to
stand with honour and unafraid at the right hand of this Lord
of Majesty, where there will be no fear or terror, but only
pure eternal comfort and joy.

For in that hour (as He says here Himself) He will separate
the sheep from the goats, so that it shall be seen openly by all
the angels, men, and creatures who are His good and righteous
Christians, and also who, on the other hand, are the false
hypocrites and the great multitude of the godless world.
This separation and selection cannot take place in the world
till that day (nor even in the company which is the Church of
Christ), but good and evil must remain here together.

Yet they have already here the comfort of the coming day
of judgement when Christ will thus separate them from the
godless, that from that day no false and evil man, and not
even death or devil will be able to touch them and tempt them
for evermore.

Sermon on the twenty-sixth Sunday after   W.A. 22. 412 f.
Trinity, 1544.

And I saw a new heaven and a new earth.
                    REVELATION xxi. 1.

This is the brightness and glory of our Lord Jesus Christ here on earth that He is despised and rejected, but He will come again and will appear in glory. He will bring a brightness so wonderful that all creatures will be made more beautiful than they are now. The light of the sun will be seven times brighter than it is now, the light of the moon will be like the present light of the sun. Trees, leaves, grass, fruit, and all things will be seven times as lovely as they are now.

The Christians will then come forth from their graves shining like the loveliest and most radiant stars. A holy martyr who now for the sake of Christ and His Gospel is persecuted and burnt to ashes like a black dull star, will then hover in the air and be drawn through the clouds towards the Lord and will go to heaven like a bright, light, and glorious star. In short, all the elect of God will be assembled in great and wonderful glory. And He Himself, the Lord Jesus, will be seated in the clouds 'upon the throne of his glory, and before him shall be gathered all nations' (Matthew xxv. 31, 32). The whole world will be transfigured and will be a thousand times more glorious than it is now.

Sermons from the year 1531.   W.A. 34. II. 126.

*The Lord himself shall descend from heaven with a
shout, with the voice of the archangel, and with the
trump of God: and the dead in Christ shall rise first.*
1 THESSALONIANS iv. 16.

What will happen then, when the voice of the Archangel
and the sound of the trumpet is heard and Christ comes?
In a flash the dead will rise in Christ; and we who are alive at
that time shall be changed in the same instant and together
with them shall be drawn on the clouds to meet the Lord in
Heaven, and we shall abide with Him for evermore. My words
are brief and poor; but who is the man to declare the meaning
concealed within these words? Let each man meditate upon
them diligently, and find in them comfort in all afflictions and
especially in the pain of death.

From that day we shall no more be tempted but shall be
delivered from all evil. There will be no more death, neither
sorrow nor crying, neither shall there be any more pain, nor
shall sin dwell in our flesh. It will be pure and clean from all
that is foul, from all evil desire and lust.

Someone may ask whether the godless will rise likewise.
The answer is yes, as well as the saints. For Christ is a Judge
over the quick and the dead, whether they are good or evil,
just or godless. But only to the faithful, that is those who have
fallen asleep in Christ, will be given the unspeakable grace
and glory, that they with Christ their Bridegroom will be led
into the new and eternal Jerusalem arrayed in a far more
wonderful glory than all the world possesses. But the godless,
who die in their unbelief, will not be drawn on the clouds to
meet the Lord in the air. They will remain here below on
earth and hear their judgement: 'Depart from me, ye cursed,
into everlasting fire' (Matthew xxv. 41). Thus the godless
will be raised like the faithful, but these unto the resurrection
of life and those unto the resurrection of judgement.

Sermons from the year 1525.   W.A. 17. i. 225.

*Then cometh the end, when he shall have delivered up
the kingdom to God, even the Father; when he shall
have put down all rule and authority and power.*

I CORINTHIANS XV. 24.

The term, the Kingdom of Heaven (as Christ Himself uses
it), applies not only to the realm where are the blessed spirits
and angels who have neither flesh nor blood, and to which
we also eventually shall attain and be united with them in
everlasting joy, but also to this life and among men. For this
difference is made between the two Kingdoms, that of the
Father and that of the Son, as St. Paul says (I Corinthians xv.
25), that Christ, God's Son, 'must reign till he hath put all
enemies under his feet. Then cometh the end, when he shall
have delivered up the kingdom to God, even the Father'.
He names here two different kingdoms: the one through
which He reigns in this life, in which He draws a veil over our
eyes, so that we cannot see Him but must believe; the other
where faith is no longer needed but we shall see Him before
our eyes. In every other respect it is the *same* thing: what we
now preach and believe we shall then look upon.

For the preaching and believing must cease and the veil
must be taken away so that we shall then live with the dear
angels eternally blessed with the beatific vision, which vision
we have here on earth only in hearing and believing. Therefore this kingdom, which is of the Word and of faith, will be
changed into a different kingdom where we shall no longer
believe, but we shall see before our eyes God the Father and
Christ the Lord. But now we must submit to the veiling of our
eyes, and we must be content to be led by faith and the Word
alone; and yet all who are baptised and believe that the Son
of God is made man and in the likeness of man are already in
the Kingdom of Heaven.

Sermons from the year 1544.   W.A. 49. 573.

And there was war in heaven: Michael and his angels
fought against the dragon; and the dragon fought and
his angels.   REVELATION xii. 7.

See then what we should learn here and what grounds we
have for comfort, namely, the knowledge that we who have
been baptised are truly blessed, and are seated in the Kingdom
of Heaven where the Son of God Himself reigns; notwithstanding that here (because we live by faith and not by sight)
the battle is still going on and the devil is among the children
of God (as he was also in Paradise in the beginning) and makes
war against the Word, the Sacrament, Baptism, and all that
belongs to Christ.

For he seeks at all times to take possession of the Kingdom
of God and to become lord of Christendom. He wills to be
seated and to rule, in the pure and holy Temple of God.

What, then, shall we do to him? This we, and especially
those who preach the Word of God, should joyfully consider, that we must hope for no peace here, but should re-
collect that we are Christ's warriors, in the field, always
equipped and ready, for when one war ends another immediately begins.

For we are called by Christ and already enrolled (in
Baptism) in the army which shall fight under Christ against
the devil. For He is the God who is a Prince of war and a true
Duke who leads His regiment in battle, not in heaven above
among the holy spirits where there is no need of battle, but
here on earth in His Church. Yes (even though He is seated
at the right hand of the Father) He is Himself with His
warriors leading them against the enemy, whom no human
power and weapons can withstand, resisting and restraining
him with His Word, which He has given to His men.

Sermons from the year 1544.   W.A. 49. 579.

Now is come salvation, and strength, and the kingdom of our God, and the power of his Christ.

REVELATION XII. 10.

When the time comes when Satan is conquered through the fighting of the Christians and he is cast out of the heavenly Kingdom of Christ, so great will be the joy that all the creatures will give thanks to God and sing: 'Now is come salvation and strength and the kingdom of our God, and the power of His Christ'. There God Himself sets both together so that the Kingdom, the power, and might of God belongs also to His Christ, that is, there is one Kingdom, power, and might of the Father and of Christ the Son.

This praise will certainly burst forth when the strife and struggle are ended, when Christendom is cleansed and purified and the lies of the devil have been put to shame.

But this praise and thanksgiving will come from those who overcome by the blood of the Lamb and who for His sake do not love their own lives. Therefore He calls for such praising and thanksgiving: 'Rejoice, O ye heavens, that is, ye Christians, that you are the kingdom of this Lord and that you are dwelling in His heaven. Ye have passed through and have won the victory over the old dragon, yet not of yourselves but by the blood of this Lamb. His blood does it and brings it to pass.'

Yet it remains true that for this victory the Christians must venture their lives, as He says: 'They loved not their lives unto death'. Therefore there must be a firm and steadfast continuing in the faith and testimony through life and death, until the devil is completely cast out through the strength and the victory of this Saviour Christ. To this end all the Scriptures point and everything has to do with this Son of God, who for us was made Man and shed His blood, that He should tread the devil with his hellish army and weapons, sin, death, and hell, under our feet, and through His joyful coming should bring us out of this war of faith into eternal safety and to the glory of the blessed vision.   Amen.

Sermons from the year 1544.   W.A. 49. 588

Harvest Thanksgiving

The Feast of the Reformation

The Day of Penitence

HARVEST THANKSGIVING

*The eyes of all wait upon thee; and thou givest them
their meat in due season.* PSALM cxlv. 15.

We should learn here that God makes the wheat grow, and
we should praise Him and give thanks to Him on that
account. We should also recognise that it is not of our working but of His giving and blessing that wheat, and grapes,
and all kinds of fruit grow, which we all need for food and
drink. The Lord's Prayer proves this when we say: 'Give us
this day our daily bread'. In the word 'give' we confess that
it is the gift of God and not our creation, and if He did not
'give', not a grain would grow and our tilling would be in
vain. . . . For how soon might all the grain in the soil go bad,
or be frozen, or rot, or be eaten by worms, or be drowned by
floods! Or if it is growing well, how soon might it be destroyed by heat, or hail, or cold, or be eaten by beetles or other
creatures! And who could count all the perils through
which the wheat must pass before it is reaped, and even then
it may be carried away, or devoured by worms? The devil
would not let a single blade or leaf shoot and grow unless
God held him in check.

Therefore, when we look at a field of wheat we should not
only think of God's goodness but also of His power and proceed to think: 'O, you dear corn, how God, out of His rich
and gentle goodness, gives you to us so plentifully, and also
with what power He protects you, from the hour when you
are sown to the time when you come to our table! . . . '

A devout and believing heart well perceives how all our
ploughing and sowing and the like would be lost, unless God's
goodness were here at work, and notwithstanding that we
must do our work diligently and seek our food from the soil
we must in no way put our trust in our work as though our
hands made the harvest. More is needed than our human
hands. God's blessing is essential to growth, and also His
mighty keeping.

Exposition of Psalm cxlvii.   W.A. 31. I. 443.

THE FEAST OF THE REFORMATION

1 CORINTHIANS iii. 11–23

*He answered and said, It is written, Man shall not
live by bread alone, but by every word that proceedeth
out of the mouth of God.* MATTHEW iv. 4.

So must we trust and be sure that the soul can live without all things except the Word of God; and without the Word of God nothing can help her. But when she has the Word she needs nothing else, for in the Word she has enough food, joy, peace, light, art, justice, truth, wisdom, and all good things superabundantly.

What is, then, this Word that bestows such high grace, and how shall I use it? Answer: It is nothing other than the actual preaching of Christ as it is contained in the Gospel. The purpose of the preaching is that you should hear your God speaking to you, telling how all your life and works are nothing before God and how you and all that is in you would perish eternally. If you truly believe how sinful you are, you will despair of yourself entirely and confess that the words of the prophet Hosea are the truth: 'O Israel, thou hast destroyed thyself; but in me is thine help' (Hosea xiii. 9). But in order that you may be saved from yourself and out of yourself —that is, out of ruin—He presents to you His dearly beloved Son Jesus Christ and bids you, through His living and comforting Word, yield yourself to Him with a cheerful heart. For the sake of such faith all your sins will be forgiven, your ruin overcome, and you will be just and true, content and devout, fulfilling all His commandments, and set free from all things.

Therefore this should be the one work and exercise of all Christians, to imprint in their souls this Word of Christ and practise and strengthen this faith unceasingly, for there is no other work which can make a Christian. Therefore a right faith in Christ means indescribable wealth, for it bestows all blessedness and takes away all wretchedness.

On the freedom of a Christian, 1520.   W.A. 7. 22 f.

THE DAY OF PENITENCE

Repent ye: MATTHEW iii. 2.

There can be no repentance where I want to pay and atone for sin by my own deeds, for since I am by nature a sinner and a child of wrath, as the Scripture says, I cannot blot out sin with sin. I can only increase it.

Repentance means that I believe the Word of God, which accuses me and tells me that I am a sinner before God and am condemned, that I am afraid, that I have always been disobedient to my God, that I have never truly regarded His commandments, and never meditated upon them, much less obeyed the greatest or the smallest. Yet I must not despair but turn to Christ, seek grace and help from Him, and firmly believe that I shall receive it. For He is the Lamb of God chosen from eternity to bear the sin of all the world and to atone for it by His death.

But if you wish to maintain that you are right, turn to other things. Turn to worldly rule, where you may well be right in opposition to your enemy who has wronged you and taken what belongs to you. There you may appeal to your rights, seek for them and demand them. But if you are dealing with God and have to stand before His judgement, do not think of your rights at all. Acknowledge that you are wrong and He is right, if you would find grace. This you do if you say with David and all the saints: 'O Lord God, I confess, feel, and believe that I am a condemned sinner; therefore, I pray thee, absolve me and wash me clean and baptise me for the sake of Christ. Then I shall know that Thou art gracious unto me, that I have been forgiven, and that I am pure and as white as snow'.

Such preaching is never without fruit. It always finds disciples who are converted and made better by means of it.

Sermon preached on the Thursday   W.A. 49. 119 f.
after Easter, 1540.